Jan 14, 1972

To Claudia

To help ensure a
Long Happy Rides without
Too many spills,
Love
Mommy & Daddy Bear

SCHOOL FOR YOUNG RIDERS

SCHOOL FOR YOUNG RIDERS

by

JANE MARSHALL DILLON

FOREWORD BY
CAPTAIN VLADIMIR S. LITTAUER

VAN NOSTRAND REINHOLD COMPANY
NEW YORK CINCINNATI TORONTO LONDON MELBOURNE

EDITED AND DESIGNED BY EUGENE V. CONNETT

Van Nostrand Reinhold Company Regional Offices:
New York Cincinnati Chicago Millbrae Dallas

Van Nostrand Reinhold Company Foreign Offices:
London Toronto Melbourne

Designed by Eugene V. Connett

Published by Van Nostrand Reinhold Company
450 West 33rd Street, New York, N. Y. 10001

Published simultaneously in Canada by
D. Van Nostrand Company (Canada), Ltd.

3 5 7 9 11 13 15 16 14 12 10 8 6 4 2

To My Husband
Who Remained Patient, Amiable and Encouraging
in the Face of a Hectic Home Life
During the Writing of This Book

Acknowledgments

To make the production of this book possible, many people contributed generously of their time and efforts. To the following individuals, I should like to express my warmest appreciation.

For technical advice and criticism:
Captain and Mrs. Vladimir S. Littauer, Syosset, Long Island.
Mrs. Howard Russell, Director of Riding, Camp Montresor, Leesburg, Va.
Miss Marion Lee   ⎤ Staff instructors at Junior Equitation School,
Mrs. Edward A. Willis ⎦ Vienna, Va.
Miss Claire Noyes, ex-chairman, Riding Committee, of the D.G.W.S.

For advice on the foxhunting chapters:
Mr. James O. Pease, MFH, Fairfax Hunt

For advice on details of correct attire:
Mrs. Stewart Bridenbaker of Stombock's Fine Riding Apparel, Washington, D. C.

For many hours spent in taking pictures at Junior Equitation School:
Mr. Bert Thayer, New York, N. Y.
Mr. and Mrs. Homer Heller, Falls Church, Va.
Mr. and Mrs. Walker Ridgely, Annandale, Va.
Col. Frank Hickman, Falls Church, Va.

For permission to use their photographs:
Marshall Hawkins
Howard B. Marler
J. D. Baxter
Cary Jackson
Thomas Neil Darling
The Washington Post Photographic Section
The Northern Virginia Sun Photographic Section

For her many lively and helpful sketches:
Mrs. Richard Ruffner, Burke, Va.

For cooperation in providing equipment pictures:
Miller Harness Company, New York
Stombock's Saddlery and Fine Riding Apparel, Washington, D. C.

viii ACKNOWLEDGMENTS

To the following pupils of Junior Equitation School, Vienna, Va.

Kathy Kusner, who plays the part of Kit Cavendish
Sara Willis, who plays the part of Sally Hilton
Judy Corcoran, who plays the part of Frances Fell
Tom Corcoran, who plays the part of Fred Compton
Nancy Hahn, who plays the part of Nancy Hadner
Peggy Hahn, who plays the part of Meg Hanover
Jill Ridgely, who plays the part of Sophie Connery
Gretchen Schiltz, who plays the part of Greta Stillway
Sarah Scheleen, who plays the part of Sara Shelly
Ridgely Rider, who plays the part of Ridgely Slater
Rebecca Ashley, who plays the part of Roberta Adams
Christine McElroy, who plays the part of Bettina McCoy
Christine Sieminski, who plays the part of Christine Solski
John Pennoyer, who plays the part of Jimmy Hudson
Mary Lou Walsh, who plays the part of Mary Lou Walters
Norma Gerstenfeld, who plays the part of Nora Durstfeld
Frankie Hickman, who doubles for "a young Tom Corcoran" in Chapters
    V and VI
Janie Samuels, who doubles for "a young Kathy Kusner" in Chapter XIV
    and who appears again in Chapter XII, vaulting and standing on her
    pony.
Jackie Heller, Terry Kidner, Jinx Snow, Jenny Lou Conner, Peggy Mayo
    and many other of our pupils whose pictures appear in these pages.
Elliott McElhinney, for permission to use her picture, on her mare,
    Catnap, in Chapter XIX.
Kathleen Noland, for permission to use her picture on her pony *Snow
    Flurry* in Chapter I.

And lastly, I would like to express my appreciation, not only to all of
our staff (secretarial, teaching and stable) for their enthusiastic support
during the writing of this book, but to all of the "riding children" of
Junior Equitation School, Full Cry Farm, for their patience while I wrote
about them!

JANE MARSHALL DILLON

Foreword

It gives me exceptional pleasure to be asked to introduce the present book; there are few works on riding to which I would rather write a foreword. This is not only because the author, Jane Marshall Dillon, is a personal friend, formerly one of my ablest pupils and presently one of my favorite teachers, but because I have a strong suspicion that the book is going to become a classic of its kind. It has all the qualifications: its clear and logical construction takes a junior rider from the moment he first mounts through to the time when he can begin to hunt and show; its theory and practice are of the most up-to-date and efficient; the true tale which runs through it gives it unusual conviction and readability, and it manages to convey precise information with a liveliness and charm which are all too frequently lacking in this sort of text.

Jane Dillon possesses a secret formula for combining serious technical explanation with the very human story of how a girl learned to ride. I know the girl well for, working periodically at the author's Junior Equitation School, I have given her lessons on various occasions and watched the development of her riding to its present level where she is a strong competitor in horse show jumping as well as amateur steeplechasing. I also know the other junior riders who appear in the illustrations and have admired the exceptional skill with which Mrs. Dillon has brought them up from rank beginners to the point where they all hunt competently and show successfully. This book tells how this was accomplished.

I first met the author several years ago when she enrolled in a special course I was giving to a group of riding teachers. From a purely material point of view she certainly didn't have to go to this trouble; she already rode well herself and her riding school was a recognized success. Now, knowing Jane Dillon well, I understand why she came to the class. She did it because she is blessed with healthy curiosity and ambition, a curiosity to know *all* the hows and whys, and an ambition to do whatever she does far better than necessity or public demand may require. It was natural for her to wish to join the ranks of those who not only make a living by teaching riding but who are interested in advancing the arts of riding and teaching. Now there are, of course, some who will ask, "What is there to advance?"

It is a common conservative belief that there is nothing new in riding and that all supposedly new theories are simply a rehashing of old tenets. But this is totally inapplicable to such modern sports as arena jumping and competitive cross-country riding. These have developed into an art only during the course of our century. Fully three-quarters of what we know about jumping and schooling jumpers has been learned during the past fifty years, and we certainly do not yet know all there is to know.

Man's memory is short and many of us are apt to forget that as late as 1891 someone could write: "When a horse leaps he throws the rider forward. The object then is to resist the impetus forward created by the horse's bound. Therefore as the horse approaches the *leap the rider should bend his body back.*" This, of course, sounds all very silly today, but the reasoning was typical of the period.

The author of this book is not the sort of person to ignore these facts nor to want to be left behind wherever riding is going. In fact she is one of those intelligent, energetic, inquiring horsewomen who are showing it the way. And her daily work with horses provides a practical proving-ground for her many ideas. It is little wonder that her mare *April Dawn* has (under her pupils) been three times Junior Hunter Champion of Virginia, and a trophy winner in such top shows as Madison Square Garden, Harrisburg and Toronto. The results of her work, however, are not limited to one horse or one rider. Her junior pupils, riding different horses, are constant winners wherever they go and she takes as many as twenty pupils out with the Fairfax Hounds. But almost more important than this: all her pupils, whether they are ambitious to hunt and show, or merely wish to learn to ride pleasantly and safely, come out of the school with a sound knowledge of horsemanship and an intelligent and sympathetic understanding of the horse which is permanently rewarding.

All this, combined with a talent for presenting her subject clearly and attractively, has gone far to make the present book what it is—the soundest and most readable text I know for juniors.

VLADIMIR S. LITTAUER

Syosset, N. Y.

Table of Contents

SCHOOL FOR YOUNG RIDERS

Introduction

Last summer my cousin, Polly Carter, came to stay with me. Polly has lived in Boston all her life. Strange as it seemed to me, she had never been to a horse show or ridden a horse. In fact, she said she had never even had a close look at anyone on a horse. As you will see from my story, I was riding a very strenuous horse show circuit at the time and between shows had to be constantly working the horses to keep them fit.

At first when I tried to explain what I was doing to Polly, it was as if I were talking in a foreign language. Expressions that were part of everyday life to me, such as hacking, hunter type, tacking up, cooling out, etc., made no sense to her.

During her visit, Polly became quite fascinated with horses and the theory of riding and schooling, and was anxious to learn all she could. I suggested that she keep a notebook, and write down my explanations of terms and comments she didn't understand. By the end of the summer, she almost had a small book. And that is what gave me the idea of writing this book.

Since there must be many people like my cousin who really want to learn about horses and riding, but have no chance to have good instruction, I have tried to explain each step and all terms I use. I hope that this won't make my book move too slowly for the group of people who already know the basics and understand the language which we who ride use. These people can just skip over them.

I realize that all too few of us have the opportunity I have at Douglas School of Horsemanship to learn riding from that starting point where I knew next to nothing to the present time when I feel equally at home schooling green horses, foxhunting or riding in jumper competitions.

Following the same program which we use at our school, I have tried to explain each step just as it was taught to us. In addition to our mounted classes and stable work, we had a regular course of lectures followed by quizzes. I have included a good many of both, so that at the end of the book (if you stick to a strict honor system!) you can give yourself an overall grade on Theory of Riding such as we received at Douglas School of Horsemanship at the end of four years.

As for the grade you receive on your practical (mounted) work, you will have to use the performance of the horse you ride to grade yourself.

And now, have fun and good luck along the way!

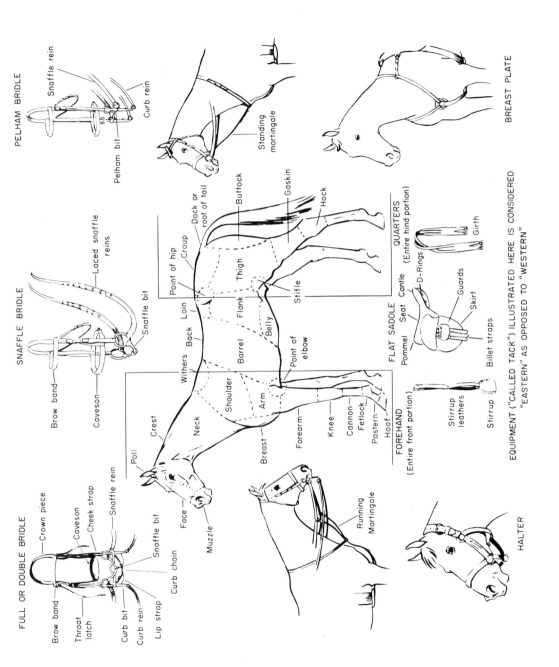

PELHAM BRIDLE

Snaffle rein

Curb rein

Pelham bit

Standing martingale

BREAST PLATE

SNAFFLE BRIDLE

Laced snaffle reins

Snaffle bit

Brow band

Caveson

FULL OR DOUBLE BRIDLE

Crown piece

Caveson

Cheek strap

Snaffle rein

Brow band

Throat latch

Curb bit

Curb rein

Lip strap

Snaffle bit

Curb chain

Poll

Crest

Neck

Face

Muzzle

Withers

Back

Shoulder

Arm

Breast

Forearm

Knee

Cannon

Fetlock

Pastern

Hoof

FOREHAND
(Entire front portion)

Point of hip

Croup

Dock or root of tail

Buttock

Gaskin

Hock

Loin

Thigh

Flank

Stifle

Barrel

Belly

Point of elbow

QUARTERS
(Entire hind portion)

D-Rings

Girth

Guards

Skirt

Billet straps

FLAT SADDLE

Pommel   Seat   Cantle

Stirrup leathers

Stirrup

Running Martingale

HALTER

EQUIPMENT ("CALLED TACK") ILLUSTRATED HERE IS CONSIDERED
"EASTERN" AS OPPOSED TO "WESTERN"

xvii

Read Carefully before Taking Quizzes

In statements dealing with the horse's mentality and nature there will always be differing opinions. Again, in any statements which deal with schooling horses or techniques of riding, there will be different ideas. Further, a different set of circumstances frequently will require any particular situation to be handled differently. Therefore, in the quizzes throughout this book, the answer to be considered and graded as *correct* is correct according to the situations, explanations and illustrations given in the text.

In the multiple choice quizzes, several answers might conceivably contain some truth. You are to select the one answer which is *the most pertinent and the most completely true* as explained in the text of this book.

In the FALSE and TRUE quizzes, you are to consider the statement *false* if any portion is false; *true* only when all parts of the statement are true as explained in your text.

In a few instances you will be asked to list particular techniques, or to draw diagrams of certain ring movements, or to correct improperly worded statements. In some quizzes you have equipment to identify.

The long quizzes, covering two or more chapters, will be graded as two or three quizzes, so that your overall grade will be fair to you. In other words, it would not be fair to give the same value to the quiz on Chapter XIV, a short chapter with a short quiz, as to the quiz on Chapter XIII, which tests you on a long and very important chapter, covering many points. Quiz for Chapter XIII, for example, will have the value of three quizzes on your overall score.

Complete instructions for scoring, together with answers, will be found in the back of the book, beginning on page 225.

INITIAL QUIZ—To be scored as two full value quizzes.

Don't take your quiz right away. Give yourself a chance to become *thoroughly familiar* with the parts of the horse and his equipment first. In the meantime you should at least look over the sketches before you start reading this book, so that you will not be lost when reference is made to "Eastern tack" or "withers" or "croup," etc. When you have studied and reviewed the sketches until you are sure you know *all the parts of the horse and equipment* indicated, give yourself the quiz.

Locate and write in at the appropriate places the following:

Brow band	Crown piece	Laced snaffle reins	Billet straps
Throat latch	Caveson	Snaffle bridle	Flat saddle
Curb bit	Cheek strap or piece	Pelham bit	Skirt
Curb rein	Snaffle rein	Pelham bridle	Forehand
Lip strap	Snaffle bit	Standing martingale	Quarters
Full bridle	Curb chain	Running martingale	Face
Stirrup leathers	Stirrup	Breastplate	Muzzle
Pommel	Seat	Cantle	Poll
D-Rings	Guards	Girth	Crest
Neck	Breast	Forearm	Knee
Cannon	Fetlock	Pastern	Hoof
Withers	Shoulder	Arm	Back
Barrel	Point of Elbow	Loin	Flank
Stifle	Point of Hip	Croup	Thigh
Hock	Dock or root of tail	Buttock	Gaskin

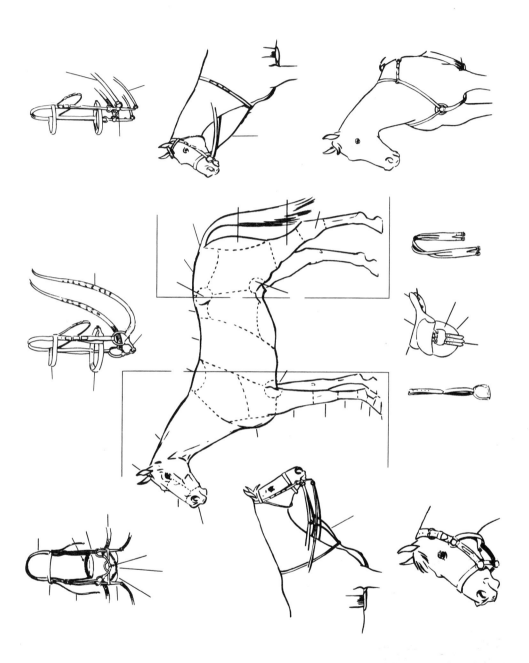

CHAPTER I

My Show Ring Debut

Horse show posters on every telephone pole had set my imagination on fire. I had dreamed of nothing else for weeks—did I dare enter a show? Each time I thought of it my heart would thump madly. I would all but choke with a sensation that was half dread, half daring. But now the die was cast. I, Kit Cavendish, would ride in the Bailey's Cross Roads Horse Show!

I was twelve that spring and had got my pony the year before. Since then, I had all but lived on his back, and *Trigger* and I had become very close. Several of the children in our neighborhood had ponies, and we all galloped around bareback or in western saddles, and tried our hands at jumping logs.

I didn't even realize that there was such a thing as a "show type" of horse or pony and that *Trigger* was a far cry from anything faintly resembling it. He looked rather like a burro, with his short, rabbitty legs and his furry ears, and was every bit as rough and shaggy. I knew that people braided their horses' manes for shows so I had worked for hours putting *Trigger's* coarse bushy mane into fat pigtails. I knew, too, that we should use eastern tack at the show, so I had borrowed a flat saddle from a neighbor who once had real show horses.

As I rode the three miles on a hard surface road to the show grounds I was sure that people in passing cars must be throwing us admiring glances since we looked so stylish, I thought. To my mind, *Trigger* looked positively stunning with his "braided" mane, and in the borrowed saddle that covered him almost from withers to croup. I must admit, too, that I was rather pleased with my own appearance. I was wearing my very first pair of jodhpurs. They had arrived just in time for the show, and were that horror of horrors—green.

When I reached the show grounds, I began to get a queer feeling in the pit of my stomach. There was no doubt about it: *Trigger* and I didn't look like the other entries. But my pride in his accomplishments and a fierce sense of loyalty drove me to the entry desk all the same. He was so clever to have learned to jump in his middle age, although he had

1

been a plow pony up until the time when I bought him, that I was determined to let people see his remarkable ability.

I studied the prize list carefully and decided to enter him first in a class which read: "Small Ponies under Saddle. To walk, trot and canter both ways of the ring. To be judged on performance, manners and way of going, 100%." After all, he *was* a small pony under a gorgeous saddle which I had sat up until 11:00 o'clock the night before to polish. Furthermore, I had with great effort taught him to walk and trot and gallop (or

Here is my "show pony" and me. This picture was taken shortly after I got him. Stunning, isn't he?

canter as they called it) when I asked him to, so I felt sure that he would win a ribbon.

The next class read, "Small Pony Working Hunter. To be held in the ring. Fences to be about two and a half feet." "Aha!" I thought with delight; "How very nice! A class for ponies of *Trigger's* type." (As you probably know, "working hunter" means a class for hunters in which their performance, manner and *style* of *galloping* and *jumping* count. Body build is not considered as it is in a conformation class. I understood none of this and assumed that "working" meant "work pony" type.) I felt that the gods were smiling on us—in some magic fashion, the class had been drawn up just for us. And the fences would be only two and a half feet high. We had been practicing over logs in the woods as well as over a little rail set up between a stump and a fence that I told myself was almost four feet. Of course I was fooling myself about the height of the jumps at home. Nonetheless I was sure that *Trigger* would have the crowd wildly applauding while he sailed over everything. I could almost see myself riding out of the ring, trophy in hand, with *Trigger* pricking up his ears for the newspaper photographer.

The great decision made to enter the two classes, I handed over my four dollars at the entry desk, and proudly tied my horse show number around my waist. I had been assigned number seven, which seemed a lucky omen to me.

We entered the ring for the under saddle (also called a "walk, trot, canter" or "hack" class) bunched up in a big group of shining, beautifully turned-out ponies. The more experienced riders immediately managed to find little gaps where they could get off by themselves so that the judge would get a good look at their mounts. I found myself pinned in between a gorgeous grey pony and an equally gorgeous chestnut pony. And so it continued. I couldn't get my pony where I could show him off or let him move on. When the command "Canter" came, I was blocked behind another handsome animal. I couldn't get by him and he cantered so slowly that *Trigger* kept breaking into a trot. So when Number Seven was not called to remain in the ring with the finalists I wasn't too surprised. What I didn't realize was that we were so outclassed that if there had been only five instead of twenty-five ponies in the ring we still wouldn't have had one of the four ribbons.

I forgave the judge for his "mistake" and waited for the hunter class to show him what a fine pony he had overlooked. Here *Trigger* would have the ring all to himself for his round over the fences, and I just knew that the judge could not fail to be impressed.

Now I was really dealt a death blow. When *Trigger* came into the ring and saw the first fence (a brush jump made of nice fresh cedar, standing up like a small forest in the supporting frame) he gave a shocked snort, planted his feet firmly down and came to a dead standstill. Then he reached out and caught a piece of the greenery in his teeth to nibble. I could feel my face growing red as I turned him for a second try, and I did know enough to ride him *hard* at the jump this time, using legs and whip. He took the jump awkwardly and reluctantly, but as we approached the next fence, we were in trouble again. This was a white picket gate and it didn't look a bit like the jumps over which we had practiced. *Trigger* would have no part of it. Again he came to an abrupt stop in front of the jump and again I circled him for another try. At this point, *Trigger* had become so disgusted with the whole (to his mind) foolish business that he wouldn't even approach the jump. And now the sad "toot, toot" that means elimination was heard and the ringmaster waved me out of the ring.

I must admit that after I left the ring I found a spot out of sight of spectators and burst into tears. Putting my arms around *Trigger's* neck, I buried my face against his rough shaggy neck and sobbed, asking him

Courtesy of Vaudine Herbster

This is what Trigger's competition looked like! Here you see the small pony who won the championship that day.

to forgive me. My feelings were hurt for him, as I knew I had made him look ridiculous. It hadn't occurred to me before that jumping the sort of obstacles over which we had practiced would be so different from taking jumps in the show ring. How did it happen that most of the other entries took them so readily?

In spite of the fact that I was quite broken hearted, something very important developed out of my disappointment.

When I cheered up enough to return to the ring side, I watched the other entries like a hawk to try to discover how it was that the other horses and ponies behaved so differently from mine.

I was particularly impressed by the horse who won the junior championship that day. He jumped like a bird and hacked like an angel, and was completely relaxed and calm in everything he did without being in the least sluggish. In fact, he and his rider seemed to be part of a little group whose horses performed very freely and happily. There was a pleasant calmness and quietness in everything they did, and I was tremendously impressed. I found that they and their horses came from a school of horsemanship not too far away, and being ever an eager beaver where horses were concerned, I went over to the director, Mrs. Douglas, to make application. I found out that the school had a long waiting list, but I was accepted and told to report the following Saturday, the first day of the school's new semester. Why I was accepted, I'll never know, unless I looked as if I needed help so badly that I could not be refused.

CHAPTER II

A Nodding Acquaintance with Terms

The next Saturday I arrived at Douglas School of Horsemanship, complete with *Trigger* in a homemade trailer rigged up by my father. My family knew absolutely nothing about horses but they were sweet about helping me with the things I liked.

After I had been greeted by my instructor, and a groom had helped unload my pony, I was introduced to Sally Hilton, who would show me where *Trigger's* stall would be when he stayed at the school. Sally, who was just a few months younger than I, had started taking lessons when the school first opened a year and a half before, so now she felt very natural in the role of hostess.

I was disappointed to find that we wouldn't ride immediately, but that the new class must spend the morning taking notes and observing. After roll call and introductions all around our instructor asked us to meet at the main ring to get what she called a "nodding acquaintance with terms" and a "bird's eye view of riding."

When we assembled in the ring she told us, first of all, that before she could teach us anything, we must understand one another's language. This morning she would explain the most common terms we would use and hear, and we would see how certain things look. Since there would be quite a bit to cover in the class period, she said, she wouldn't try to explain *why* certain things were true or certain terms were used, or go into any subject very deeply. All that would come later. We were to take careful notes and review them after we got home. Next week we would have a written quiz on the material covered today.

Frances Fell, who had done some riding before she came to Douglas School of Horsemanship (DSH, as it was called) and was considered the school's most advanced rider, led her own horse, *Glennwood,* to the ring. Little Meg Hanover led up the pony, *Sauce Box.* These two would be our models.

From the notes I took that morning I have tried to tell what the instructor said, and what we saw during that class. This is about the way it went:

This is a horse (pointing to *Woody*). He is a grown up male horse of

Photo by Marler

Here is *Saucy,* one ear up and one ear back, being measured.

Photo by Marler

Frances shows *Woody* the measuring stick, which he carefully investigates. After all, he must make sure it won't bite him!

the type used for riding. Such an animal is called a gelding. Male horses of the type used for breeding (that is, to be fathers, or, properly termed, sires) are called stallions or studs. They are seldom used for our sort of riding except in books. There are countries where stallions are used for general riding, and in our country they are used for racing.

Until *Woody* was five he was a colt. If he were female instead of male he would be a mare, and until he was five would have been a filly.

Here is a *pony* gelding (indicating *Saucy*). In the case of *Woody* and *Saucy*, you see quite a difference in size, but suppose *Saucy* were a very large pony, how would you determine whether he was a pony or a horse? The decision, according to the American Horse Shows Association Rule Book, is made by height. The animal who measures 14 hands and 2 inches or less from the withers to the ground is a pony. If he is a fraction of an inch over, he is a horse. You measure, keeping the "arm" of your measuring stick exactly level, as I am doing now. As you see by the stick, a hand is four inches. We see that *Saucy* stands 11 hands and ½ inch. Of course there is no doubt in anybody's mind that *Saucy* is a pony, but we have several animals in the stable that are on the border line, and might be mistaken for horses. Undoubtedly they have some "horse blood," but because of their height, they must be classified as ponies. Now we will measure *Glennwood* and we find that he is 15 hands and 2 inches.

Measuring stick

While we are discussing types I would like to mention that we consider all of our horses and ponies "hunter type." There is no *breed* of hunters, although, amongst horses the hunter generally has *some* thoroughbred blood in his veins. *Pony* hunters may be of almost any breed. Any horse that hunts successfully a certain number of times a season can claim to be a "qualified hunter," but all the same you do look for a certain *type*. We expect to find an animal who moves with long low strides which cover the ground with the least output of energy, since hunters in the field (that is, out foxhunting) often have to maintain fast gaits for rather long periods of time, and cover a lot of ground. You don't expect to find very high head carriage in the hunter. If his head is up in the air he

Photo by Marler

Woody is a very nice illustration of a good hunter type, moving freely and quietly on loose reins, head and neck extended.

In sharp contrast is this horse of saddle type.

cannot watch the ground and handle himself well over all sorts of rough country, through gullies and streams and over logs and fences. The horse with the high head carriage and high action—that is, way of picking up his legs—is generally considered a "Saddle type." This means that he resembles, or sometimes belongs to a breed classified as the *American Saddle Horse*. This is not a breed or type that is practical for us to use in the sort of riding we teach and do. Among other things, we consider jumping a part of riding, and the horse we described first is generally better adapted to handling himself over jumps when going cross country, for

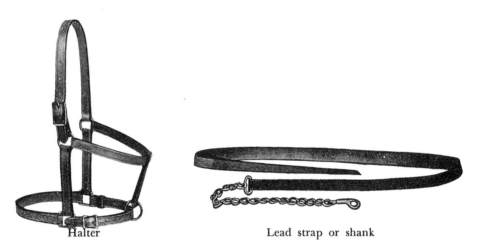

Halter   Lead strap or shank

the same reasons that he is a better cross country horse generally. There are, however, instances where saddle horses have made outstanding jumpers in the show ring. This is the exception rather than the rule, and even those few who can jump high fences would not be very comfortable to ride to hounds.

When you see us looking at a horse and saying that he "looks a little saddle-ish" we probably mean that his neck looks long and head is carried high, or that his tail is set on high, or that his action is short and high—or we might mean all of these things and a few others too.

So much for these two general types at the moment. Next, I would like you to observe a horse being "tacked." When we put the horse's saddle and bridle (and any other equipment which he may wear, such as a breastplate) on him, we say we are "tacking up." We call this equipment his tack. We led *Woody* up to the ring in a halter; that is what the horse wears in the stall, or turned out in the field, to make it easier to catch and handle him. That strap with the brass chain and clip at the end that is attached to the halter is known as a lead shank or lead strap.

Now, as you see, Frances is putting the saddle on *Woody*. This is a forward seat saddle, suitable for the sort of riding we do. Notice how she starts it well forward and lets it ease *down* on the horse's back, rather than sliding it forward against the hairs. Now she tightens the girth, but not terribly snugly at this moment. Next, she slips the halter off but leaves it hanging around *Woody's* neck so that he can't walk off if he takes the notion. Now, you see, she slips the bridle reins over his head. And now watch the way she takes the crown piece of the bridle in her right hand and the bit in her left. See, she actually slips her fingers in the sides of

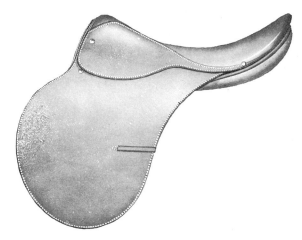

Forward seat saddle

Woody's mouth—there are no teeth back there—to persuade him to open his mouth, and there! the bit is in, and the crown piece over his ears. That is the throat latch she is adjusting now, and she leaves it loose enough to be able to slip her hand between it and *Woody's* throat, or throttle as it is called. She is now tightening the girth again; horses aren't too keen on having them drawn up tight all at once. Can anyone guess why she slipped her hand under the pommel (front) of the saddle? No? Only to make sure that it doesn't "sit down" on the withers and pinch or bruise. Now she is checking all the little keepers—that is, those little loops that keep the loose ends of the various parts of the bridle from flapping around. You probably noticed that the stirrups were slipped up to the top of the stirrup leathers, and now, as you see, she is snapping them down and taking a rough estimate against her arm of the length she will want to ride them. They measured a little short, so she is letting the leathers down a notch. And now you see *Woody*, tacked and ready to be mounted.

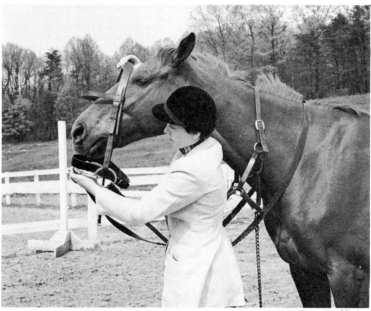

Photo by Marler

Bridling. "Now watch the way she takes the crown piece in her right hand and the bit in her left."

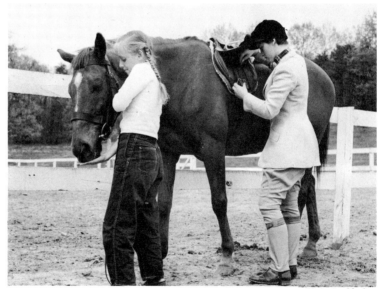

Photo by Marler

Saddling. "She tightens the girth but not terribly snugly at this point."

That was a very nice demonstration, Frances. Next will you show us the proper way to mount? You see, she stands at the shoulder and faces the quarters. In this way, if *Woody* tries to move around, she is more or less in the center of his pivot. If he tries to move forward, he moves right into her. If she stood facing around the other way (demonstrate this for a minute, please, Frances) and he took a step forward, she would find

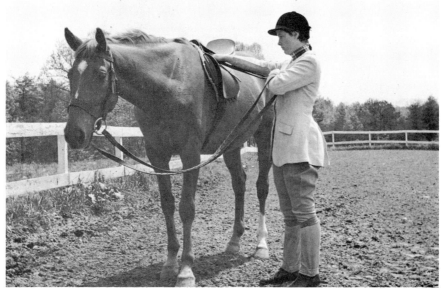

Photo by Marler

Measuring your stirrup leathers. "Now, as you see, she is snapping them down and taking a rough measure against her arm of the length she will want to ride them."

herself hopping along behind him. Who can think of the situation where it might be better to stand at the quarters and face the forehand (front)? Right, Kit, if the horse had the habit of trying to back as you mount. Of course, the best bet is to teach your horse to stand still while he is being mounted!

Notice that Frances has shortened the reins on the off (right) side just a little so that *Woody* can't take a nip at the seat of her pants while her back is turned—many horses consider this great sport. Notice too that she has flipped the "bight" of the rein—that is, the left over portion above her hand—to the offside so that she can't possibly tangle up in the ends of her reins as she mounts. Now please observe closely how, as she puts her left foot in the stirrup and prepares to mount, she slides her toe *through* and *down* as far as she can. There are two reasons for this—one, so that her foot is less likely to slip back out of the stirrup and the other, so she

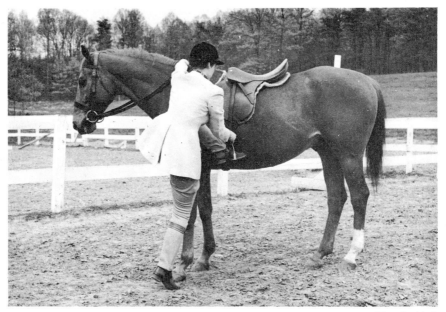

Photo by Marler

Mounting. "As she puts her left foot in the stirrup she slides her toe through and down."

Photo by Marler

Mounting. "Did you notice that her right leg swung through the air clear of the horse's quarters?"

won't "gouge" her horse in the side with her toe. This is the only instance
I can think of where it is correct in riding to have the heel up and toe
down!

Now she has her left foot in the stirrup, the reins and a piece of mane
in her left hand, and her right hand on the cantle (back part) of the saddle.
Now watch . . . as she swings herself up and her right leg is about level
with her left, she moves her right hand forward to the front of the saddle.
Did you notice that her right leg swung through the air clear of the
horse's quarters, instead of being dragged across his rump, and how softly
she settled in the saddle? In all these little things, it is possible to make
your horse comfortable or uncomfortable, and as a result, calm or jittery.
You did that very nicely in slow motion, Frances.

Make a note of one other point before we leave "Mounting." Frances
got on from the left side, you noticed. That is the side normally used for
mounting, dismounting, leading the horse, tacking him, etc. It is the side
on which the throat latch of the bridle and the buckle of the halter fasten.
It is called the "near" side. The right side is known as the "off" side. I
can think of some rather complicated reasons why this has developed as
it has, but I don't think them important enough to discuss, so just accept
it as a custom. Here at our school, we think it is a good idea to have the
horses learn to be mounted from both sides, but in all your normal riding,
you might as well go along with the tradition and mount from the left.

Now that you have seen how one mounts a horse, it might be a good
idea to show dismounting before we go further.

It is *almost,* but not quite, the same process in reverse. (Please demonstrate, Frances.) Notice in dismounting, the rider again swings the right
leg across the horse's quarters without *dragging* it over his rump. Now,
as the right foot is about level with the left, the rider leans for a moment
on her hands and slips her left foot out of the stirrup. Then she jumps
lightly down. In the old method of dismounting, the left foot was left
in the stirrup until the right foot was on the ground, but this practice has
been abandoned. You can imagine what an awkward spot you would
be in if the horse suddenly moved forward at that point.

Would you like to see what we call an *"emergency* dismount"? Will you
show us, Frances? We practice this in class at all gaits—first at a walk,
then at a trot and finally at a canter—so that getting off a horse quickly
and safely becomes easy. In class the command is given "Fall, please!"
Riders *slip feet out of both stirrups* immediately, and just slide, or vault
off. You practice landing on the balls of your feet, with knees bent, and
you move in the same direction that the horse moves, so that you will
not jar yourself. Of course, you keep the bridle reins in your hands. There

Photos by Marler

Dismounting. As the right foot is about level with the left, she leans for a moment
on her hands and slips her left foot out of the stirrup.

are times when the rider needs to get off in a hurry and you may find that this practice stands you in good stead. Also, it seems to take away the fear of falling which some people have. Okay, Frances, show us from a trot. . . . Whee! That was really fast, wasn't it?

Photo by Marler

Holding reins. "As you see, her thumbs are on top, and she has run the reins *up* through her hands and *across* the palms of her hands." (Photo shows reins being held a little too close together.)

Well, so much for dismounting and "emergency dismounts." Now that Frances is on her horse again, let's observe the way she picks up the reins.

As you see, her thumbs are on top, and she has run the reins *up* through her hands and *across* the palms of her hands. She holds down the part of the reins that comes across her forefinger with her thumb and flips the bight to the off side. There is another way to hold the reins, called the "driving hold" that you will see later for special purposes, but the way Frances has them now is the way we will have you hold them for some time.

We are now ready to see the horse move. When this horse moves, the various ways in which he moves his legs are termed his *gaits*. The horse's natural gaits are the walk, trot and canter, or gallop, which is just a faster canter although the horse does put his feet down a little differently at the canter and at the gallop—but more of that when we study the mechanics of the gaits. At the moment, just observe the following things: (please have the horse walk, Frances). What you see now is the horse's slowest gait. He is walking and the walk is quite smooth. The rider just sits in the saddle. (Now a trot and please don't post for a minute.) As you see, the horse is moving faster, and what he does now is a very springy gait that bounces the rider around if she just sits. Let's see what she can do to avoid the bouncing. Ah! Now she no longer bounces but is going up and down as one of the horse's front legs goes up and down. Your eye may not be able to catch it at this point, but actually as the right leg is in the air, she is in the air; when it comes back on the ground, she is in the saddle. This is known as posting and it is what you do to avoid bump-bump-bumping on your rears. In learning to post, you don't have to bother about what the horse's legs are doing. It's very simple to catch the rhythm. You can steady yourself with your hands on the horse's neck and at first actually pull yourself up and down. You will soon find that if you relax and more or less let it "do itself" it's much easier to post than to sit an ordinary trot without posting.

Let's look at a faster gait still. What the horse is doing now is cantering. His legs work in a rather complicated way at the canter, and we won't discuss the mechanics of the gait at present; but as you see, the rider again is sitting. She doesn't sit as still as she did at the walk; in order to move in one piece with her horse, her upper body moves a little more. Now, we'll look at one more thing (gallop the horse, please). Notice that at a gallop the rider gets up out of the saddle in a position which we call a "gallop" or "jump" position. Her weight is down in her stirrups, which really act as a floor under her and she doesn't sit in the saddle at all. In this way she isn't bounced around by the fast movement as she would be if she attempted to sit in the saddle. Okay, that is enough, Frances.

Now then, you have seen the horse at a walk, a trot (with the rider posting), a canter and a gallop. When the horse moves at gaits, as we call it, he is said to be "hacking." In a horse show, a "hack" class is one in which the horse is shown at gaits only, as opposed to a jumping class. If your horse moves well and has good manners, you might say that he is a nice "hack." When you go out for a general ride along roads or bridle path, you say that you are going hacking, or that you are going for a hack. You might say that you are going to hack to the hunt meet, rather than send your horse in a van.

Well, let's see. We have discussed horses versus ponies and the way you distinguish between the two when there is no obvious difference in size, and the way they are measured. We have discussed the two main types of horses, at least as *we* think of them. Of course, there are many types as well as breeds of horses and ponies too, and some day we will spend a class discussing them, but we won't get into such a discussion today. I don't think we will go into colors and markings today, either, other than to tell you that *Woody's* bright copper gold shade is called chestnut; *Saucy's* reddish tan is called bay.

You have seen the equipment in which the horse is ridden and watched a rider tack up and mount properly, and you have observed the horse moving at gaits. They are, you remember, walk, trot and canter, and a faster canter called a gallop. You have seen how the rider sits to the saddle at a walk and a canter, posts at a trot and rides in a gallop position at a gallop.

I haven't discussed the rider's position, as we will go into that in detail when you yourselves mount, but perhaps you noticed that the rider looked balanced over her feet the whole time she was riding, rather than "propped up" by her horse. Did you notice, too, that as she rode faster, she leaned further forward, as you do when you run fast?

Now, before we go any further, would you like to put away your notebooks and pencils and take a breather? Then we'll ask Sally to take you around to see the various rings and hunter courses. Suppose we plan to meet again in about half an hour.

Most of the group were glad enough to have a break here, as part of the new pupils were complete beginners and they said their heads were bursting with the new terms and ideas. As for me, while I was interested in the way these terms were explained, I was consumed with impatience to mount and ride! Well, that would come eventually.

CHAPTER III

A Bird's Eye View of Riding

When we met again after our little "breather" we found a different horse and rider in the ring.

It developed that the blacksmith had arrived a few minutes before and *Woody* was being reshod. Our instructor explained to the group that horses' feet grow constantly, just as our fingernails do. Within four to six weeks from the time that they have last been shod, their feet will grow out a little over their shoes, and they will need to be reshod. Sometimes the iron shoes are worn thin, and they will get a new set. If they have worked mainly on soft ground, the shoes may be perfectly all right. In that case, the blacksmith will "pull" them, trim the horny walls of the hooves (which is just like trimming fingernails) and put the same shoes back on—this is called "resetting."

Nancy Hadner was to fill in on *Which One*, an attractive bay gelding that had been "in school" since D.S.H. first opened. Nancy had not ridden as long as Frances, and the instructor explained that it might be a little difficult for her to demonstrate all the things she had planned to show us. Particularly in jumping, she wasn't as far along as Frances, so we might run into a little trouble when we got to that point, but we would see.

Our lecture and demonstration commenced once more, and again I will tell what the instructor said, putting it into lecture form as well as I can from my notes:

Here at DSH, we think of riding on three levels. When I say "here at our school" I don't mean to imply that this is the only place where this is true. Not at all. Most modern schools of horsemanship now follow the same general idea.

Now it may surprise you to hear that we sometimes say that a pupil rides "on a beginner level" even though he may have been riding as long as a year, or even longer. Please demonstrate, Nancy. You see, she is riding with the reins completely loose, and only uses one rein or the other when she needs to, in order to hold the horse on the rail or change her direction. Now if she were a *complete* beginner, we would ask her to hold onto the mane to steady herself, keeping the reins looping. Those of you who

20

haven't ridden at all will be asked to ride this way until your seats are completely secure. Not only will it help you establish a correct position but we want to be sure that you do not do something which we call "catching the horse in the mouth." This is an expression you will hear many times, and it is important that you understand what we mean and also that you know when it happens. So please listen and watch closely. As Nancy rides with her reins looping and her hands on his mane, the horse can move his head around all he wants and still won't be jerked in the mouth by the bit which is attached to those reins, will he? Now shorten your reins, please, and take your hands off the neck and pretend to be a beginner, learning to post the *wrong way*. . . . There, you see what we mean. . . . As she rose into the "up" part of the posting beat she pulled herself up on the reins. The reins of course, are attached to the bit, and so the bit hit the horse on the "bars" of the mouth. In other words, she "caught the horse in the mouth." This happens many times and in many ways other than the illustration we just showed you, but I don't like to abuse the horse in order to make my point. Just remember, any time that the reins snap tight, when you didn't plan to make them tight to give your horse an order, you "caught him" or "hit him in the mouth."

All during the time that you are establishing a secure and steady seat you will be asked to ride on loose reins, which is what we call riding "on a beginner level." You see, during that time your hands will do things you don't tell them to do. If you lost your balance even slightly and the reins were not loose, your hands very probably would fly up and jerk the reins, catching the horse in the mouth. Of course, you will want to see how you will control your horse during this period. To begin with, all of our horses are voice trained, but you should know how to start, guide and stop your horse with hands and legs too. While you are riding on a beginner level, it is done in the simplest possible way and just as common sense would tell you.

1. When you want your horse to move straight ahead, have the reins even, "cluck" to him and squeeze him with your legs.
2. When you want him to go to the left, take your left hand off the mane, and pull the left rein enough to turn him as far that way as you wish him to go. It's as simple as that.
3. If he tries to disobey you, and cut into the center of the ring, instead of staying on the rail, use the rein on the rail side to give a short quick jerk, that says, "No, no, horse. You stay here."
4. When you want him to stop, keep the reins even and pull straight back until he obeys, and then immediately loosen them.

A little later, when your position is fairly secure, you will still ride on loose reins, but you won't keep your hands on the mane except when you particularly need to steady yourself. You will find that you will need the support of the neck longer at a trot and at a canter than at a walk. At this stage, you must be careful that when you pull the left rein to tell the horse to go to the left, you loosen the right rein, and also keep it on the right side. Don't cross it over to the left side. Now, Nancy, will you demonstrate starting, guiding, and stopping the horse on the beginner level?

All right, you have seen how we expect you to ride your horses, and why it is necessary to ride them that way until your seats are so strong and steady that your hands can work independently of the rest of your bodies.

Let's take a look at the next step. Please establish contact at a walk, Nancy. Now you see the reins are no longer loose and yet Nancy does not jerk the horse's mouth. And notice something else—her hands and arms are moving back and forth and the reins have no slack in them. Let's see why the hands move. Look at the horse's head; it is moving with every stride and pulling her hands forward and back. The horse is making what are called "balancing gestures" with his head and neck. What the rider is doing is called "riding on contact." Now let's watch at a trot. This is interesting, isn't it? Before, at a walk, Nancy sat still and her hands moved; now her body goes up and down and her hands are staying still. Let's take a look at the horse's head again. No, it doesn't make balancing gestures at a trot, does it? Since the horse's head is "steady" now, the rider's hands must be steady too when she maintains contact. Then that is the answer. Now the canter, and watch what happens this time. Well, her hands and arms are moving again, so his head must be moving and pulling them—look and see. Yes, it really is, isn't it? Fine, bring your horse back to a walk. What you just saw, which is called "riding on contact" or riding with following hands and arms, is the big step between riding on a beginner level and on an intermediate level. We won't go into starting, turning and halting on contact; I only wanted you to see what contact looks like. Naturally, you realize that it isn't practical to do all your riding at all times and on all occasions on loose reins. And if you don't want the reins loose all the time and yet don't want to abuse the horse's mouth, you must let your hands be moved by the movement of the horse's head. If the reins are tight and your hands stay fixed in one spot as his head moves, again you will catch the horse in the mouth every time he tries to reach out his head. Demonstrate for just a minute, Nancy. A minute is all I can bear to watch. . . . That's enough, but you saw

The walk.

The trot.

The canter.

Nancy Hadner shows how each gait looks on contact. Her hands are a little too low at the trot. Excellent at walk and canter. (*Photos by Marler*)

how the horse caught himself on the bit with every stride, didn't you? It hurts his mouth.

Very well, you have seen how the rider handles the reins at all gaits on the beginner and intermediate level. It would hardly be worth while to show how the horse moves when ridden on an advanced level, even if Nancy could demonstrate it. You have to watch the way horses move for a long time before your eye begins to see movement of high quality as opposed to movement of average quality. And the difference between

Photo by Marler

Jumping a low fence from a trot, at a beginner level. "She gets up in what we explained was 'jump position' and leaving the reins loose, catches the mane."

intermediate riding and advanced riding is mainly seen in that way. You see, at that level, the rider uses his hands and legs so subtly that you hardly see what he is doing to get results. Well, enough on that subject.

You have watched the horse at gaits on loose reins and on contact. You have seen him ridden on a beginner and an intermediate level. Don't imagine, however, that you will always ride on contact when you have reached the intermediate level, any more than that it would be practical to do all your riding on loose reins forever. You will do probably half of your riding on loose reins always. Loose rein riding helps keep your horse's mouth fresh and responsive.

Let's take a look at the various levels over jumps, or fences, as we call them. Nancy, please demonstrate jumping on a beginner level. Take the horse over that little low jump, approaching at a trot and keeping completely loose reins. . . . She's trotting him around the ring once to get him settled down and "listening" to her. Now as you see, a few strides before the jump she gets up in what we explained was "jump" position, and leaving the reins loose, catches the mane. She stays up out of the saddle over the jump and for a few strides on the landing side. Look how calm and undisturbed the horse remained throughout. Please demonstrate the same thing for us once more. . . . Fine.

Now let's show the class the next step. This is for the rider who is still *jumping* on the beginner level, but riding at gaits on an intermediate level, which sometimes is the case. As you see, Nancy approaches keeping a

Photo by Marler

"No, that didn't work, did it? Instead of sliding her hands and arms forward along the sides of the horse's neck, she put them up almost on the mane."

little "feel" on the horse's mouth; that is, riding on contact. Several strides before the jump, she gets up in jump position, catches the mane and jumps that way, with the reins looping. An advanced rider might do the same thing on a "green"—that is, unschooled—colt. We'll explain why when we get into schooling. At this point, I just want you to see the several steps, if Nancy can show them.

Next, let's try the jump on an intermediate level. This may not come out too well as Nancy is just *beginning* to attempt this in her own classes, but we'll see how it goes. This time she will attempt to let her hands *slide along the sides of the horse's neck,* following the gestures (the movement, that is) of the horse's head, and taking a very slight support from the neck. Go ahead, Nancy, and try. It's a little easier to get the feel moving at a canter than at a trot and also over a little higher jump; that's why she is cantering toward that post and rail jump. . . . No, that didn't work, did it? Could you all see what happened? Instead of sliding her hands

and arms forward along the sides of the horse's neck, she put them up
almost on the mane. It isn't easy to make the transition, when it has been
practiced so many months the other way. Nancy will be working on this
particular technique in her own classes for quite a while before she can
manage to jump with hands and arms sliding forward, *habitually* following the gesture of the horse's head and neck.

Photo by Cosner

Colonel Alex Sysin on *Light Heart demonstrates* "following hands and arms"
beautifully.

Let's give credit where it is due, though—she did manage to stay up out
of the saddle all through the jump, and in landing, and did not interfere
in any way with the horse's free movement.

Try once again, Nancy. That was better, although far from perfect. We
won't spend any more time trying to demonstrate this technique today.

Well, you have seen the jump on the beginner level and an attempt
at the intermediate level, and of course we will have to omit the advanced
level. I'll explain it to you, but none of our riders are up to demonstrating it just yet. This is "following through the air" over a jump, and it takes
quite a few years of practice to do it well. On an advanced level, not only
must the rider keep his seat out of the saddle in jumping position through-

out, but at the same time must have the seat and legs so strong and secure that he is able to maintain the position while his arms reach out and follow the gestures of the horse's head and neck through the air. Therefore he gets no support either from the saddle or from the horse's neck. I asked Sally to bring up a photo that illustrates these points very nicely. Gather around and take a look. Until you try it yourself, you can't begin to appreciate how much practice such form takes. I will be pleased if any of you can do this well in four years.

Well, riders, that is it for the morning. Thank you very much, Nancy. You were nice to leave your own class and come and fill in for Frances. I expect you have had enough and I'm sure everyone's brains are crammed sufficiently for one session. Let's go have some lunch.

She was right. Our brains were crammed, and the prospect of lunch sounded wonderful.

QUIZ FOR CHAPTERS II AND III

To be scored as two (2) quizzes, one of sixteen (16) parts, and the other of seventeen (17) parts.

Mark as correct *one statement only.*

1. An adult male horse of the type used for general riding is called a:
    a. gilding
    b. gelding
    c. stallion
2. An adult female horse is called a:
    a. lady
    b. mare
    c. vixen
3. A female horse is called a filly until she is:
    a. three
    b. five
    c. seven
4. Stallions are used mainly for:
    a. foxhunting
    b. breeding—that is to be fathers, or sires
    c. nice pleasure hacks
5. Until he is five, the male horse is a:
    a. foal
    b. yearling
    c. colt

6. In measuring a horse you measure from the:
   a. poll to the ground
   b. croup to the ground
   c. withers to the ground

7. In measuring a horse you say he is 15 or 16:
   a. feet
   b. hands
   c. fingers

8. A hand is:
   a. six inches
   b. four inches
   c. two inches

9. The horse spoken of as a hunter is a:
   a. breed
   b. type
   c. color

10. The saddle horse or saddle type can be spotted by:
    a. his way of moving with long low efficient strides
    b. his high head carriage and high action
    c. his ability as a cross country horse
    d. the fact that he wears a saddle

11. Ponies are distinguished from horses by:
    a. a dividing line on size
    b. small ears and fine muzzles
    c. fine silky coats

12. A pony may not be more than:
    a. 15 hands
    b. 14 hands 2 inches
    c. 12 hands 2 inches

13. The horse's natural gaits are the:
    a. trot, rack and canter or gallop
    b. trot, pace and canter or gallop
    c. walk, trot and canter or gallop

14. The rider normally posts at the:
    a. walk
    b. trot
    c. rack
    d. canter

15. Posting means:
    a. bouncing naturally on the end of your spine
    b. going up and down with the rhythm of the beat of the trot
    c. riding up out of the saddle as if you had thumb tacks in it

16. When you say that your horse is a "nice hack" you mean that he is:
    a. particularly good at jumping

    b. a good foxhunter

    c. a pleasant mount at gaits

17. The beginner should ride with:

    a. loose reins because it looks so casual

    b. with the reins tight to have something on which to balance

    c. with reins loose, catching mane where necessary to steady himself, so that the horse can move his head and neck freely

18. Riding on contact means:

    a. riding with tight reins so that the horse can't run away with you

    b. shortening the reins until the slack is taken up and then letting the horse pull your hands back and forth by the movement of head and neck

    c. riding so that you sit very close to your horse.

19. The horse's head and neck move the least at the:

    a. walk

    b. trot

    c. canter

    d. gallop

20. Jumping on an intermediate level means that you:

    a. jump with the reins looping

    b. let your hands slide along the horse's neck, following the gestures of the head and neck

    c. can now jump high jumps

21. When you jump properly on "an advanced level" you:

    a. follow the gestures of the horse's head and neck through the air without steadying yourself on his neck

    b. grab the mane so that you will not interfere with the gestures of head and neck

    c. jump big fences on high ground

22. As you go over the jump you should:

    a. sit down in the saddle

    b. come down with a definite thud so the horse knows he has a rider on him who will demand obedience

    c. stay up with your seat out of the saddle in jumping position

23. When you put the horse's saddle and bridle on you say that you are:

    a. hacking up

    b. dressing him

    c. tacking up

24. A halter is what one puts on the horse's head to use for:

    a. riding him

    b. catching, handling or leading him

    c. throwing him while his feet are being cleaned

25. When you put the saddle on, it is a good idea to:

    a. tighten the girth quickly so that the horse can't buck the saddle off

      b. tighten the girth softly and slowly

      c. jerk the girth up abruptly to let him know who is boss

26. When you put the saddle on you should:

      a. put it in the middle of his back and slip it forward

      b. place it on the horse's back well forward and close to the withers so that as it settles into place it will not rub the hairs the wrong way

27. When you put the bridle on you should open the horse's mouth by:

      a. banging the bit against his teeth

      b. blowing up his nose

      c. slipping your fingers in the sides of his mouth where he has no teeth

28. As you prepare to mount you measure the length you will want your stirrups against:

      a. your arm's length

      b. your eye's guess

      c. a yard measure

29. As you mount you normally stand at the:

      a. shoulder, facing the quarters

      b. quarters, facing the forehand

30. You normally mount from the:

      a. left side

      b. right side

      c. leap-frogging over the rump

31. As you prepare to mount:

      a. have the reins exactly even

      b. shorten the rein on the mounting side so that the horse can watch what you are doing

      c. shorten the rein on the off side so the horse can't take a nip out of the seat of your pants

32. The left side is called the:

      a. near side

      b. off side

      c. close side

33. The "bight" of the reins means the part:

      a. horses love to nibble

      b. that joins the bit

      c. that, in riding, is "left over" between your hands and the end of the reins

CHAPTER IV

Get There with *Your Horse!*

Lunch hour was over and at last we were to ride! If I hadn't been so terribly keen to learn everything I could about horses and riding, it would have been a blow to be put in a class of "Advanced Beginners"—that is, riders who were just beginning to be fairly steady at a canter, when I knew I could stick on like a bur at a gallop or ride over a three foot fence. The difference was, of course, that these riders had had help and criticism from the very beginning and so had not had a chance to acquire the bad habits I had. It was explained to me that first day that while I was a far stronger rider than most of the others in our group, I must spend a few weeks (or months, perhaps?) in what was termed a "position" group.

A little at a time, the teaching methods of the school began to make sense to me. The starting point for all new untrained riders like myself, and for all beginners, *was first of all* to establish a "seat" that was strong and secure; that would not disturb the horse, and that would make it possible to use what are termed "the aids" efficiently. I learned that "aids" meant my hands, legs and voice. I discovered that good style and form in riding *did not mean* riding to look pretty; it meant riding in a way that made it possible for the horse to perform at his best. That idea appealed to me.

In the year I had had *Trigger,* I had learned everything I knew from my young "cowboy" companions, and I did all sorts of dreadful things— I "flapped" like mad as I cantered, arms working back and forth like wings; I rocked back in the saddle and, of course, I hurt my pony's mouth as a result. I had ridden bareback so much that I was used to wrapping my legs around my mount with toes pointing down, instead of taking advantage of the stirrups. I found that I did ABSOLUTELY EVERYTHING WRONG!

To make things worse, I was taken off *Trigger,* because the instructor said he wasn't completely "stabilized." This means that he wouldn't work in a ring with a group of other horses and ponies holding nice steady gaits while the reins remained loose. Well, of course he wouldn't, I told myself defensively; after all you don't canter or even trot much when you

31

Photo by Marler

Terry Milton demonstrates stabilization. Here *Gazelle* maintains an even canter on completely loose reins.

Courtesy of Frances and Homer Heller

Mary Lou Walters on *Little Mingo* shows that her mare will maintain even speed and gait even when the rider folds her arms.

are a plow pony. He was wonderful to do it at all, even though I did have to use a little switch to make him gallop—or canter as they called it in the school.

While I was secretly offended at the slight to *Trigger,* it was easy to see the advantage of having the sort of "stabilized" horses the school used in these "position" classes. As you will find in Chapter VIII you will be able to "stabilize" your horse or pony at home. It isn't very difficult and it's fun to do. Since I was to concentrate on *me* it was wonderful to be on a horse who seemed to "go by himself." These horses kept their position in class with reins completely loose, and responded to voice commands. Can you believe it? It fascinated me, too, that they could be got in such a *frame of mind* that they would stay agreeable when I knew that legs nudging them and seats pounding them (as beginners do) could not be too comfortable. Of course, I was just beginning to see these things when they were pointed out to me, and I was constantly amazed that I had never noticed all the things which had been going on under my very nose!

Incidentally, as far as the horses' attitudes were concerned I soon began to learn that no one should ride a horse very long without beginning to understand what made him "tick."

But for the moment, we must drill, drill, drill on POSITION. We were insulted, praised, ridiculed, encouraged, needled, and in general whipped into some sort of shape. A few couldn't stand the gaff and dropped out, but most of our group began to develop what the school called "a pretty decent design" before the spring was over.

In order to understand why we sit on our horses as we do, we found that we must understand what happens when the horse moves. Just as with us when we walk and our weight falls first on one foot and then on the other, so the weight of the horse, when moving, constantly switches back and forth. Just the same, there is such a thing as the average point of the horse's balance if he is allowed to move naturally, as he moves when unbothered by a rider. *This point of balance is not in the middle of the horse's body,* as I had imagined, but *closer to the front, just behind the withers.* And since the horse's front (forehand) is also his strongest part, it certainly made sense to hear that the rider's weight should be as far forward and close to the pommel (the front) of the saddle as possible. This is where the horse will feel it the least, and where it will be directly over his balance line. I accepted this idea with great enthusiasm, as I knew that soon I would be getting too big for my pony, and certainly wanted to do everything I could to make his job of carrying me around simpler.

Then it was pointed out to us that we must not only sit so that our

Behind feet   Over balanced   Balanced over feet in
                                             the position one would
                                             have at a standstill

Sketches by Mrs. Richard Ruffner

weight was right over our mount's center balance point, but that we ourselves must be balanced over our feet in such a way that if the horse mysteriously vanished into thin air we would land on the ground on our feet, not our faces or our backs.

I can see our instructor now, demonstrating BALANCE OVER THE FEET in a dozen different ways. She would pretend to be hitting a tennis ball, throwing a basket ball, ice skating, bicycling, to show how one must stay balanced over his feet or topple either forwards or backwards.

Courtesy of Gertrude and Walker Ridgely

Rider nicely balanced over her feet. "Then a good rider demonstrated these same points on a horse."

And then she would demonstate how, as one runs or moves faster, he leans more forward, and as he slows down how the weight comes back to its original position. On rainy days or in rest periods we studied pictures of people on skis and then compared them with pictures of people on horses. We made a little stick man from pipe cleaners. First a flap was made for his feet, which would serve as his "base of support." Then, because he was to be crouching a little, a bend was made for his knees and then we saw that to keep him from toppling over, another bend must be made for his hips. We could see that if you pushed him together a little in one place, you must push him together in another, too—in other words, if he was still to stand alone, all the angles became sharper—the same as with us on our horses, if we stayed balanced over our feet when stirrups were shortened. As someone said, when our stirrups were shortened, we were like "pushed together accordions" and when lengthened we should become "pulled out accordions."

The other point that was stressed over and over again, along with balance and the FORWARDNESS of it, was a term that I used earlier and that gradually came to take on real meaning, and that was having a secure "base of support."

This meant, just as with our stick man, having something under you to put your feet on and to support your weight, like a floor. On ice skates, the skates form your base of support; on a bicycle (when you get up and pump, clearing the seat) the pedals; when you run, the ground; and when you ride, the stirrups. Now our pipe cleaner man was put on a miniature toy horse kept to demonstrate, and we couldn't help seeing that his position, balanced in the stirrups, was just the same as when we stood him up in his crouching position on a table. We saw that his stirrup leathers would hang straight down and his lower leg would be a little back. Then a good rider demonstrated these same points on a horse.

Only a complete moron could have failed to get the idea of being balanced over the feet, keeping a secure base of support by having lots of weight down in the stirrups and leaning farther forward to stay balanced when moving faster.

CHAPTER V

Drive Your Heels Down and Weight Forward!

Yes, only a complete moron could fail to *see* it, but doing it was another story. To try to get it, we had to practice riding in what was called "gallop" or "jump" position, part of every class period. This is what we were told to do. "Catch a piece of mane in your hands about half way up the horse's neck (that is, at the crest) and stand up in your stirrups. Now, still holding the mane to steady yourself, sink down so that you have a bend at your knees and your seat *just* clears the saddle. As you ride, pretend that you have thumb tacks, points up, in your saddle. Don't sit on those thumb tacks!"

We found, riding this way, we could not use our horses to prop us up. We realized that this is what happens when we get "behind our feet"—that is, behind that balance point we have been talking so much about.

We must hold this position, keeping the ankle joints soft and springy; we must keep our heels driven well down with our feet lying against the inside of our stirrups and the tread of the stirrup just back of the balls of our feet. Our toes should turn *slightly* out—about 35° we were told. We

Approximately correct

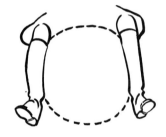

Legs approximately correct – feet approximately 30° or 35° East and West. Feet could have a little greater "break" at the ankle.

Sketches in Chapter Courtesy of Mrs. Richard Ruffner

must keep our heads up, shoulders open and backs hollow. Our upper legs, inner surfaces of knees and upper part of calves must lie snugly against the sides of the saddle.

At first we practiced this exercise steadying ourselves on the horse's neck, but very soon we were expected to do it with hands on either side of, but not touching, the horse's withers. If you do this for any length of time you begin to find the balance point in yourself. It's like standing alone on a seesaw and balancing it. Incidentally, it is possible to maintain a gallop position with the legs wrong—either too far in front of you or too far behind you—by pinching like fury with the knees, because that is what I started doing. But you can't maintain it very long. As you begin to get tired and relax a little, and try to really find your balance, usually everything falls into place. The good design becomes the line of least resistance. When you can be relaxed and comfortable and hold this position for five or ten minutes at a time, I'll bet you that things will fall into place. Your overall "design" will be about correct.

All during these position classes, we were required to ride with the reins loose, using our voices as much as possible to control our horses. If

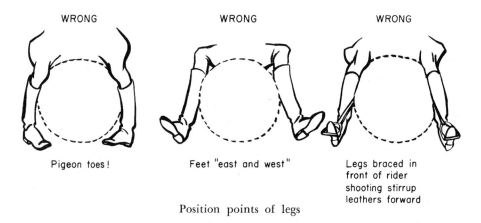

WRONG   WRONG   WRONG

Pigeon toes!   Feet "east and west"   Legs braced in
                                                    front of rider
                                                    shooting stirrup
                                                    leathers forward

Position points of legs

voice didn't work (for example, if the horse didn't stop on the command "Ho!") then we must give a short quick tug or little jerk on the reins, hard enough to make the horse pay attention to what we told him. We were never to be any rougher than we had to be, but we were to be *just exactly as rough as the horse made us be*. In other words, we must never *nag* and encourage *disobedience* by constantly pulling and hauling at our horses. We must demand and get obedience in the first place. We must mean what we say and stick to it through thick or thin, *never* letting the horse imagine that he could "bluff us out" of what we said in the beginning.

Have you ever seen a small child on a pony, pulling and struggling to get the pony to go where she wants him to, and the pony setting his jaw and pulling back, knowing that he stands a 50–50 chance of getting his own way? Riding him becomes a constant struggle between the two, and a smart pony, with a typical pony sense of humor, may even try to rub his rider off on every tree.

I had seen a lot of this, so I took to heart the instructions: "Don't nag. If, for example, the horse tries to cut into the center of the ring, give as sharp a jerk as you need and then *right away* let the reins go loose again so that he sees that life is more pleasant when he obeys." This made good sense to me.

I said that during position classes we were to ride with reins loose as much as possible. Remember, I explained that most of the group, when I joined them, were just beginning to get fairly steady at a canter, and nobody's seat and legs were completely fixed. If the bottom of the whole

thing (the base of support) isn't fixed and steady naturally the top couldn't be. This meant that the upper body would undoubtedly wobble and the hands fly around and do things they weren't meant to do.

We were required to keep our hands on the horse's neck when first practicing posting and cantering in a correct forward position. Have you ever seen a rider *using the reins to steady himself?* I guess he just never thought about the fact that the reins are attached to a bit, the bit is in the horse's mouth, and that each time he rises, pulling himself up by the reins, all his weight goes Whambo! right against the horse's mouth.

For this reason we were required to ride with loose reins until our legs and seats were completely steady, secure and fixed in a good strong position, because then and only then would we be able to *make our hands behave exactly as we wanted them to without regard to what the rest of our bodies were doing.* When that time arrived, we would be ready to start learning CONTACT. This will be explained in detail when we get to it.

All this time, it was still drill, drill, drill, on POSITION. We had to
take turns acting as leader in the class, holding a steady posting trot

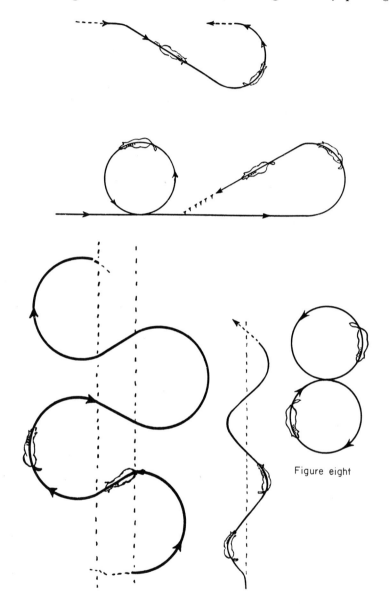

Figure eight

round and round the ring, leading large "figure eights" made by executing two "Change direction" commands (see diagram), then circling to the
rear and the next rider leading. We practiced position at a canter, singly,
in groups of two or three, and then, if that went well, as an entire class.

We made elementary half circles, very large, at first at a walk, then at a trot (see diagram). We rode large fat serpentines, zigzags, and circles (diagram). These were called lessons in GUIDANCE as well as in POSITION.

It was constantly stressed that no matter what the top of our bodies did, our legs and seats must stay put, over a strong base of support. Trying to keep heels down and legs still with lots of weight in the stirrups, we rode bending down and touching our toes. We rode in jumping position with our arms outstretched. We dropped stirrups and picked them up without hitching the knee up, just raising the toes and feeling for the stirrup, so that we would not alter our body position at all. We were told we must learn to sit in such a way that if the horse bucked, shied, or if we lost a stirrup over a fence, our seats would stay secure and our hands would be able to do exactly what we wanted them to do.

Frequently our class was divided into two sections and we had to observe and "judge" one another. Was the rider's head up and looking straight ahead, or was it crooked, throwing the whole picture out of focus? Was the back hollow, inclined a little forward in a nice active

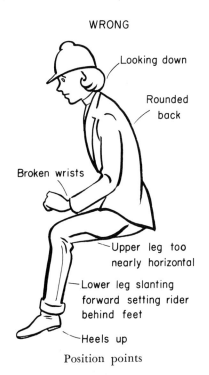

WRONG

Looking down

Rounded back

Broken wrists

Upper leg too nearly horizontal

Lower leg slanting forward setting rider behind feet

Heels up

Position points

position, or did a rounded back spoil the design? Did the arms hang loosely to the elbow, or were the arms rigid and hands dropped too low? Was there a nice smooth line through the wrist, or did the rider have "broken wrists" (diagram) which would rob his hands of any elasticity? Was the rider forward on the front of his seat (pelvic bones) or did he sit on his tail bone, again throwing the whole structure out of balance? And then the legs and feet—were the feet a little behind the knees with the rider's lower leg back just enough to permit the stirrup to serve as a floor? Were his feet in the stirrups with the tread under (or just behind) the balls of his feet, in that ideal position to balance? We found that feet thrust too far in the stirrup robbed the ankle of any elasticity or spring; if they were not far enough in, there would be all sorts of spring (enough, in fact, to bounce you all over your horse), but no steadi-

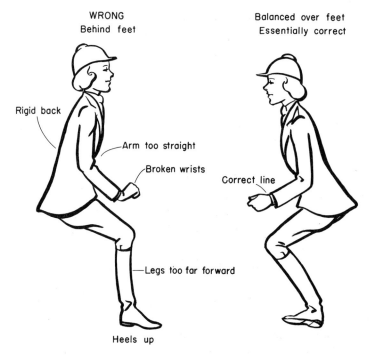

Position points

Photo by Marler

Sophie Connery, with knees sticking out. Just look at the daylight between her knees and the saddle!

ness. Were the feet lying close against the inside of the irons, with a little bend at the ankles that rolled the soles of the feet out, and the knees in? Were the inside portions of upper legs (thighs), knees and upper calves lying snugly against the sides of the saddle?

We began to develop quite an eye for seeing what was wrong, and were supposed to make suggestions as to what might help the faults we found in each other.

Sophie Connery's knees would stick out, away from her saddle— what might help? Make her post without stirrups about ten minutes out of each class period, came someone's heartless suggestion. Show her how to lean down and pull the round muscle of the upper leg back and flatten the knee against the side of the saddle.

Meg Hanover, looking at the ground, with back rounded and heels coming up!

Meg Hanover had quite a trick of looking at the ground. We urged Meg to fix her eyes on the dairy barn across the valley as she rode down the track, and on the cupola of our stable coming back. But Meg had to learn the hard way, as you will find out in the next chapter.

"Fred Compton, so relaxed that his back was rather like wet spaghetti, and who was always behind his feet . . ." Notice how the pony's mouth is being pulled as a result.

Fred Compton, who was so relaxed that his back was rather like wet spaghetti, and who was always behind his feet, got the classic cure: "gallop position" with arms outstretched for fifteen minutes out of every hour.

Greta Stillway, who had ridden in Japan before she came to Douglas School of Horsemanship, had a very snappy design, but it was too stiff—sort of frozen looking—as though if she should be removed from her horse by a huge pair of tongs, she would come off still in the same position. Get up in gallop position, Greta, we suggested, and then bounce a little as you stay up—sort of jiggle at the knees. Now sit down and drop your stirrups and ride a while that way. Now back in gallop position jiggling at the knees.

As for me, I had all sorts of problems. My stirrups rattled, because of the way I pinched with my knees and failed to use my lower legs or put any weight in the stirrups. Loosen up at the knee joint, Kit, I was told, and let your weight drop down into your stirrups. Ride in gallop position. Stop flapping your elbows! Stay in gallop position and ride with your arms folded and your elbows in against your sides. Stop twisting, Kit. That isn't helping the horse to move. Your lower leg is swinging back, Kit; get it out of the horse's ribs! And so it went, day after day. A little at a time my position began to improve although five years later, riding in advanced horsemanship classes, I still have my problems. You'll probably see my lower leg too far back in all my later pictures.

QUIZ FOR CHAPTERS IV AND V

To be scored as two (2) quizzes of ten (10) parts each.

In some instances all three answers may be true but you are to select the *one statement* that is the *most pertinent*.

1. Mastery of basic form is important because it:
    a. makes the rider look pretty
    b. enables the rider to do a more competent job
    c. gives the horse a sense of security
2. A horse at a standstill carries about:
    a. sixty (60) percent of his weight on his forehand
    b. one half his weight on his forehand
    c. forty (40) percent of his weight on his forehand
3. His center of balance at gaits is:
    a. toward his front, just back of the withers
    b. directly through his center line
    c. in the general direction of his quarters
4. The rider, in order to unite his center of balance with that of the horse should sit:

    a. as close to the withers and to the pommel of the saddle as possible

    b. exactly centered over the middle of the horse

    c. a little back toward the cantle so that his weight will be over the horse's loins

5. Another reason that the rider will sit as you have indicated in the previous statement is due to the fact that the horse's strongest portion is:

    a. toward the forehand, immediately behind the withers

    b. about the center of the horse's body

    c. toward the quarters and over the loins

6. The rider should not only unite his center of balance with the horse but he should sit:

    a. a little behind his feet to insure greater security

    b. directly over his feet to be balanced himself

    c. a little in front of his feet to make it easier to grab mane

7. Your stirrup leathers should always:

    a. slant a little forward

    b. hang approximately vertical

    c. slant back towards horse's ribs

There are certain points of position which you should know by heart together with the reasons.

8. The head should be:

    a. tilted a little forward and down so that you may watch the terrain

    b. a little to the side so that you will not risk being bumped in the nose if the horse throws his head up

    c. erect and straight so that you may watch the horse's head and neck, maintain proper balance and see where your horse is going

9. Shoulders should be:

    a. comfortably rounded for proper relaxation

    b. open to aid balance and help keep body in an alert position

    c. held stiffly back so that one has a military bearing

10. Arms should:

    a. hang to elbow and be bent at the elbow

    b. be held straight forward in front of the rider, forming a straight line from shoulder to wrist

    c. with elbows just a little back of rider's body

11. Torso (upper body):

    a. stiff and erect

    b. relaxed and alert and inclined a little forward

    c. rounded and swaying a little to the rear

12. The rider should sit:

    a. a little forward on pelvic bones

    b. on tail bone with buttocks tucked under him

13. Thigh, inner surface of knee and upper calf should:
    a. lie just a little away from the horse's side and the saddle so that their contact will not upset the horse
    b. maintain contact with the saddle to create a firm leg
14. The foot should be placed in the stirrup with the tread of the stirrup:
    a. under the instep
    b. under or slightly behind the ball of the foot
    c. with the toe only in the stirrup so that rider will not tangle up if he falls
15. Rider's feet should lie against the:
    a. inside of his irons to keep legs steady
    b. on the outside of the irons so that he may use the inside of his irons as spurs
16. Toes should be:
    a. exactly parallel with horse's body
    b. turned in
    c. turned out about thirty-five (35) degrees
17. Heels should be:
    a. up to give rider more spring
    b. down to harden calf and provide a secure base of support
18. The beginner and low intermediate should ride with reins:
    a. tight in order to steady himself
    b. loose to permit the horse free use of his head and neck
    c. tight to keep the horse from stumbling
19. As the horse moves faster the rider should:
    a. increase the forward leaning of the body in order to remain in balance with his mount
    b. stay straight and erect as he was at the slower gait
    c. lean a little backwards to lessen the effects of the wind in his face
20. When you say that a horse is stabilized you mean:
    a. that he always is thinking of, and wanting to go home to the stable
    b. that he will maintain even speeds at all gaits on loose reins

CHAPTER VI

Even Beginners Jump

I had been in for all sorts of surprises at DSH, one of the biggest being that these other children who had just learned to canter had begun what the school called "pre-jumping" or "crossing little rails" even before they cantered, and they looked much better at it than I did.

This is the way it would go. As we trotted around the ring, the class would get the command "Get up in gallop (or jump) position. Grab the mane as you do it." Fifteen or twenty seconds later we would get the command, "Resume posting." When everyone was doing this automatically, one or two little rails would be set out on the track, with one end on the ground, the other at the dizzy height of about a foot. Now we would get the command "Jumping position" about ten feet before the rail, and "Resume posting" some ten feet on the other side of it. Woe and double woe to him who failed to hang onto his "hunk of mane" and snapped back on the reins and caught his horse in the mouth. That was CRIME NUMBER ONE. I can hear the Voice ringing out like a pistol shot, "Either gr-rab the mane, or get off the horse. No matter how good you think you are, grab it and hang on to it! I will not have the horse's mouth abused because you want to show off." The Voice could sound unbelievably vicious; we would be electrified into doing what it said, and then the whole matter would begin to come out better.

Starting over those tiny jumps that the horses couldn't possibly object to crossing, made it so simple that it wasn't long before the whole class was "jumping" two foot jumps. Then we would start riding miniature courses (that is, four or more jumps, rather than just single obstacles) about two feet high, and would trot over them as a drill—doing it round and round. This seemed to hypnotize the horses into remaining calm and adopting an "Oh! What-the-heck-this-is-rather-dull-and-certainly-very-simple-business" attitude. Sometimes the horses would become really bored and careless and not bother to pick up their feet. Then an instructor would stand beside various jumps with a long whip in hand, or give the rider a little crop to carry.

We also did hours of "cavaletti," which seemed to me, personally, to provide the best situation in which to practice the form I needed so badly.

47

This is the way cavaletti works. Six or eight poles are laid on the ground about four feet three inches apart (or at whatever distance best fits the horse's stride), and opposite the last will be a pair of standards. The horse is supposed to trot, trot, trot, putting one foot down between each pole. If he puts in an extra stride between poles, the cavaletti is too long for him, and the poles have to be brought a little closer together—or he has to be waked up a little if he was getting in the extra stride because he was just "loafing" along so that he didn't move his legs properly.

Photo by Marler

Class riding over cavaletti. Note the loose reins permitting the ponies free use of head and neck.

The rider gets up in jumping position a few feet before the first pole, grabs the mane, leaving the reins looping, drives his heels down, and looks up. He must stay *just like that* until a few strides after the last pole, when he resumes posting again. He must hold a nice steady trot all the way around and again a nice steady trot through the cavaletti.

About now someone on the ground will raise one end of the last pole onto the lowest peg of the standard, approximately a foot off the ground. Horse and rider will continue to do just what they have been doing. Then the other end is raised, and as this is done, making a little jump, the person handling the rails must increase the space between the last rail on the ground and the jump. How much it is increased depends on the stride of the horse, and this you can learn only by watching from the ground. You want to give the horse sufficient room for a comfortable little jump. That's all. As the jump is raised a little more, the person on the ground continues to increase the distance between the last pole on the ground and the jump, so that a "just right" arc for a jump of each size is permitted. Doing it this way, the rails are sort of sneaked up on you, and neither the horse nor rider realizes that they are beginning to jump a little higher. Riders and horses all get hypnotized together. It was over cavaletti that the jumps first reached the height of three feet for the class as a group.

It was over cavaletti, too, that we seemed best able to work on avoiding CRIME NUMBER TWO: Thumping down on the horse's back. Incidentally, I think it is remarkable to notice how many riders do this in ad-

Photo by Marler

This is the way the jump looks with the last pole raised to about three feet.

vanced horsemanship classes, over big jumps, or out hunting. Of course, it's not the easiest thing in the world to keep your seat out of the saddle (who should know better than I?) as the horse begins the descent, lands and gallops away, but surely if it is practiced from the very beginning, it's not really impossible! (Captain Ringrose, of the Irish Army Team demonstrates that fact better than anyone I have ever watched.) In addition to the fact that you may give your horse a sore back, "thumping down" many times will knock the horse's hind legs right into the jump.

After the two foot jumps taken as a class drill and the three foot cavaletti had become routine, our next assignment was to jump individually. This, of course, was harder; in class formation, if you had a good leader, the horses found it easier to follow than not, but now for the first time over jumps riders had to "ride" their mounts a little, or introduce a certain amount of CONTROL. Everyone had previously taken turns at leading figure eights, etc., on the flat, but even these little jumps made the situation quite different. I had generally acted as leader in the drill classes over rails, as my control was a little stronger than my position.

Now, at last, the chance was being offered me to "ride a course" individually, and I became carried away with my idea of what was to be a brilliant, flashing round—although I knew we weren't supposed to be brilliant. The jumps had been set up to two feet nine inches in honor of my greater experience, and I was back on my heart's love, *Trigger*. In my eagerness, I began to "gun" my pony in my best cowboy style, flap my elbows, throw my legs and heels up into poor *Trigger's* ribs, and in general must have looked like Ichabod Crane doing acrobatics. I was not the star of the class that day.

We had excellent opportunities in these beginner jumping classes to see what happens when the basic rules of "form" are ignored. These classes made it much clearer that the real purpose of "form" was to enable you and the horse to do the job better.

In class with us was eight-year-old, Meg Hanover, who was so tiny, blonde and fragile in appearance that she made you think of a little Dresden china doll. Her personality was altogether different; she had all the courage and determination in the world, and everyone felt that she had the makings of a real rider. She was generally assigned to *Sauce Box,* the jumpingest jumping bean in the shape of an 11 hand pony anyone ever saw. *Saucy* was so steady and consistent that he was used in these beginner jumping classes, but when his short pony neck reached out and down over a jump, he was hard to stick on. If Meg looked down instead of up (and this was her besetting sin) and let her legs slide even a little bit back out of place with heels coming up, it was as if a curve was commenced which could end only one place—on the ground. It would, too, every time. While it was an excellent demonstration to those of us who watched, because we could really *see* what happened when the head goes down and heels come up, it was a rugged way of learning for poor Meg! She was off *Saucy* three times one afternoon before she finally got the knack of driving heels down hard and fixing her eyes on some point over his head. Since she had such a tough time in the beginning, I think it's nice to know that in the next two years *Saucy* and Meg became a winning combination in all small pony jumper classes in our state.

We also saw what happens from the opposite fault—sitting back and getting "left." Fred, the boy whom I said before was so "relaxed," got caught sitting on the end of his spine at the take-off and simply could not make a forward thrust with his pony. He was bounced off her and tossed neatly through the air more than once before he finally got the feel of stepping down in his stirrups, gripping with his legs and leaning forward.

These two riders demonstrated falls from two mistakes that were exactly opposite—one rider getting too far forward and toppling over the pony's head; the other being "left behind" so that the jump flipped him off.

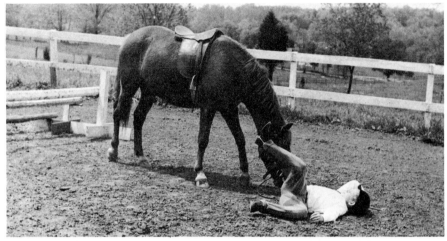

"He was bounced off and tossed neatly through the air more than once until . . ."

"He finally got the feel of stepping down in the stirrups, gripping with his knees and leaning forward."

The way I have put this, it sounds as if our next step from doing cavaletti and crossing little rails in class formation was to ride courses, but this was not exactly the case.

Before we rode anything that could be called a course we rode over individual low jumps by ourselves; then over two, and sometimes these two formed little in-and-outs (two jumps set just far enough apart to allow the horse one stride between), with the first bar of the in-and-out

Courtesy of Gertrude and Walker Ridgely

Sophie Connery demonstrates jumping on a beginner level, reins looping and holding the mane, to spare the mouth. But few things come out perfectly—as you see, the knees still stick out! Also, Sophie is jumping without a hard hat on, which is contrary to our school rules.

generally keeping one end on the ground. I mention this to show how slowly we were allowed to take each new step. While I was all impatience at the time, I realize now that this must have been the reason that when we went to shows our riders and horses performed quietly and confidently, and made such a nice appearance. We were always told that *it didn't matter how long it took us to accomplish the next step, as long as we did each step well.*

CHAPTER VII

Horse Sense

When I had been taking lessons at DSH for several weeks, I got up one Saturday morning to hear a steady rain beating on my windowpane. "Timed just right," I told myself. We were a little overdue for a "theory" class in the club room at the stable. This one was to be a lecture on how the horse's mind works and how it follows that he can be trained to do what we wish him to do.

I was sure that I understood how *Trigger* felt on every subject, but I was anxious to find out if he was typical, or if he was the unusual "character" I believed him to be.

When we were all comfortably situated with paper and pencil in our club room, just down the aisle from the stalls, the lecture commenced. From the shocked expressions on the faces of some of my friends it was easy to see that they were a bit outraged, just as I was, at what we all felt were slighting comments on our horses' mental powers. But the longer I listened, the more I had to admit that what was said made sense, and that perhaps we had all been "wishing" qualities into our adored mounts.

Here is the gist of the lecture which I have tried to put together from the notes I took that day:

Horses are not the most intelligent of animals. They can't reason out their problems very carefully. If the stable catches on fire, for example, and you open the stall doors, they will not try to escape. They cannot seem to understand the obvious fact that staying in means death, and just outside the open door is safety.

If your horse slipped away from you out on a trail where you had dismounted, let's say, to fasten a gate, and trotted merrily off without you (which he might do, hungry and eager to get home to supper) at no point on his route home will he stop and say "Goodness! My old friend who feeds me is back there on the trail I had better go back and get him." He will continue on home and if no one is there will stand for hours outside the closed stable door, pawing impatiently. He is unable to understand that the person he left miles out on the trail isn't there to feed him.

The fact that horses aren't highly intelligent does not make them any less fun for us. Indeed it makes them more fun. Undoubtedly, but for that fact and a few other qualities we will discuss, they wouldn't permit us to ride them long hours at times when they would prefer to be grazing, or over high fences which they have no interest in taking. After all, horses are beautiful, graceful, trainable. They provide us with some of the happiest moments of life. So let's understand and appreciate them as they are, not as we would like to pretend that they are.

Sketches in Chapter Courtesy of Mrs. Richard Ruffner

First of all, *horses are timid.* Their main protection, when wild, was flight. Try waving a flapping cloth at a group of horses in a field, and generally they will gallop madly away. Dogs, in the same case, in all probability would come up and catch the cloth in their teeth to play. If you are riding, and your horse hears a rustling in the bushes, his first impulse is to *run.* From his point of view, that rustling might mean that a panther is lurking, ready to pounce on his back. Run first, and check into the situation later, says instinct.

Horses have wonderful memories. They often *remember* the place along the trail where they were frightened the day before and will be all prepared to run again. They remember which stall is theirs in the long string of stalls, all exactly alike. They remember that they are allowed to stop at the watering trough on the way out of the stable. They remember the route back home, even when the rider cannot.

Horses are very much creatures of habit. This is closely connected with their good memories. They get into the *habit* of going to a certain stall.

They get into the habit of stopping at the watering trough, even when they aren't thirsty. They get into the habit of being turned out in the field in front of the stable instead of the field behind it. When it's time to rotate the fields you are using for pasture, they are most reluctant to accept the change. It's as if they are saying, "No, no! Don't you remember? *This* is our grazing field."

Horses are gregarious (like company). Turn two horses out in a field, and they will, invariably, be found hobnobbing around together. When

Horses are gregarious.

"There seems to be no such thing as a lone wolf horse." In spite of the feeling one gets in this picture of aloneness in the dawn of day, *Jumping Giraffe* actually has his devoted friend, *Tango,* close at hand, but just out of the picture.

horses were wild they moved in herds for protection. Now, when you turn a group of horses out in a field, they will generally be found in companionable little groups. There seems to be no such thing as a "lone wolf" horse.

Horses are great imitators. If you are riding along a road at the head of a line of horses and your horse "shies" at (jumps away from) a piece of paper blowing along the road's edge, the horses behind him generally do the same thing. If one horse begins to buck and play in high spirits, as a group are riding, the other horses find the temptation to join the fun almost irresistible.

Horses have a strong "homing" instinct. Let's say once again that your horse gets loose, while you are off on a trail ride. He very probably will make his way straight home and right to his own stall, even though you rode out over a new trail. And undoubtedly he will take the most direct route, rather than return over a roundabout path you may have followed when you came away from the stable. (This is assuming that you are riding alone. If riding in company, the horse's herd instinct most likely will persuade him to stay around his friends until you have a chance to recover the bridle reins!)

So we have said that horses are timid, that they have good memories and easily acquire habits (good or bad), that they like company and are highly imitative, and that they have a strong homing instinct.

Then, of course, there are all sorts of other personality traits that are present in varying degrees. Horses seem to have considerable curiosity.

Watch them look over the horse newcomer the first day he appears in the riding ring with them. The new horse is definitely the "new kid at school" and is sometimes given a rough time.

Horses make strong friendships amongst themselves. You will find in your grazing groups the devoted friends who are almost inseparable. Some-

times a third horse tries to win away the friendship of one of such a pair, and then there may be real fireworks.

Horses seem capable of a certain rather limited affection for humans who understand them and treat them intelligently and well. And they

certainly grow to trust you. While your horse will never swim out into the lake where you might be screaming for help and save you, he will rub his head against you and come to your whistle if he connects you with pleasant things. He won't go even this far if he fears and dislikes you and connects you primarily with pain.

Some horses, and more frequently ponies, can figure out very simple problems. Here you find the greatest variation. A few horses, and many ponies, will be able to solve the method by which the bolt on their stall door works, and how to take it in their teeth and slide it open. The majority of horses will never even tackle this problem, but stand in their stalls, looking longingly but passively out at the green fields.

Some horses (and again more frequently ponies) have a quality which, for want of a better term, we will call "sense of humor" or whimsey. These

animals may give you a gentle and playful nip in the seat of your pants, while in the friendliest possible mood. They may then jump guiltily away as you straighten up in real or mock resentment. And in another minute they may be softly nuzzling you again to show it was all in fun anyhow. Or was it just to attract attention? Again, your horse may buck you off in an excess of high spirits and then immediately turn and look at you with big innocent, interested eyes as if to say, "My goodness! What are you doing down there?" In all probability he will stand perfectly quiet as you remount. Or, back in the stall, he may persist in picking up in his teeth the curry comb, which you momentarily laid down, and tossing it on the floor. Playing with you? It's a little hard to say, although we do know that amongst themselves the instinct to play is very strong. Just watch a group of horse "youngsters" in the field, standing up batting away at one another, nipping and madly chasing each other in all sorts of wild harum-scarum games.

We mention these personality traits so that no one will imagine that because we say that horses aren't highly intelligent animals that we mean that they are four-legged machines without personality. This is not the case at all.

You will make use of all the understanding you can acquire of your horse's instincts and personality traits in schooling him. And most of all, you will make use of one other trait that belongs to humans as well as horses. Horses, like humans, like being comfortable and do not like being hurt. *This is the basis of training, when used intelligently by the trainer.* Naturally, to do this intelligently, you must understand the other quali-ties we have described too.

The horse doesn't want to be hurt any more than you do. Since he is by nature timid and not exactly a fighter, he probably will go along with what you tell him as long as you make every step very plain and also make every step easy, physically. Be careful that you don't get your horse into a panic (he panics all too readily) because he doesn't understand what you mean, or you ask too much of him or ask it too fast.

Since he has a good memory, he will remember the things that hurt, such as a jab in the mouth because the rider "snapped back" and swung on the reins over a jump. The next time he sees a jump a little red light flicks on in his memory and says, "Better stop. Jumps hurt." And the rider is in for all sorts of trouble reassuring him on that score. On the other hand, if he is never *punished* for doing what he was asked to do (jumping in this case) but is rewarded for doing it, he will readily acquire the *habit* of taking a jump when asked. Naturally, you will not ask him to jump a fence that is too difficult for him at his stage of training. If you do, no matter how well you ride him over that fence, you *are* punishing him. If it is too high for him, he is afraid to try it. If he does try it, because you force him to, and it really is too big for him to take with physical ease, he will take it awkwardly, land awkwardly and no doubt hurt himself. Then jumping has become a punishment. And you are in for trouble which you could have avoided by using your head.

Of course, nothing will ever "follow the book" 100% and we cannot say that you will never have to use your whip in schooling a horse over fences. There may be times when he takes a notion that he would much rather "spook" at a jump than go over it. Or he may be in a lazy frame of mind, one warm spring day, and decide that it is easier to stop than to take a certain jump. In these cases, quite possibly you will have to use your whip to insist. But just be very sure that you are not punishing your horse for *your* mistake, either in judgment of his ability or through your actual riding.

Two other personality traits we mentioned earlier, gregariousness and the tendency to imitate, will act both as a help and a hindrance in riding and training. It is a great *help* that the young or excitable horse feels re-assured and soothed by working in the ring or along the trails with a quiet, steady old friend. It is a great *help* that he gains confidence to negotiate a tricky stream crossing by following another horse. It is a *hindrance* that his tendency is to gallop off because the horse in front of him did. Later on, when we have hunter exercises in the field, you will be working specifically to overcome this herd instinct.

All the other personality traits we mentioned contribute to the fascination our horses hold for us. These quirks of personality make them more interesting and ever so much fun to work with, and help keep us on our toes in adapting our schooling program to the particular horse.

Of course (concluded our lecture), none of you riders are ready to "school" a horse in any but the most elementary sense. However, it is never too soon to start *understanding* the horse you ride.

At this point I think our instructor must have noticed that we were beginning to squirm a little and look out the window at the sun which was just beginning to break through the clouds.

We were dismissed for a luncheon break and asked to meet again in an hour to go to the longeing ring. After lunch we were to observe some simple illustrations of step by step training.

QUIZ FOR CHAPTERS VI AND VII

To be scored as one (1) quiz of twelve (12) parts.
Mark as correct *one statement only.*

1. In beginning to jump, it is important that horse and rider start riding over:
    a. fairly good sized obstacles from the very beginning to learn what jumping feels like
    b. very small obstacles, taking each new step slowly
2. When doing cavaletti with a small jump at the end the horse should:
    a. canter over the bars on the ground
    b. trot over the bars on the ground
    c. walk over the bars on the ground
3. In approaching and taking a jump, it is important to:
    a. look down at the ground and the obstacle, letting the legs slide a little back towards the horse's ribs
    b. lean a little back, and shoot the legs forward
    c. maintain a forward position with head up, legs in place and heels down
4. If startled, horses are more likely to:
    a. run than to attack
    b. attack than to run

5. In general horses are:
    a. quick to forget
    b. slow to forget
6. Most horses:
    a. look eagerly for new experiences and resent routine
    b. are very much creatures of habit
7. At heart, most horses:
    a. are "lone wolves"
    b. like company
8. Horses in general are:
    a. so highly individual that if one horse does one thing, the next in line will probably do just the reverse to assert his independence
    b. highly imitative, the second frequently following the behavior of the first in line
9. If the rider becomes lost while riding and leaves it up to the horse to find the way:
    a. the horse's sense of humor will probably induce him to take the rider on a long roundabout ride
    b. the horse will probably head straight for home
10. Horses':
    a. ability to reason out their problems makes them unique amongst animals
    b. reasoning ability is, in general, rather limited
11. Horses, in general, are:
    a. somewhat limited in their affection and loyalty for a particular human
    b. so intense in their loyalty and affection for their owners that a change of owners often causes great emotional difficulties, even if the new owner treats the horse in the same manner as the former owner
12. Horses actually are:
    a. just four-legged machines without individual differences
    b. individuals in spite of somewhat limited mentality and many characteristics in common

CHAPTER VIII

Putting Horse Sense to Work

When we met after lunch, Sally Hilton was asked to bring *Penny Ante* out of her stall and explain what she was teaching her. Sally, who was one of the school's original pupils, was considered amongst its most promising riders. She had acquired the cute, cobby little mare *Penny* that spring, sold as a four-year-old, "broken to ride," but having had no systematic schooling. *Penny* was now nearing the end of her first six weeks' training.

Each horse's "kindergarten" lesson was "voice commands on a longe" (also spelled lunge), and since this method of schooling may be unfamiliar to the reader of this book, as it was to many of us, I'll try to explain it just as it was demonstrated.

Penny was led out in a "longeing caveson" (see illustration) with longe line attached. The longe line is a web line about 25 feet long, with a loop

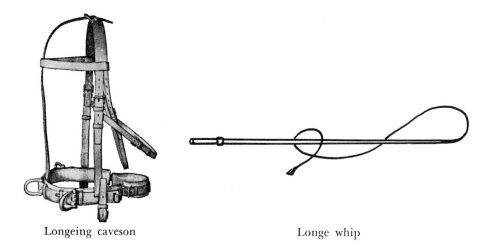

Longeing caveson   Longe whip

on one end for the "trainer's" hand and a swivel clip on the other end. The clip snaps into a ring on the nose band of the caveson.

Sally had the loop end of the line in her right hand; in her left she carried her "longeing whip" (a long whip to "back up" what she said) and in her pockets she had carrots, cut up into small pieces.

She led *Penny,* with us following, to an enclosed ring about 60 feet in diameter. Then she stood in the center of the ring and let the mare go out to the end of the line, and walk, trot, gallop, buck or play around exactly as she wished for a few minutes. It was explained that it is a good idea to let a horse get the high spirits out of his system before asking him to settle down to work.

However, the point was also made that in the case of an unbroken colt or an animal unused to much handling this would not be feasible. Such

Here Greta Stillway longes *Foolish Son* and lets him work off a little steam before he is ridden.

an animal might tangle up in the line and throw himself into a wild panic. The colt would have to work off his high spirits playing "free" in the ring. Then, too, when you first put him on the line it would be necessary to walk around with him until he got the whole idea *on a much shorter line,* and only gradually "feed it out" as he became accustomed to the feel of it. In *Penny's* case, this had not been necessary even at first because she was perfectly used to being handled and would not become upset.

(By this time Sally's mare already understood voice commands on a longe quite well, but to demonstrate to us, the lesson was presented as it had been the first day. *Penny,* having had six weeks' work could show us several consecutive steps, which brought out the points discussed better than just watching the very beginning.)

When the little mare had romped around as much as she wanted, Sally walked over to her as she had the first day to "introduce her" to the longeing whip. You do this, it was explained, so that your horse pupil will not be panicky about the whip, but will respect it. She ran the whip over *Penny's* body, and the mare remained quite unconcerned. (The first day, Sally said, she had done considerable snorting and backing away from it!)

Then Sally went back to the center of the ring, and since *Penny* happened to be turned to the left at that moment, she shifted the end of the

Photo by Marler

"She shifted her longe line into her left hand and her whip into her right."

longe line into her left hand and her whip to her right. (*Penny* longed quite well in both directions now, but again Sally was showing how the first lessons were given.) Standing in the middle of the ring she raised the line in her left hand so that it would more or less "lead" the horse. The right hand followed *Penny* up with the whip pointed at her quarters just enough to induce her to start walking; at the same second she said "walk" in a clear distinct voice. As the mare circled the ring and was almost back to the gate she had entered, it was easy to see that she was slowing down and considering stopping (the old homing instinct at work!), So instead of urging her on as she actually had in later classes, Sally quickly said "Ho!" in a low clear voice. *Penny* stopped, as she had hoped to do anyway, and as she did, Sally immediately moved over to her, and gave her a carrot piece, patting and praising her.

In *Penny's* first lesson, these two words were all that were worked on, over and over, at first always giving her the command "Ho" at that moment at the gate where it was her inclination to stop anyway. Each time she stopped, the voice command was given just before she managed to stop of her own accord and then she was rewarded.

It didn't take long for her to figure that each time she heard that particular sound and stopped, a tidbit was coming. You could almost see the little mare thinking "Hm! Most interesting. Every time I hear 'Ho' and stop for it, I get a treat." Next, to be sure that she understood, Sally had begun to say "Ho" at a time when *Penny* had not been thinking of stopping. And now if she slowed down at the gate or at any time other than on command, she would be urged on by the word "walk" and the whip pointing.

The next step is to add the word "trot" to your horse's working vocabulary. Sally made this a short, sharp sound, and always used the same tone of voice. *Penny* understood, of course, but Sally showed how she had pointed the whip at her a little more vigorously to make her understand at first. The same thing had been true with the command "canter." She had at first had to "touch her up" with the whip to make her understand that she was to move still faster. Even now, if *Penny* got a little lazy, Sally would use the whip.

It had taken her about two weeks, working almost every day, to teach *Penny* to understand these four words and what to do about them. During that time she had been careful to use the same tone of voice for each word, over and over. (I don't think I made that very clear. All four words were not said in the same tone. Just the opposite. Each must have a different sound from the others to make it easier for the horse to understand, but those different sounds must be the same every time.)

She also longed the mare as much to the right as to the left, so that she would not develop one side more than the other. You see, if she always worked in a circle in the same direction, she would develop the muscles of her legs unevenly.

Penny was still being reviewed on this lesson every day before Sally rode her. Sally commented that she felt that her horse had learned to pay attention to her, the trainer, during this period, and to realize that things would go well if she would try to *work with* her trainer—that is, to cooperate.

The instructor interrupted here to say that Sally was quite right. This kindergarten lesson was the foundation on which her later training would be built. In it she learned *one very simple thing at a time thoroughly* before a new point was introduced. It was so much easier to obey than disobey. Obey—tidbit. Disobey—a jerk or the whip. Which would any sensible horse choose?

At this point, *Penny's* saddle and bridle were brought to the ring. Slipping off the caveson, Sally tacked up her mare.

Now she mounted and demonstrated for us riding on loose reins, and using her voice to control her horse.

Eventually, when your horse understands both voice commands and longing perfectly, you can begin to "free longe." (That is, exercise your horse in a ring, at whatever gaits you command, without the use of a line.) Here Mary Lou Walters "free longes" *Little Mingo* over a 4′6″ single pole. Notice how well the mare folds her legs, and the excellent use of head and neck.

Then Sally showed us the next step. This is combining voice signals, which *Penny* now knew, with hand and leg signals. These hand and leg signals at present were being given in the most elementary way. This time as Sally said "walk" she squeezed *Penny's* sides with her legs and, as the mare moved off, she patted and praised her. After this had been done a few dozen times, no horse could fail to understand that the soft squeeze and the sound "walk" meant the same thing.

Now as she said "Ho" she pulled on the reins just hard enough to stop her so that *Penny* would put *these* two things together. In this way she learned that the sharp, definite pull on the reins, which of course pulled on the bit in her mouth, meant exactly the same thing as the sound "Ho." Again as she stopped, she was given her tidbit.

"Trot" and "canter" had been taught in the same way as "walk," using increasingly vigorous leg signals to make the difference clear. Whenever necessary, Sally used her whip to enforce what she had said with her legs and her voice.

This was the stage of schooling which *Penny* had reached in the six weeks. Sally was still using voice *along with* hand and leg signals until *Penny* completely understood the signals without the use of voice. When she *completely understood,* Sally would not have to stop her either by voice *or* by pulling hard on the reins. *Penny* would understand both signals that meant stop. Nor would Sally have to kick hard with her legs to tell her to move on. Gentle squeezes would do it. In this way, a horse is taught to be quickly responsive to legs that say "move on" and hands that say "slow down" or "stop."

Much later, our instructor said, when *Penny* was completely stabilized (this, you remember, means that the horse holds even speeds at all gaits on loose reins) and responded quickly to hand and leg signals given in this simple way, Sally should begin to ride her on "contact." Contact belonged to later classes for us as well as for this particular horse.

Our instructor pointed out that she had asked us to watch this demonstration so that we would see how the horse's learning processes work. We had seen how each simple step was added to the step before. Each new step had to be first combined with and built on something the horse already understood.

Now, I think it will be easier for anyone reading this book to understand how it was that our class horses behaved as they did. Class horses generally had about a year of training before they were used as "beginner" or "position" horses. Some, because of their temperaments, would never be used for beginners. Some, because of a different temperament (a very quiet, steady, unexcitable nature), might be used sooner. Those used sooner generally would come from the ranks of older horses, not youngsters.

As I write this, explaining how it was all done at DSH I realize that many people have to learn to ride on rented horses who are ridden by all sorts of people in all sorts of ways. Of course, if you are one of these people, your job is much harder. If you can possibly arrange to take lessons from a capable instructor on horses schooled as described, you will be money ahead. If you can't, your best bet is to ask the stable to give you a quiet, steady horse, on which you can practice your basic lesson. This is, of course, POSITION.

If you ride a rented horse, this particular chapter can only help you by enabling you to understand the horse you ride. You will be less likely to become upset or think the horse is mean if he doesn't obey you properly. Remember, he is undoubtedly confused. He has had riders on him who steady themselves by hanging onto the reins (which really says "stop"). At the same time their legs are unsteady and nudge him when they don't mean to (really saying "go"). So perhaps for years he has had riders on him who say "Horse, go on. Horse, stop" all in the same breath. If he is high strung, he has become a nervous wreck. If he's unexcitable, he may become sullen and, in your opinion, "stubborn."

In any case, don't go out of an enclosed ring on your rented horse without an instructor or someone from the stable to take care of you until you have developed a good seat and a reasonable amount of control. It is so easy to get into a situation on a bridle trail that you can't manage and have an accident which can spoil all your future pleasure with horses.

If you have your own horse or pony, most assuredly you should put this chapter to use. You will not only have great fun teaching your mount these simple things (what you are teaching is the beginnings of stabilization) but the two of you will grow to understand one another's language and learn to work together. In addition, you will be building a good foundation for all of your horse's more advanced schooling.

My cute little old friend *Trigger* had been taking such a "kindergarten" course during the time that I had been working on position on the school's horses. And it was all turning out very well indeed for both *Trigger* and me.

CHAPTER IX

Our Big Promotion

Hallelulia! Happy Day! School was out (academic school, I mean) and life was pure enchantment. I had three months to eat, sleep, dream and ride horses. *Trigger* came to Gaymeadows to board for the summer, and we riders who kept our horses at DSH might stay all day, every day.

Class was held every morning now, Mondays through Fridays. I had been promoted out of the group in which I had started, and had joined the magic circle of horse and pony owners, most of whom were considered "intermediates."

In my new group were many of the riders who were to become my close friends over the next few years. Fred Compton, Sophie Connery and Greta Stillway, who had been in the "position" group because of special position problems, were now in the new class too. We all felt vastly honored that we were up in class with Sally Hilton. It was Sally, you will remember, who had demonstrated longeing, voice commands and combining voice with leg and hand signals on her own little mare, *Penny Ante*.

We were now considered steady enough and good enough on position to begin work on "contact" instead of riding almost entirely on loose reins. This was the big step between riding on an "elementary level" and on an "intermediate level."

You probably remember that on the first day we came to DSH we had a demonstration of riding on contact (see Chapter III) but at that time we only saw how it looked—we didn't learn how to do it, or why.

In order to make you understand how this business of "following hands and arms" or "contact" works, you should first understand how the horse's head works at the different gaits. You may remember that we observed that at a walk, the horse's head made "balancing gestures" and again at a canter and gallop, but not at a trot. This is because the trot is a two beat gait (the diagonal pairs of legs work together—that is, the left front with the right hind and vice versa) so that the horse is supported by legs *at each end* of his body instead of by one, or by three, as occurs in the course of each cantering or galloping stride. Thus at the trot, the horse's balance is much steadier. (See diagram on p. 70.)

The walk is a four beat gait. If you start with the left hind, the next leg to move is the left front; then the right hind moves, and lastly the right

69

front. (This is the way you count the beats at a walk. Actually, the horse will move a front leg first—in the case mentioned, the right front—and the other legs will move in the sequence described.) This way of moving

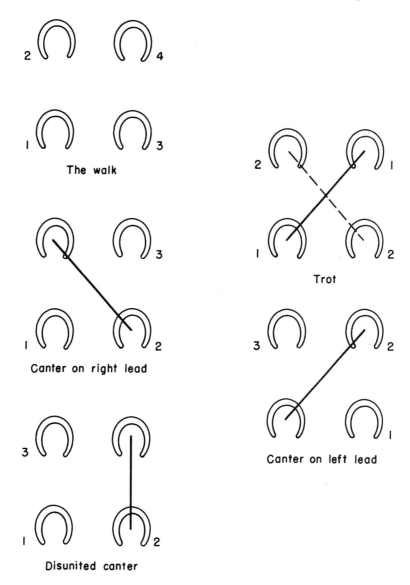

The walk

Trot

Canter on right lead

Canter on left lead

Disunited canter

his legs in four separate beats produces what we call a less stable (steady) gait, as far as the horse's balance is concerned. So he uses his head and neck as a "balancer," just as we use our arms when we walk. The canter and the gallop are even less stable gaits, due primarily to the faster speed.

The canter. Here the right hind has lifted, the right diagonal pair is on the ground, and lastly, the left fore leg prepares to strike the ground.

These photos of Jimmy Hudson on *Sh-Boom*, illustrate very nice contact. At the trot Jimmy's hands are a little low, and the straight line from bit to elbow is broken. Also, half-Arab *Sh-Boom* does not travel with head and neck extended as we would wish. Contrast this canter with *Which One's* on page 23. And since we all agree that nothing is perfect, we might as well mention that Jimmy's back is a little hunched!

Courtesy of Frances and Homer Heller

The walk. *Sh-Boom* has just "pushed off" with the left hind and prepares to follow with the left front.

The trot. Note how the diagonal pairs of legs work together.

As we use our "balancers" (our arms) more when we run than when we walk, so does the horse use *his* "balancer" more at faster speeds.

At a canter, which is a three beat gait, the sequence of beats is as follows: one hind leg comes forward and grounds; then the other hind leg and its opposite foreleg come forward and hit the ground together (this is called the "diagonal pair"); lastly the horse strikes the ground with the remaining foreleg. I'm explainng all this first so that you will understand why, in riding on contact, the hands and arms move at the walk, canter and gallop, but remain rather still at a trot.

This is the way we were told to start working on contact. We were told to "creep up on the reins" until we had practically all the slack out of them, and then to try to urge the horse on until he took the last tiny bit of slack out of the reins himself. He does this by moving more energetically in response to our legs urging him and, as a result, reaches out with head and neck. This is called "accepting the bit" or "moving on the bit" and at faster gaits "leaning on the bit." Now that there is no slack in the reins the rider's hands will be pulled gently forward and back as the horse walks, making balancing gestures of head and neck. As explained above, the same thing will be true, and to a greater extent, at a canter and at a gallop. It's harder at these faster gaits to ride with following hands and arms without jerks or loss of contact, because it is harder to keep the position secure and perfect so that your hands can do exactly what you want them to do.

It sounds so simple, but really it requires considerable skill to do it well. We tried all sorts of devices to help us acquire the knack. We took the reins between forefinger and thumb to lighten and soften our hands. Sometimes we would try riding on contact with our eyes shut to see if that would help us get the "feel." Sometimes we would tie red bows on our horses' manes, about at the withers, and fix our eyes on them to see if our hands and arms moved back and forth as they should at a walk, canter, and gallop.

To ride well on contact really requires a great deal of practice, and is the essence of having "good hands." It's terribly easy to lose contact (get a little slack in the reins) or to jerk the horse's mouth. As we rode around the ring, the instructor would call out, if we lost contact or jerked, "loose— jerk" to sharpen our consciousness of it. We were told to pretend that the reins were silk threads and that if they became slack our horses would gallop over a precipice—we were supposed to ride as if this were really true when we worked on "following."

We discovered several other things about contact, as we worked. We found that it is much easier to maintain contact on a big striding horse

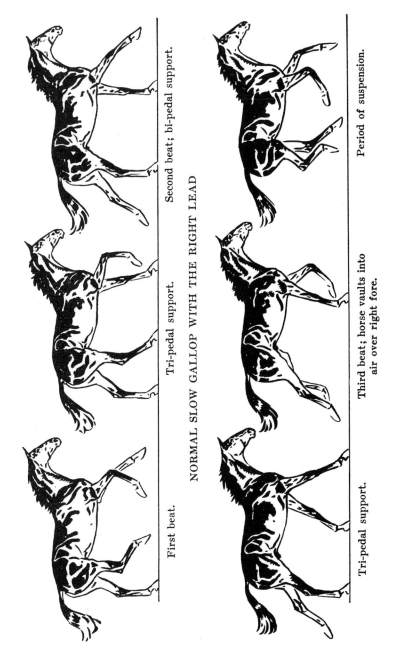

First beat.

Tri-pedal support.

Second beat; bi-pedal support.

NORMAL SLOW GALLOP WITH THE RIGHT LEAD

Tri-pedal support.

Third beat; horse vaults into air over right fore.

Period of suspension.

Taken from *Training Hunters, Jumpers and Hacks* by Brig. Gen. Harry D. Chamberlin.

who makes a strong gesture of head and neck. On such a horse, it's easy to feel the pull. Some horses make very slight gestures and of course it is much harder to get the "feel" in this case. Also, we noticed that the horse who had a small gesture of head and neck generally had a poor walk. Then it was pointed out that bad riding of this particular kind (riding with tight reins and not following) discourages the free natural movement of the horse's head and neck. The horse, in an effort to avoid being jerked in the mouth, will try *not* to use his balancer and the result is that he walks less freely and well. Therefore, we were warned over and over not to practice for long periods at one time because in our first efforts to learn contact, we were bound to be clumsy and make mistakes and too many such mistakes would make our horses fearful of accepting the bit. They would then lose the good natural gesture and their movement would suffer.

For about a month we spent part of almost every class period working on contact but always for short periods only, and only *establishing contact after we had our horses moving on loose reins at a specific gait.* The next step was to really *use* contact in our riding. In other words, instead of starting, stopping and turning our horses, and changing gaits in our old so-called "primitive way," we now began to practice these things while riding on contact.

Our instructions now went about this way:

Commence the walk on loose reins. Creep up on the reins and urge the horse with your legs until all the slack is gone and then begin to follow. That is a nice walk, Greta. Good, everybody. Now, class, when you hear the command, "Halt!" I want to see how softly it is accomplished. If your horse's head comes up, you have been rough. To get your halt, instead of the sharp definite pull you used to give when riding on loose reins, if your horse ignored your voice, you will now try to get the horse to halt as you close your fingers on the reins. The very second he obeys, relax the feel on his mouth, but don't throw the reins away. Increasing the feel of the bit on the bars of the mouth (taking) and immediately relaxing this feel on the mouth (giving) when the horse responds to the increased pressure, is considered a definite technique. It is called "give and take." There may be a series of such "taking" and "giving" actions; or if the horse obeys immediately, you need to "take" only the one time, and then promptly "give."

As you halt, your upper body comes back to the position it has when you are at a standstill. The change in your position will be very slight, as you don't lean forward very much for a walk. Now, all halt! That was nice, Fred. Kit, *Trigger's* head came up and his mouth opened—you were rough. I know his mouth isn't very soft or responsive, so try little vibrations of the bit. Really, it can be a very mild form of seesawing the bit in the mouth. Remember, a horse pays more attention to a bit that slides around in his mouth than to a steady pull. Or I might put it this way— it takes less pulling if the feel of the metal against the bars of his mouth not only presses harder, but moves from side to side. It is a more effective way to attract the attention of the horse whose mouth is a little hard. Try again; all walk, and on the command halt, I want to see every horse come to a standstill with head and neck in about the same attitude that it has at the walk. That will be our ideal. All halt! Better, Kit, but still a little rough. Of course, it's hard to do it well on your pony, but at least his head didn't come up in the air this time, although his mouth opened a little. We'll keep working on it. In your particular case, it might be good strategy to give a soft little "ho" at the same second you start the small vibrations of the bit. Fred and Sally both got very nice halts. Will you two please demonstrate. Commence the walk. Now halt! Did you notice that both horses stopped in a perfectly relaxed manner without either tucking their chins in, opening their mouths or throwing their heads in the air? Obviously they aren't in the least afraid of their riders' hands, and obviously, too, both riders use their hands very softly or their horses *would* become afraid of the bit, and attempt to evade it in some manner. That's what horses are doing, of course, when they throw their heads up, or open their mouths, or tuck their chins in, dropping the bit, as you slow down or stop.

As I write this, I think of the hours we put in on just this one point. I know our instructors didn't expect perfection at this time, but hoped to see us do it at least half way decently. I found good halts almost harder than any of the other techniques we tackled that summer. To go from walk to trot without loss of contact was easier. We were told to do it this way:

As you get ready for the faster gait, you will do the same two things relating to position that you do when riding on an elementary level— load the stirrups (that is, drop more weight in the stirrups), and lean further forward *a fraction of a second before* the horse's change of speed. You do this, as you know, so that you will not "snap back" as the horse changes the speed with which he is moving—instead you are "getting the drop on him." So much for the two things you do, position-wise. Now for the things you do control-wise—that is, in connection with your signals to your horse. In going from walk to trot, prepare for the change by creeping up on the reins and shortening them a little. Your reins won't need to be as long to maintain contact at a trot because at this gait, the horse's head comes up. A fraction of a second later close your legs on your horse in the signal to move on faster. Only when the horse has commenced the trot will you start posting; and now you must be careful that your hands really belong to the horse's mouth more than to your body. They must remain steady, even though your body is going up and down, in rhythm with the beat of the trot.

Well, going from walk to trot without loss of contact was fairly simple, and the only hard part was keeping the hands steady while posting. But, oh my! Change from trot to canter without loss of contact, or jerking the horse's mouth was a different story! Believe me, this is hard. In fact, just watch riders in advanced horsemanship classes in big shows, and you will see very few who do it well, which gives some idea of how difficult it is. And then, there was the eternal problem that we couldn't practice too much because it *is* hard and we would make mistakes and then we would spoil our horses' gestures of head and neck. Sort of a vicious circle! Anyway, this is the way the transition from trot to canter on contact is supposed to be done:

Cease posting. Close your legs on your horse, which says, "horse, faster." Your horse's tendency will be to trot faster, but instead of letting the energy your legs have created escape in a faster trot, your hands check your horse, and in a sense you "bottle up" his energy. Your legs continue to urge until your horse is ready to break into a canter. As he takes the first cantering stride, your hands *immediately* give, and you begin to follow the gestures of head and neck.

When this is fairly smoothly done, you don't see any of this, as it takes much longer to describe it than to do it. It is sort of: one, legs urge; two, hands check; three, legs urge and hands give and follow as horse moves forward in a canter.

Of course, this way of using your aids becomes a signal to your horse very soon, so he understands perfectly well when you want a canter. In the case of a lazy horse you have to use rather vigorous legs, and hands checking, until you feel you have sparked him just enough so that he will move forward in a *faster gait* rather than merely increasing the speed of his trot. That would be his natural inclination, if you weren't sufficiently emphatic about what you are asking him. And you can see how much synchronizing this takes—just enough leg, just enough hand—to get a smooth canter departure without loss of contact. You don't want him to bound forward into a canter like a scared rabbit; but again, you don't want him to move off in a faster trot. You have to use your legs and restrain with your hands until you feel that he is ready to *change* his gait, and then you have to try to get him to do it smoothly—and *then* you have to be ready to move forward with him, without snapping back and jerking his mouth, or losing contact!

I can't believe that this was ever easy for anybody, and certainly it wasn't for any of us. None of us did it well by the end of the summer, although of course we did begin to get the "feel," at least enough to realize when we were doing it wrong—which was most of the time!

Slowing down from canter to trot and trot to walk was comparatively easy. You do this by soft flexing of fingers and wrists just enough to induce the horse to come to the slower gait, and as he slows down, your upper body "drifts" back to the position it has at slower gaits.

About the same time we began to work on wide turns at a trot and a canter, keeping the horse on contact. This is done about as your common sense would tell you. If you are going to make the turn to the left, for example, you take your left hand outwards, and in a sense, *lead* the horse to the left. In fact, the rein used in this way is called a "leading rein." When you do this, you usually give as much with the right rein as you take with the left. You will also find that you and your horse stay in balance better if you step down on your inside stirrup (left one, in this case). If the horse tries to "fall in" on the portion of a circle you are riding (that is, to cut down the size you had planned), you will use your inside leg against the girth to discourage this idea. And then, too, you don't want him to move with body stiff, like a poker, letting his quarters "skid" outside the path his front legs took. Some horses have a tendency to do this, and to discourage it you use your inside leg against the girth and at the same time you move your outside (right leg, in this case) behind the girth, against him. We used to think of it as pushing his quarters over just a little.

All the time we were practicing these changes in gaits, turns, etc., it was stressed over and over that when our horses were walking, trotting, or cantering, we must require them to maintain even speed. So there again, we had to learn how much leg to how much hand—how much we could urge with leg if the horse lagged—how much we should restrain with our hands to keep him from breaking gait. Then we discovered if we used too much hand, our horses would begin to tuck their chins in; others may "lug" on the bit. All this is really quite a difficult matter of balance between legs and hands. And both were to be used as lightly as possible at this stage of the game.

We were told that the real purpose of riding on contact, beyond the obvious advantage of having more control, is to develop in the horse a better way of moving. We weren't ready, our instructor told us, to make use of it in this way. Hands have to be really good before that can happen. We worked on these assignments now just as techniques, and eventually we would be able to use this knowledge in "connecting" or "putting together" the horse who moves in a coltish or lackadaisical, disorganized way.

QUIZ FOR CHAPTERS VIII AND IX

To be scored as two (2) quizzes of eight (8) parts each.
Mark as correct *one statement only*.

1. "Longeing" (sometimes spelled "lunging") means:
    a. that the rider repeatedly "lunges" at the horse with a long whip
    b. teaching or exercising the horse on a long line
2. In teaching the horse voice commands on the longe it is important to teach him:
    a. the words walk, trot, canter and ho at the same time, so he can learn to distinguish between the sounds readily
    b. one or two words at a time before going on to more
3. After the horse understands the voice commands, the rider teaches leg and hand signals by:
    a. really beating up the horse if he ignores the use of legs and hands
    b. combining soft leg and hand signals with the voice commands which he already understands
4. When the horse performs his lesson well it is:
    a. sensible to reward him, so that he grows to connect the habit of obedience with pleasant things happening
    b. a mistake to reward him, or he might refuse to perform without bribes
5. The big step forward, as explained in this book, from riding on a beginner level to riding on an intermediate level lies in the fact that the rider now should be able to:
    a. jump high fences
    b. ride on contact, with hands and arms following the gestures of the horse's head and neck
    c. go foxhunting
6. When riding on contact, you will note that the horse's head, and hence the rider's hands, remain rather steady at:
    a. a walk
    b. a trot
    c. a canter
7. The trot is a:
    a. two beat gait

     b. three beat gait

     c. four beat gait

8. In a trot, the:

     a. legs on the same side move together

     b. diagonal pairs move together

     c. each hind leg pushes off, followed by the corresponding front leg

9. At a walk the legs move as follows:

     a. after the first preparatory step with, say the right front, then left hind, then right front, then right hind and then left front

     b. after the first preparatory step with, say, the right front, it will be followed by the left hind, then by the left front, then the right hind and lastly the right front

     c. diagonal pairs moving together

10. At a canter the legs move as follows:

     a. right hind, right front, left hind, left front (when on the left lead)

     b. right hind, right diagonal pair (right front and left hind together) and lastly left front (when on the left lead)

     c. when on the left lead, first the right diagonal pair (right front and left hind) and then the left diagonal pair (left front and right hind together)

11. When riding with following hands and arms the rider should:

     a. set his hands to stop the motion of the horse's head

     b. move his hands quickly back and forth in such a way that he pulls the horse's head back and forth, thereby encouraging the animal to develop a big gesture of head and neck

     c. allow his hands to be pulled forward and back by the movement of the horse's head and neck

12. As you halt your horse his:

     a. head should come up and mouth open slightly

     b. head and neck should remain in a natural attitude and mouth should remain closed

13. Give and take means:

     a. increasing and decreasing the tension (feel-pull) of the bit on the bars of the mouth

     b. *giving* a treat for obedience and *taking* a whip to the horse for disobedience

14. To commence a canter on contact the rider should:

     a. use the whip until the horse begins the canter

     b. one, legs urge; two, hands check; three, legs urge and hands give and follow as horse moves forward in a canter

     c. pull the horse's head to the outside and kick with the inside leg

15. To make a wide turn to the left you normally would:

     a. move both hands to the left until the right has crossed the neck to the left side

     b. take your left rein outwards in a leading rein, with the right hand giving as much as the left takes

     c. take both reins in your left hand and swing the horse to the left

16. The real and eventual purpose of riding on contact is to:

     a. develop collection in your horse

     b. improve the carriage of his head

     c. to better his way of moving

CHAPTER X

The Enchanted Land Across the Road

Even the most eager and serious pupils need a change of pace from time to time. Our instructors realized this, and so every now and then we would have a more casual type of class. In fact, to us it really didn't seem a class at all, but just a lark. This would be a ride out over the dirt roads and through woods, trails, and open fields. Sometimes we would take a ride that wound around through neighbors' farms and then brought us back to our own. We had a lot of wonderful country open to us. While this sort of riding was mainly for pure delight, of course we were learning all the time.

The type of ride we took was always geared to the ability of the weakest riders. If we had riders along who had just been promoted to going on trails, we couldn't have as fast and exciting a trip as we could when we had what was called a "strong group." If we had a large group that included "low intermediates" (the usual step after "advanced beginner") we probably wouldn't have a chance to gallop, or even canter. With ten or twelve horses and ponies cantering together, no matter how well schooled they are, a few are bound to get carried away by the spirit of the thing—galloping all together as they used to in a herd when they were wild—and while a capable rider can settle his horse down and enjoy the fun too, the weaker riders can't. If one or two let their horses get out of hand, trouble can start for everybody.

One thing that made even the slower rides more interesting was this: riders from intermediate ranks took turns leading the group. The instructor rode along beside the line of horses and riders or towards the back, and observed the judgment of the leader. When we led, we were responsible for the safety of the entire class and were graded on our judgment of pace and consideration of all members, horse and human.

The first day I was invited to lead a ride was on a lovely cool morning in July—a rare thing in Virginia. It had been raining almost steadily for several days before that, so we knew that the ground would be soft and the going a little deep down the banks of Difficult Run, which we had to cross to take the ride we planned. We knew, too, that the horses would be quite fresh and full of themselves after standing up most of the week, due to the wet weather.

The instructor discussed the way the class had best be arranged with the leader. The two that we were a little worried about (the weakest riders) would be on the quietest horses (*Riptide* and *Little Red*), and would be directly behind me. I was to ride *Trigger,* who made an excellent lead pony. Greta Stillway, riding *Tango,* should be somewhere near the front, as *Tango* fretted and bounced around if kept too far back. Greta had become quite a tactful rider, and she got along well with over-eager horses. Next, Sally Hilton was to take *Penny,* who went nicely anywhere you put her. Directly behind *Penny* we put two of the small ponies, *Fancy Flight* and *Sauce Box.* Sally could keep an eye on these two with their younger riders, and *Penny* would act as a good influence on *Fancy,* who was a bit of a devil. *Pink Lady* was assigned the position behind the two little ponies. *Pinkie* took a fairly strong rider, as she would become temperamental if the horse behind rode up on her. So behind her was Sophie Connery on *Wayward.* Sophie could keep her pony wherever she wanted her, and would not let her creep up on the heels of the horse in front of her. Behind her was Betty McCoy on *Storm Cloud.* The instructor would have to keep an eye on this mare, as she was a little spooky about trucks, and the first part of the ride would be on the road. Fred Compton was to watch the group from the rear, and call up to me if there was any difficulty along the line. He had just acquired his own horse, a wonderful old mare called *Wireless.* Since he was anxious to teach her to stay back anyway, this assignment suited him very well. Mrs. Douglas was coming with us on *April Dawn,* who was a complete angel in the show ring but a perfect scamp on the trail. She loved to feign terror at the most ordinary objects along the trails, such as innocent white rocks or old rotten logs. She would roll her big brown eyes, snort and prance around as if she expected the log to come to life and leap out at her. On the other hand, if the log had been painted in purple, green and red stripes and set up five feet high across the trail as part of a jump course, it would settle her nerves—she would prick up her ears, look the situation over, and sail calmly over it!

I must seem to be going into a lot of detail over who rode what and where. The point I want to bring out is that even the best behaved horses have their little personality quirks, and all this has to be taken into consideration. The capabilities of the different riders must also be understood, and all these factors put together in deciding the line-up for a trail ride. The instructor really did the deciding, but she would confer with the "leader" so that he (or she) would start taking in all the things to be considered when responsible for a group.

When horses and positions had been assigned, I was trying to review in my mind all the things that I must remember. Most of them were just common sense, and common courtesy, but I must remember them all and remind the group.

When horses were brought out, each rider must check his equipment to be sure that all tack fitted properly. Throat latch should be loose enough

Courtesy of Lt. Col. Franklin Hickman

"When horses are brought out each rider must check his equipment to be sure that all tack is fitted properly." Note rider on far left cleaning out her horse's hoof. Another tightens his pony's girth, and the rider to his right checks her mount's curb chain. Still another permits her mount to have a drink before starting out.

for the rider's hand to pass between it and the horse's throat. Bit must lie just to the corners of the horse's mouth. If the horse is in a pelham bridle, the curb chain must not be twisted, and should be loose enough to allow the rider to pass two fingers between it and the groove of the chin. All billet (loose) ends of straps must be slipped through the keepers. Girths must be snug. There must be no twisted straps anywhere. Saddles should not "sit down" on horses' withers. This checking only takes a minute if it has become a habit, but today it is my responsibility to see that it is done.

Now we are mounted, stirrups adjusted and girths checked once more. Everyone drops in as planned. Riders are cautioned not to "ride up" on each other. Everyone is to keep about one horse's length apart. (The distance should be greater if we were going to ride fast, which we weren't.)

We always walked the first ten or fifteen minutes, so that the horses would warm up slowly and quietly, and have a chance to settle down to work in a relaxed frame of mind. Then when we were to begin to trot, I called back to the group so that they could shorten reins and be prepared to move on faster. Any instructions or warnings were always passed back down the whole line. I glanced back and saw that all the horses were behaving very well, and riders seemed comfortable and confident. Just as I was congratulating them inwardly, a big sand truck rounded the bend. I held up my hand to indicate to the group behind a quick slowing down (you do this, and the whole line follows suit so the people at the back take in what is happening and won't pile up), and then waved my crop back and forth in a signal to the truck to slow down and stop. The driver was nice enough to do it. We always made a big gesture of stopping to thank the drivers for their courtesy, and as a result, most were kind enough to pull up and wait until the column passed. This was fortunate, as *Storm Cloud,* who was perfect in every other way, just did *not* care for clanging trucks.

When we passed cars or trucks along the road, we were careful that all riders stayed on the same side. Its pretty confusing for the driver to try to run the gauntlet through a group of horses milling around on both sides of the road.

We had one more slight hazard to meet before getting off the road, and that was to pass between two houses in each of which lived a thoroughly disagreeable dog. I passed back a warning here to shorten reins and sit tight as the dogs might startle someone's horse, and of course slowed down to a walk again before getting to "The Lion's Den," as we called it. As usual the dogs came bounding out with a great barking and snapping. Although they didn't really bite our horses they would sometimes manage to get them fussed up, and several of us "stronger riders" would get after the unpleasant animals with our crops to run them off. On this first day of my big responsibility we managed to get by without mishap. Shortly after this unpopular spot we turned onto our woods trail, where I drew a sigh of relief. Here we ride through a lovely little alley-way where honeysuckle covers an old fence line, and trees meet overhead. At the end of this pretty section is Difficult Run, a fair sized stream. As we expected, the banks were quite steep and slippery. Here I called back the reminder (as the leader is supposed to do) to be sure that horses had free use of head and neck. Riders were supposed to get forward where their weight would interfere the least with the action of horses' quarters and catch mane to steady themselves. If mounts hesitated, legs were to be used strongly to urge them right on, before they got the idea of stopping. Really, our horses were awfully good; not one hesitated, even the little ponies (or I should say, least of all, the little ponies!). We splashed merrily through and up the opposite bank without any trouble at all. Riders got forward and out of the saddle again to make it easier for the horses to clamber up the bank. We were always careful to insist that our horses walked through such crossings, as rushing can cause accidents. Horses who want to leap and bound up slippery banks are apt to pull tendons, and it is bad manners anyway. We had a rule that as each horse scrambled up the bank, the one in front of him should stop and block the trail. Then he would move

on and that horse stop and wait for the horse behind *him* to negotiate the crossing. If you don't do it this way, it's hard to keep things from getting faster and faster at the end of the line, and the last horses start rushing. Well, we were all across, and the younger riders on the smaller ponies were feeling like real dare devils. It *is* exciting on a small pony, when the stream comes up almost to your feet!

Next we make our way across a boggy meadow, and here we must walk, or chance pulling a shoe or a tendon in the bog. And now the ground begins to rise, and we are in the woods. All through this trail we have built little brush jumps at intervals (nature also had made us a few from fallen logs), none more than two and a half feet. Today, since we have the younger and weaker riders with us, we must hold the pace down to a lazy trot, so that our mounts won't get too eager. Again, I call back to remind riders of the little jumps coming up and to get up and grab mane. Also, that no one is to let his horse get beyond a trot.

This is the part of the ride we all love the most. In the woods along these winding, wild looking trails, we feel that we have found an enchanted forest, and that no one else knows it is there. Then eventually we come out into bright sunshine again, and into a field with a very nice rail fence jump, and to its right, a gate. This is ideal, as the fence is too big for some of our group today, so I open the gate and hold it for the ones not ready for a jump of that height. When they are safely through, I can

Sketches in Chapter Courtesy of Mrs. Richard Ruffner

Penny Ante canters smoothly over a chicken coop.

go back, and *Trigger, Wireless, Wayward* and *Penny Ante* (and of course *April Dawn*) canter smoothly down to the fence and over it. There is no question about it—ponies are remarkable jumpers! This fence is about three feet, three inches, and *Trigger* takes it with as little effort as the horses. From here, we go on up a hill, at the top of which is a gap for the younger riders and a chicken coop jump for the same four of us. Here Mrs. Douglas says she will take the younger group through the gap, so we four can canter on up and over.

On the far side of the chicken coop we have a slight surprise. A tractor is sitting there, and *Trigger* decides to make a case of it, and pretend it is a bear or a tiger. Disgusted with him for being so silly, I try to push him on, but Mrs. Douglas calls to me to let him and any others who want to take exception to it, stop and have a good look and sniff at it. This way, they may get the notion out of their heads that there is something scary about such an object!

This matter settled, we are ready to start the trip home, as this is about as far as we can go without coming out on a hard surfaced road, which Mrs. Douglas doesn't want us to do with this particular group. Anyway, the morning will be gone by the time we are home.

We start back, and those of us who want to take the coop again are advised to trot to it this time. It's low enough to take from a trot, and

since it's heading home, and on the landing side we start abruptly down the hill again, we don't want to get up much speed. As it is, *Wayward* and *Wireless* begin to play a little after they go over and Mrs. D. calls out a sharp "walk" command to settle them down. Now down to the rail fence jump, where *Wireless* and *Wayward* are asked to go through the gate and only *Penny* and *Trigger* are permitted to jump. I must say, I was about to burst with pride at my pony's good manners and good jumping.

We started trotting on home at a good clip, this time skirting the woods trail and circling around the edge of the woods through some fields. I turned around in the saddle and glanced back to be sure that all mounts were behaving and staying put in line when suddenly there was no pony under me! A rabbit had jumped up under *Trigger's* feet. He took a quick bound to the side and I landed on the ground! Directly behind him, *Riptide,* who probably hadn't seen the rabbit at all, but only *Trigger's* sudden bound, followed suit and his rider was off too. Behind him, *Little*

Red had decided to play it safe until he could find out where the danger lay, and had taken a small sideways hop, and his rider was sitting on his neck.

I have never felt so foolish in my whole life! *Trigger* was standing over me and I give you my word as he snuffled and blew through his nose and poked me he was laughing at me! So was the whole group of riders, as it was easy to see that we two were only startled but not in the least hurt.

Photo by Marler

"A rabbit had jumped up under *Trigger's* feet."

I had landed with my bridle reins still in my hands, and scrambled to my feet much embarrassed. *Riptide* was trotting around the group and Mrs. Douglas had dismounted and was trying to lure him with a sugar lump. He accepted the bribe and in another minute everybody was back in the saddle.

I was completely chagrined and sure that I would never be trusted to lead a group again. But Mrs. Douglas only laughed and assured everyone that the same thing would have happened to her or any one of us under the same conditions. This soothed my ruffled feelings considerably. In fact she went further and praised my light landing, and pointed out that this is one of the reasons why we practice "emergency dismounts" from almost our first day in class. By the law of averages, we were going to have some falls, but it was unlikely that we would get hurt unless we landed stiffly from being frightened in the first place. It is the tense rider who is likely to have a painful landing. Even *Riptide's* rider, Christine, who had only been riding about six months, and had landed flat on her back, got up laughing. Christine said that this was her first bona fide fall and she was glad it had happened as she had found out that falling off a horse is just nothing.

After this little excitement, we walked our horses for quite a while. Back through the bog and across the stream we would have to walk anyway, and then instead of returning by the road we cut across a neighbor's farm. In a tenant house on the farm was one of our favorite friends—a

wonderful old colored man who always greeted us with great sweeps of his battered felt hat and lots of conversation. In a small field beside his cabin was a mule that looked about the same age as his owner. He was over at the knees, stiff and sad looking, and we used to bring him tidbits. Old Sam, our friend, was pleased by this attention to *Nebuchadnezzer*, the mule, and used to let us pick apples and berries as a return courtesy.

From here we went on across open fields. Pastured in these fields were cattle, with horns which looked formidable. Now cattle are not quarrelsome creatures, and only stand and stare at you when you ride through, but to riders who are not used to them they look very threatening. Children out for their first trail rides always used to ask: "Will they chase us?" This was quite a joke to the ones who knew that cattle are even less aggressive than horses.

The last lap of this particular ride took us through several gates, and over sliding bars. Those of us who were considered the better riders divided up the job of gate opening and closing, and lowering bars. This is excellent practice for both horse and rider, particularly for those who plan to hunt eventually.

Back at our own stable horses were checked to be sure they were cool and dry before being put up. On the sort of slow ride I have described, naturally the horses would come in cool. If the ride is faster, you make it a point to walk the last ten or fifteen minutes so that your horse won't come in hot. If for some reason this can't be done, when you reach the stable the horses must be untacked and walked on foot before being put up.

The faster rides, in which about half a dozen of us went out with an instructor, were more exciting. We could move on and get in a few

gallops without being afraid someone would come off his horse. Sometimes we would go out and find the hilliest sections we could over which to work our mounts. This is wonderful "muscling up" for your horse. Then, too, working over uneven ground at fairly fast gaits is good for mature horses to develop better balance and ability to handle themselves. When we went out for this sort of ride, we didn't have as many gates to open, either. Several were low enough to jump, and this is an excellent way to teach your mount to jump whatever and wherever you ask him. Of course, all this is assuming that you use your head and never ask your horse to take a jump that is too stiff for him. Nothing is worse psychology than to force your horse to do something that he can't do without hurting himself.

We were reminded that we should *use* the techniques we learned in the ring and on the slower rides. Hands and arms should "follow" at walk, canter and gallop. We should try to slow down and stop softly. We should get up out of the saddle when we really galloped in a field. When galloping, we should keep several horses' lengths apart. Of course, we should get up off the horse's back both up and down steep hills or banks. We should think ahead and not put our horses in situations that would upset them—

for example, between the houses where the dogs used to run out at us, we should slow down *before* we got there, even if we didn't think we would fall off should the horses shy. We should let them take a good look at queer objects, such as odd pieces of equipment, or laundry flapping on a line. If a horse becomes slightly gimpy (lame) we should get off and check to see if he has picked up a stone. This can happen quite easily. If you find nothing wedged in between shoe and hoof, the horse may have momentarily bruised the sole of his foot, and perhaps walking a minute or two will take care of it. If he continues lame for any length of time, he must be taken in. If you get a loose shoe your horse should be taken home. Even on fast rides, you don't go charging through streams or through bogs. This can pull a shoe or strain a tendon. You should always use your head and consider the condition of your horse—if he hasn't been getting much exercise, then he shouldn't be taken out and given a very strenuous ride. He shouldn't be trotted or galloped on a hard surfaced road—not only is there danger of slipping, but hooves hitting the hard surface fast (and therefore *harder*) is bad for your horse's feet and legs. Normally, he shouldn't be ridden fast down steep hills—this is a difficult feat for a horse. Nor should he be galloped up steep hills, unless terribly, terribly fit.

The rider must not only consider his horse but the other members of his group, no matter how able they are. If you see a companion's horse becoming "fussed up" as he waits his turn for a jump, it is polite to ask him to go ahead. The other rider may decline, feeling that his horse must learn to wait his turn, but give him the chance. If you come on any hazard as you ride, such as broken glass, old wire or perhaps an unexpected hole, be sure to call back and point it out to your companions.

Really, most of the things we were to do were just good manners and thoughtfulness of both riders and horses. In fact, add to these two things a little knowledge and common sense, patience, courage and coordination and you have the qualities that make a first class rider.

QUIZ FOR CHAPTER X

To be scored as one (1) quiz of fifteen (15) parts.
Mark as correct *one statement only.*

1. In arranging a group ride, one will always gear the speed and stiffness of the ride:
   a. to the ability of the strongest riders
   b. to the ability of the weakest riders

2. In riding out on a trail it is important:
   a. that horses stay "nose to tail" in close formation, to discourage any running away
   b. that riders keep at least a horse's length apart on slow rides; greater distance on faster rides

3. When you commence a ride you always:
   a. warm up by a brisk trot or canter at the beginning to limber up the horse's legs
   b. warm up slowly by walking the first ten or fifteen minutes

4. Instructions or warnings called back to you should be:
   a. passed back down the entire line
   b. absorbed by you quietly without comment; if the ones at the back don't hear that is their own fault

5. In preparing to pass any strange object that may frighten the horses the group should:
   a. gallop on to get the hazardous situation out of the way as quickly as possible
   b. shorten reins and slow down

6. In riding *down* a steep bank or hill the rider should:
   a. tighten the reins to keep the horse's head up and equalize his balance
   b. lean well back to lessen the chance of toppling over the horse's head
   c. lean forward and allow the horse free use of his head and neck

7. Through streams and bogs it is a good idea to:
   a. gallop so the horse won't sink as far and risk pulling a shoe or a tendon
   b. walk so that the horse will not risk pulling a shoe or a tendon

8. In falling off a horse in most instances you are unlikely to get hurt:
   a. if you are relaxed
   b. if you tense up your muscles and brace yourself

9. If you find yourself riding through a field of cattle:
   a. gallop away quickly before they attack your horses
   b. you don't need to worry; the cattle will not attack you

10. The last ten minutes or so of your ride:
    a. walk your horse to bring him in cool
    b. have a good gallop to be sure that the horse has gotten enough exercise

11. In riding on trails and fields:
    a. hands and arms should not attempt to follow the gestures of the horse's head and neck
    b. hands and arms should follow wherever possible

12. If your horse becomes lame on a ride, or loses a shoe, or a shoe becomes loose:
    a. you should take your horse in
    b. the best policy is to ignore the difficulty; the horse should not be pampered

13. Riding on hard surfaced roads at fast gaits is:
    a. an excellent way to develop your horse's agility
    b. hazardous, both from the point of view of slipping and from the point of view of damaging the horse's feet and legs
14. In riding on the road, when a line of horses passes a car:
    a. separate the group so that half will be on one side, half on the other
    b. keep all horses on the same side
15. When you are riding with a group of able riders, you:
    a. will not need to consider the difficulties that may occur to the advanced rider
    b. still consider the problems which any one may have with his horse

CHAPTER XI

Every Horse Is Different

A big part of the fascination of working with horses undoubtedly lies in the fact that each is an individual. In spite of the fact that there are certain standard aids to be used, the way you use them must vary with the situation. Horses aren't like modern gadgets. You can't set certain dials the way one might set the automatic washing machine and then go off and read a book and return to find your horse all schooled. Your horse gets ideas of his own. Some of his ideas we can't quite follow—but a lot of the fun of schooling is trying to figure out what is in his mind. It's as if you try to get inside his brain and see what he is thinking and why.

For example, does he buck after going over a jump because he is a little sore and something hurts, and so he becomes upset and resentful? Or does he do it because he is in high spirits? Or is it a sort of rebellion because he was confused and didn't like it?

Did he refuse (stop at a fence) because he has been jabbed in the mouth and so is afraid of being hurt again? Or is he a little lazy and finds it easier to stop than to go on? Has he been allowed to stop by an over sympathetic rider until it has become a habit? Or is the fence a little high for him and he lacks confidence in himself? Does he stop because he is young and awkward and hasn't "found himself" with a rider on his back?

As you work with different horses, you may discover foolhardiness, caution, boldness, "chicken heartedness," stubbornness, cooperativeness, resentfulness, amiability, craftiness, panic, cleverness, rebellion, laziness— one could go on forever describing the different qualities that may crop up in different horses. The important thing, of course, is to try to understand *why* a certain horse behaves in a certain way, and what to do about it to make things come out right.

In some instances it's simple to see what has happened to a horse and why he behaves as he does; but erasing the bad memory from the horse's mind is much harder, and sometimes can never be done. In other instances you never can figure out just what *has* happened to a particular horse before you got him. Then there are times when you completely misunderstand why a horse is behaving in a certain way, no matter how closely you watch and try to figure. Sometimes you have to make guesses, and if one guess is wrong, try another.

We were told that we would never become real horsemen and horsewomen without using our brains and without the quality of *sympathy* with the horse's outlook. We were encouraged to observe and criticize each other, discuss and experiment. Riding at DSH was always stimulating *mentally,* besides being fun in every other way. Perhaps you'd like to hear about some of the specific horses that we worked with that summer, and how some of them turned out.

Courtesy of Mrs. Richard Ruffner

Does he buck because something hurts him?

There was little *Foolish Son,* a beautiful dark brown pony, sensitive, able, highstrung and, when he came over to us, a nervous wreck. *Foolish* was an undersized thoroughbred, who by an odd chance never grew beyond 14:1, and so was classified as a pony, although every inch thoroughbred by temperament. In his case, it was simple enough to see what had happened to him. *Foolish Son* and the boy who owned him were sent over to our school because the pony was refusing his fences all the time. He would have been crazy to jump, as every time he *did* jump, Bobby, who was away behind his legs anyway, was badly left. He would positively *swing* on the reins. You would hear the reins snap, and see poor little *Foolish's* head go up in the air and the awkward and painful landing that followed. Then, not being a glutton for more punishment, he would try to protect himself by quitting at the next fence. Wham! would go the crop—after all, Bobby announced, it was just stubbornness! The pony had been jumping four-foot fences and hunting like a breeze when he had bought him. He had pictures to prove it!

It was hard for us to see how anyone could be as *blind* as this boy was: Needless to say, he was taken off *Foolish Son* in record time and, to his great annoyance, forced to grab mane on one of our school horses over two-foot fences.

Foolish Son was assigned to one of our older riders, who began to walk and trot him over rails on the ground. When he would do this on loose reins, he was stopped and given a tidbit, and praised to the skies. Unfortunately Bobby's family wanted a quick miracle, and this was the sort of situation in which no quick miracle is possible. When, at the end of two weeks, the rails were still on the ground at one end, and no more than a foot high at the other, they were disappointed and took the pony home again.

We saw them often at shows that summer. *Foolish* never once got around a course of jumps the whole season, and it made us quite sad to watch him. It was sort of an equine version of the "Poor Little Rich Boy" tale, as the pony had the most plush quarters and meticulous stable care at home. We were sure that he'd be much happier in the less plush quarters of Gaymeadows where people would understand his jitteryness and would not punish him for stupid human mistakes. He did eventually come to live with us, but that is part of a later story.

Tango, the cute little chestnut mare that I have mentioned before, had lots of bounce, but her style over fences was not good. She not only traveled but jumped with her chin tucked in. She was twelve when we got her, and must have been ridden by someone who never released her mouth even over a fence. But *Tango* was of a very different temperament from *Foolish Son.* She had adjusted to the situation and made the best of it. She just tucked that chin in to try to evade the bit and went right on jumping perfectly willingly. The only way that she indicated that she wasn't completely happy about the situation was by rushing her fences a bit, in an effort to "have it over with." In her case, it was decided that miniature spread fences would induce her to extend head and neck somewhat. She was required to take all jumps from a trot only, so that she could not make use of the momentum of speed, and encouraged to go on loose reins. Of course, we had to work and work to persuade her to jump on loose reins, and we kept fences very, very low. By the end of the summer she was using herself somewhat better, although she never completely overcame the overflexed poll which causes the "tucked-in" chin and vertical face. Or you could put it the other way around. After all,

this attitude of head and neck was the habit of years. She did improve
enough to hunt safely that winter, and the next summer managed to pick
up ribbons in most of the big shows in Virginia. But in spite of this, I
know that Mrs. D. was never completely happy about her jumping.

Another of our horse pupils that summer was *Pied Piper*. *Pied* was a
young horse, strong, sensible and with a nice attitude. He was inclined

Courtesy of J. D. Baxter

Tango jumping with "tucked in" chin.

to be rather clumsy and awkward in learning to jump—he just naturally
wasn't one of the quick, cat-like jumpers. His worst fault was getting in
close and "climbing" his fences. That summer he was allowed to jump
only "in-and-outs," as in this way you can teach the horse to take off
and jump where you say. In this sort of corrective jumping, you put the
second element of the in-and-out too close for the horse to get in an extra
stride, but at a distance that requires him to take off a little further back
than he would if left to make the decision himself. This helps establish
the *habit* of a better takeoff. After hundreds of such jumps, his muscles
and brain become accustomed to doing it this way. *Pied* became one of our
very nicest hunters and jumpers, and only occasionally reverted to his old
fault—as any horse will. The photo shows a jump where he got in too

close at a show a couple of years later. However, he was consistently in the ribbons that season, so you will realize he didn't make this mistake often.

One mare that I loved and was allowed to work with that summer was *Cornflakes*. This is a pleasant tale to recount, because *Cornflakes* seemed almost hopeless when she came, and has turned out so well. She was one of those unfortunate horses whom people have tried to "quick make" for

Courtesy of J. D. Baxter

Pied Piper "got in too close." Notice how tightly he must fold and the extra strong use of head and neck to get himself out of his dilemna.

open jumping. She does have lots of jump, but when we got her she was in a state of hopeless confusion. When she approached a jump, she would begin to rush. Apparently her mind was saying, "Shall I take it? Shall I try to run out? Shall I put on the brakes and try to dump the character seated on my back?" When she did take a fence, she never took off twice from the same distance. She seemed to be so much of two (or maybe three) minds about how she would handle the situation that her jumps were dangerous and erratic. It was as if she would sometimes change her mind even after the take-off, and so one leg would go one way, one another, in a sort of wild scramble.

As soon as she was ours (she was with us as a boarder at first, and then a little later was given to the school) she was stopped from jumping com-

pletely, until her frame of mind improved. I was given the job of stabiliz-
ing her. I took her on long walks alone or with one quiet horse in the
afternoons. I would work her round and round the ring, trying to induce
her to go on loose reins, using my voice to soothe her, patting her, talking
to her constantly. I was always loaded with treats for her, stopped her
frequently and then rewarded her. Sometimes I would persuade her to
stand still for three or four minutes doing nothing before I would give her
a tidbit. Sometimes no tidbit after the halt, just patting and praise. I spent
a lot of time fooling around her stall, playing with her, primping her,
riding her bareback. My idea was to do anything and everything to con-
vince her that her bad experiences were over and that from now on life
was to be a lazy, relaxed sort of affair. She was a mare of tremendous energy,
so this was not easy, but she really had a sweet nature, and became affectionate and friendly in her stall. It was six weeks before she began to
relax under saddle, and to work quietly on loose reins in the ring. All
during this time she was not allowed to take one fence, but was trotted,
walked or cantered around them, between them and sometimes up to
them and then halted and patted and praised. At first the very sight of
a jump would send her into a tailspin—they obviously reminded her of
poling (being hit with a pole while in the air), wiring (a fine piece of
wire strung up just above the jump), and all the other devices to "quick
make" the open jumper. These memories are hard to erase.

So it was the end of the summer before we began to trot her over poles
on the ground, and fall before we began to sneak them up a little. We
used cavaletti extensively, and in the fall began to use all sorts of tiny
jumps singly and in combinations.

It was wonderful to see the improvement, even though it was slow. This
type of horse will always require a most tactful rider, because one real
mistake can fuss her up for the rest of the day. The next summer Greta
Stillway began to take her around to horse shows, and she performed
brilliantly under Greta's quiet handling.

Another horse that we found most attractive and interesting was *Dark
Knight*. Here was an entirely different temperament, although he had
had a small dose of the same medicine that *Cornflakes* had had for so much
longer. We never found out about *Dark Knight's* early life. He had the
lip number (number tattooed on the inside of upper lip for identification)
of the thoroughbred who has been on the track. We felt that he should
have been fast when he was young, as he was a magnificent mover and
the length of his stride was simply fantastic.

We knew a little about his *immediate* past history. He came to us from
a dealer, a professional who plans (if the horse shows any natural aptitude)

to teach a horse to jump in one afternoon. Apparently he had gotten the
works in that afternoon. When *Dark Knight* came he really knew nothing
about how to take off and land and handle himself over a jump. He would
run out or stop when he got a chance, but when he did jump he soared
'way over the fence. But because he was by nature of a somewhat calm
temperament he had not become jittery as a result of that afternoon—he
was just confused and temporarily charged up.

Courtesy of J. D. Baxter

"When he did jump, he soared 'way over a fence." (*Dark Knight* with Ridgely Slater)

We resorted to the old system of making the lesson easy for him and
one that he need not fear—tiny jumps in all sorts of combinations to
teach him to handle himself and learn to estimate the amount of effort
he must make. It was interesting to see the way he had reacted to the
poling—he had a tremendous amount of natural spring anyway, so he just
figured to jump higher, and his leaps looked for all the world like those
of a deer. The problem was to teach him to estimate the situation correctly and it took a long time to see any improvement. He was still bounding about three feet over every little one-foot fence at the end of the
summer, and sometimes getting confused about where to take off. It
seemed as if jumping was no effort to him, but what he didn't understand
was how to shorten his stride to "get in right" on the approach to a jump—

he seemed to feel that he must take off and leap from wherever he saw the fence!

He was a hard horse to ride over jumps because of this terrific spring, and progress was so slow that it was a little discouraging. He was assigned to a young rider who adored him, and worked with endless patience. Unlike *Cornflakes*, who was a bundle of energy under saddle but friendly in her stall, he was very aloof and never showed affection. But happily for him, Ridgely Slater found him charming and romantic and loved him dearly. By the next summer, in Ridgely's hands, he managed to win ribbons in hack classes, but only rarely in classes over fences. He still had not become completely consistent in jumping. But once in a while he would turn in a round in his slow, deliberate, effortless style, soaring over each fence in a fashion that won the judge's approval and a ribbon for him and for Ridgely. Two seasons later he was hunting—never too well in the back of the field, but extremely well when he could be up front! Like so many horses, his temperament changed when he went out hunting, and from being a calm, quiet animal he seemed to feel that a hunt was a steeple-chase. So when I say that he hunted well, even up front, it was really a great accomplishment for horse and rider.

It's impossible to discuss the style of different Gaymeadows horses without mentioning that most unique of animals—*April Dawn*. There were no problems connected with *Dawn's* jumping—or at least the only problem was that you couldn't turn her out in a field, because she would go fence-hopping just for the fun of it. *Dawn* was, and still is, that rarity amongst horses—a natural jumper. She is a little mare (15 hands ½ inch) possessed of the most astonishing spring and bounce, but it was her other qualities made her even more remarkable. She was completely consistent, willing, eager and yet calm in her jumping. The only way I can explain it is to say that jumping seemed no effort to her, that she would just as soon jump a fence as go around it, and since she had a most amiable nature and knew that you were asking her to jump, that was it. Apparently it just never occured to her that there was any other path open. She seemed to say, "Well, why not? It's certainly no trouble to me!"

I couldn't help laughing one day when one of the stable men had turned her out in the field with *Sprite*, a little pony, to act as "nurse-maid" and try to keep her occupied. *Dawn* loved to play with the ponies, and sometimes this system would induce her to stay out. When it was time to bring her in, Nat, the groom, opened the gate to let *Dawn* and *Sprite* through. *Sprite* was a little in front of *Dawn* and went through first. *Dawn*, instead of waiting long enough for *Sprite* to get out of her way, just hopped over the 4½-foot fence beside the gate, rather than waiting to go through the gate being held open for her. There were dozens of such instances. We built a fence five feet six inches at the end of the field that was her regular "jumping in" place, in an effort to have some way of keeping her where we wanted her. Ten minutes later, on the first day we turned her into this field, she became bored. In she came, not laying toe to it. After that, we gave up, and when we wanted to turn her out, would have someone "baby sit" her.

Her style over a fence was simply flawless. You will see on page 219 one of *Dawn's* effortless bird-like jumps, feet tucked neatly up, head and neck extended. In the next few years her winnings were really staggering in both hunter and jumper classes. In fact, I doubt that there is a horse in the United States ridden by a junior (rider under eighteen) who has continued to win, or won so much in such a diversity of competitions over the years. You'll hear more of this remarkable mare throughout this book, as she was, and still is, the real star of our stable, and one of the few truly memorable horses I have ever known.

Should she be called "great"? No, somehow "great" is the wrong word. Perhaps it would be more accurate to say that *Dawn* was endowed with tremendous natural ability and terrific personality.

You probably want to know what makes such a jumper—so do I, and so does everyone who breeds, raises and schools horses. Certainly, we could find no clue in her breeding. That was as contradictory as everything else about this mare. By a five-gaited Saddle Horse sire, out of a nondescript dam, *Dawn* looked distinctly Arabian! But generally Arabs are not the best jumpers; their conformation is against it in the first place; so here was another puzzle. Like the Arab, she was short-coupled and compact, with a straight, rather flat croup—all of which should not produce a jumper. And how did she get that Arab look, anyway? From the American Saddle Horse sire or the plain dam? A pure golden color, she is endowed with a fine intelligent head, brilliant wide-set eyes, fine muzzle, small ears. She is affectionate, delighted to anticipate and fulfill the rider's desires as long as they don't cross with her own—but the most headstrong mare in the world if it is a matter about which she feels strongly! She could learn anything—two-track, the turn on haunches, flying change, extended trot, in record time, and was always a most willing pupil. She seemed very happy to do these things (simple and fun, she seemed to be saying graciously) and the only time she became a self-willed headstrong *brat* was when she was out hunting! "Here," she seemed to say, as she reared and whirled in her eagerness to take the fence and out-distance the foremost hound, *"let me go!* Now I want to have a little fun and do what *I* want to do, for a change!" You could neither reason with her, nor discipline her in this matter. So we discovered that we had to accept her as she was on this one score, and just be happy that she would go on winning state championships, "Three Day Events" and classes at national shows.

I have talked about some of the problem horses, and of our very special "rare one," but haven't mentioned that string of loyal, dependable school horses, neither brilliant nor glamorous, to whom we owe so much. The longer I know them, the more I respect them. Some were slow in learning. They tell me that *Riptide* was awkward and fell over several fences when he started jumping, but now he is almost foolproof. *Storm Cloud* had quite a lot of natural ability over a fence, but her disposition had been quite poor when she first came. Now, you couldn't ask for a nicer, more capable animal. *Little Red* had lots of natural ability at jumping, but not much heart for jumping in a ring. He seemed to say "What a stupid pursuit! You end right where you start." But out on the hunter course or cross country he was perfect and made the loveliest fences in the world. *Jumping Giraffe,* who had been a funny combination of awkwardness and grace in learning to jump, had become a most willing, careful jumper, although his style was not that of the hunter. *West Wind,* a common clumsy-looking mare, was a very capable and consistent jumper. In fact, while the natural ability differed considerably, practically all of our school string jumped safely, calmly and willingly as a result of the way they were schooled. Like the human pupils they were given all the time they needed to learn each step thoroughly and carefully. The school felt that it was perfectly natural to take a year to make a successful class horse. Each horse was considered and studied as an individual, just as I explained when discussing some specific cases. As for the ponies, they seemed to know how to jump even before they had had much schooling. Ponies mature faster and learn much faster than horses and, in addition, have a great deal more natural jumping ability.

A few horses and ponies didn't "pan out." If, after six or eight months, they remained unreliable without showing signs of improvement, they were considered poor prospects for class and the school disposed of them.

QUIZ FOR CHAPTER XI

To be scored as one (1) quiz of six (6) parts.
Mark as correct *one statement only.*

1. One of the most interesting aspects of working with horses is the fact that:
   a. all the rider has to do is to learn a set of signals; if he applies them in the same way, every horse will react in the same way

    b. each horse is an individual. The rider must study his particular horse pupil to learn how to get along with him best

2. If the horse is inclined to refuse a fence:
    a. the rider must try to discover whether he is stopping because he is upset, lazy, apprehensive, etc. He will then adapt his method of correcting the fault to the situation
    b. the disobedience can be traced to stubbornness only. Therefore the rider must, in every instance, apply crop and spurs until he gets results

3. The horse that is inclined to jump with a "tucked in" chin can probably be improved by:
    a. use of a standing martingale
    b. taking the jumps at greater speed
    c. lots of work over small spread fences

4. One method which may correct the jumping of a horse who "gets in too close" is to school:
    a. over high straight fences
    b. over in-and-outs that are set altogether too far apart for the horse to take comfortably
    c. over in-and-outs that are set in such a way that the horse must take off a little further back than he would if left to make the decision himself

5. With the horse who is inclined to rush his fences it may be wise to:
    a. push him at the fences even faster so that he will develop a distaste for rushing and hence will slow down of his own accord
    b. make the jumps so high that he will slow down to look at them
    c. discontinue jumping until he is calmer, and then commence re-schooling over low and easy obstacles, jumping mainly from a trot

6. One fundamental necessity in schooling a horse is:
    a. speed in accomplishing one's goal
    b. establishing an absolutely set schedule and then never deviating from it
    c. taking all the time you need to do the job, and employing patience, sympathy and an effort to understand the horse

CHAPTER XII

Time Out for Pranks

The old saying about all work and no play holds good in connection with riding too. We worked so hard in morning class that in the afternoons during our free time we turned into complete harum-scarum wild Indians, explorers, anything and everything but calm intelligent little pupils! The farm was an ideal location from which to launch exploring parties. On weekends, since there was no riding class, we who had our own horses and ponies used to pack lunches and set forth to explore the country. We

did every possible hare-brained stunt. We rode over to the Potomac River and forded it where our ponies must swim a few strokes. We considered this a thrilling pastime. We knew where there was an old gravel pit that extended for a mile or so, and this made a wonderful place for wild games of "hide and seek" on our ponies. The gravel trucks, going in and out and scooping up sand, left narrow roads leading up to promontories. From these look-outs the person who was "it" had a vantage point from which to spy on the riders trying to sneak to base, and then there would be a wild race for "home."

Four of us (Sally, Greta, Berta, and I) formed a secret organization known as the "Safari Club" which was very well named. It is hard to explain about our secret hide-outs all stocked with provisions. Nobody could understand the sort of spooky enchantment we found in these hidden rendezvous in the woods—but as I write and think about those

Vaulting on over the tail.   This is a nice way to ride, too.

Pair jumping minus tack is fun. This picture, taken two years later when I was almost 15, shows *Trigger* with his mane hogged. I finally gave up on it! When the mane is too coarse and bushy, this sometimes is the best bet.

early summers I begin to feel sort of sad that I am seventeen now and probably nothing will ever be as thrilling again.

I know Mrs. Douglas would have had a spasm if she had known some of the chancy things we used to do with our horses and ponies on these outings. However, some of our afternoon games were right on the farm, and these she considered perfectly harmless and fun too. She encouraged us in our so-called "circus tricks." I learned to jump *Trigger* bareback and without even a halter on. By the next summer I could take him over any course that way. We learned to vault on our ponies over their tails. We learned to ride standing up on their rumps. Berta and I worked up a clowning acrobatic act, but since we could never get any "pay customers" we finally had to give it free!

We staged impromptu horse shows, adjusting the rules to fit the situation. For example, such and such horses should jump the lower pony jumps because they were not ready for the higher fences, but would be judged on an equal basis with the horses. We worked out a handicap system which was really a fairer way to make odds equal than can be done at regular horse shows. The height each horse and pony should jump must be agreed upon by all before a class started. We made up little sets of ribbons and charged ten cents a class entry fee to cover the cost. One of the ribbons that meant as much to me as any I have ever received in a big show was a "jumper championship" ribbon which *Trigger* won from points accumulated in these little afternoon get-togethers.

Various members of our group took turns judging, and we were very careful and professional in our decisions. Again, Mrs. D. approved of these pursuits, and used to help us with them.

Another of our favorite afternoon pastimes was playing with the pony foals. That spring three of the pony mares had foaled and the babies were simply adorable.

In the case of the youngest, nature had slipped up a cog, and the dam refused to accept her foal. We had to take over with bottle and formula. The baby, *Firecracker,* would come flying when he saw the bottle and really grew to behave like a human infant. He seemed to like to sit around in people's laps. But we never could find a formula that suited him, or possibly he was loved and petted to death—or perhaps it was a combination of the two. In any case, he did not survive and while it was a real tragedy at the time, I'm not sure that he ever could have grown up to be treated as a mount after the hours he had spent being cuddled in people's laps!

The other two were strong and sassy enough to suit anyone. They were halter broken practically from birth, and we used to take them for little jaunts on lead lines and jump with them over low, and always soft, brush jumps. We took them for rides in the pony trailer, behind the jeep, so that they would never be afraid of being loaded and traveling. Both were sold as yearlings to old friends of the Douglases and we heard regularly from their new families. We were all delighted that our "pony children" turned out extremely well, hunting and showing very creditably.

What gluttons for punishment we were! After a strenuous morning class, an afternoon playing around with our ponies, we sometimes came

Here Randy Douglas has the honor of serving *Firecracker* his evening meal.

back to have "human horse shows" in the evenings! This was serious business, too, with carefully worked out courses and prize lists. I can laugh right now, thinking how funny my friends looked as "Pairs of Hacks" or "Hunters over the Outside Course." One of the few accidents we ever had at DSH was a fractured collarbone as a result of a fall over a little triple bar in a human open jumper class!

The greatest treat of all was to bring supplies and cook over a campfire and then sleep in the stable. We generally asked permission to do this for birthday celebrations. What we liked to do best was to sleep in the stalls with our horses, but Mrs. D. put the "quabosh" on this, on the grounds that a hoof might, by accident, be planted in someone's face one fine night! We compromised and agreed to sleep in the hayloft if we might stay.

Once when we were having such an overnight lark in the stable, a group of riders was spending the night up in the farmhouse the same weekend. They decided to have some fun at our expense. About midnight the five of them got rigged up in all-black costumes, even including gloves and improvised masks and sneaked up on us. We were bedded down in the straw, still talking, settling the affairs of the world—horse world, that is. Suddenly, in the darkness, we were set upon by weird apparitions, and at the same time felt revolting soft wet SOMETHINGS(?) licking our faces! What were they? Tongues of monstrous wild animals? Creatures from the supernatural world? Our screams pierced the skies. The joke

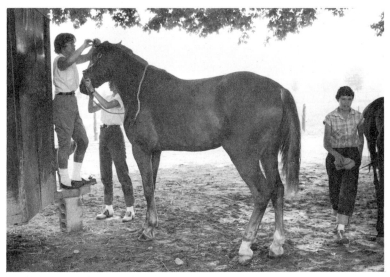

Here Tina McCoy is trimming out *Baby Bonjie's* ears with small curved scissors.

was so successful that the marauders had to identify themselves quickly and show us what had "licked" our faces—wet sponges!

Some of our free time was devoted to doing quieter things. Afternoons were ideal times to get our mounts out and primp and polish them under the trees. With small curved scissors we trimmed the hair out of the insides of ears. Chin whiskers must be kept cut too. Fetlocks and the little fringe of hair around the coronary band (Do you know where that is? If not, look back at your diagram on page xvii) must be kept trimmed off for a neat appearance. Every three or four weeks, manes must be pulled. They are never cut, but "pulled" to a length of about three inches. This is slow work. You take a few strands of mane at a time, wind them around your finger or a mane comb, and then pull. This thins and pulls a little at the same time. The finished job will be *approximately* even, but without the sliced off, stubby appearance that cutting would create.

Hooves must be cleaned out with hoof picks every day and a good hoof dressing worked in every now and then to keep them in proper condition. There is a knack in learning to clean out the feet. At first, you may have to pinch your horse a little on the tendons behind the cannon bone to make him understand that you want him to pick up his foot. And sometimes you may find it works out well to push the horse a little off balance and lean against him, so he won't lean on you! When your horse is used to having his feet cleaned, you probably will do no more than put your

"There's a bit of knack to learning to clean out the feet."

hand on the pastern and he will pick up his foot politely and hand it to you. Hold the hoof with one hand, take the hoof pick in the other and scrape carefully around frog, heel and sole to leave the hoof thoroughly clean. It's a good idea, too, to clean *away* from the heel, which bruises easily.

In hot weather, a bath in warm soapy water is a good way to get your horse thoroughly clean. It doesn't take too long to get him dry, if one first goes over him with a sweat scraper, before starting to walk him. But most of all, for a real sheen on the coat, the rider must polish and polish and polish!

As we gathered under the trees in the afternoons busy over these pursuits, we had long discussions of equipment.

About saddles, the big argument seemed to be between Pariani's and Crosby's. These two seemed to be the makes leading in popularity in our league at that particular time, although one or two held out for Smith Worthington. Most of the group, like myself, were saving their money for good forward-seat saddles, and had not quite made up their minds as to which make would be their final choice.

We had long discusions about bridles. Most of us hoped to start hunting that fall, and it was everyone's ideal to hunt in a snaffle. The Egg Butt

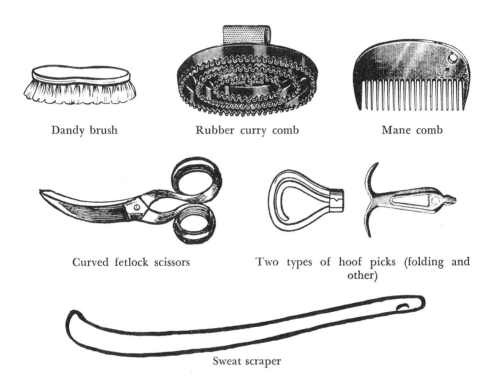

Dandy brush   Rubber curry comb   Mane comb

Curved fetlock scissors   Two types of hoof picks (folding and other)

Sweat scraper

or Barrel Head snaffle bits were generally agreed to be the best, but one or two liked the idea of the Racing Dee. Someone else had seen a full cheek snaffle and that was the "neatest bit ever." We were pretty sure that on a nippy day some of our horses would feel too good to hunt quietly in snaffles, and that we might have to use Pelhams for added control. But if one used a Pelham, it must be a Tom Thumb hard rubber Pelham—any other kind just wasn't in society! And how did everyone feel about the Kimberwicke bit? This is a bit which presumably combines the action of the snaffle and curb (see page 112). You have a sort of Pelham bit but only one rein to manage. None of us thought that this made much sense.

Did the others know that Don Bevins had sent away and ordered a standing martingale for *Lady Uppercrust?* Just wait until Mrs. Douglas saw that! Naturally, anyone knew that a standing martingale, tying the horse's head down, was just a clear admission that the rider had rough hands and didn't know how to school!

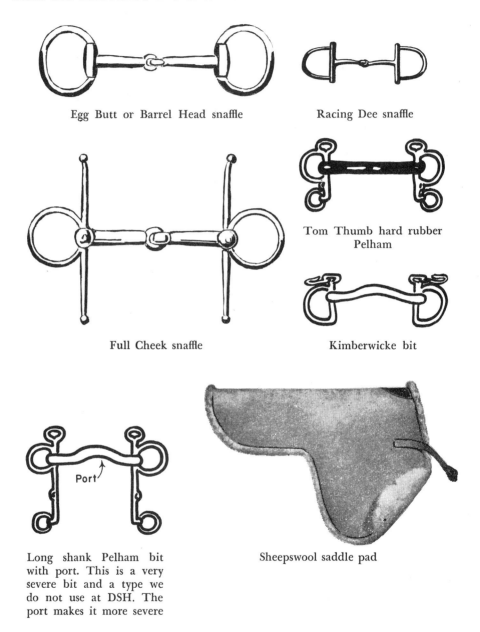

Egg Butt or Barrel Head snaffle

Racing Dee snaffle

Full Cheek snaffle

Tom Thumb hard rubber Pelham

Kimberwicke bit

Long shank Pelham bit with port. This is a very severe bit and a type we do not use at DSH. The port makes it more severe

Sheepswool saddle pad

What did everyone think of the elastic-end girth Sally Hilton had gotten for *Penny Ante?* Neat, wasn't it? And how about the nice fluffy sheepswool saddle pad Frances Fell had gotten for her birthday? Well, they are sharp looking, but nuisances to keep clean. Sophie Connery had got the new halter she had been saving up for all summer. It was a beauty, with three rows of stitching, rounded throat latch and brass buckles on both sides, and brass name plate with *Wayward's* name on it, riveted to the cheekpiece.

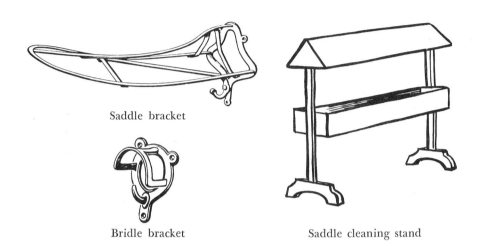

Saddle bracket

Bridle bracket   Saddle cleaning stand

Wasn't it keen about the new saddle and bridle racks that Mrs. Douglas had ordered for the tack rooms? They would be those metal jobs that let the saddles air out on the underside, and they were going to be in our stable colors, too.

So we chattered on as we worked. We were inclined to be a little bit "faddy" about styles for our horses, but we learned a lot about equipment from this swapping of information and ideas.

QUIZ FOR CHAPTER XII

To be scored as (1) quiz of sixteen (16) parts.
Identify the following:

1. curved fetlock scissors
2. saddle cleaning stand
3. mane comb
4. Dandy brush
5. rubber curry
6. saddle bracket
7. hoof pick
8. sweat scraper
9. bridle bracket
10. Egg Butt or Barrel Head snaffle
11. Racing Dee snaffle
12. Full Cheek snaffle
13. Tom Thumb hard rubber Pelham
14. Kimberwicke bit
15. long shank Pelham bit with port
16. sheepswool saddle pad

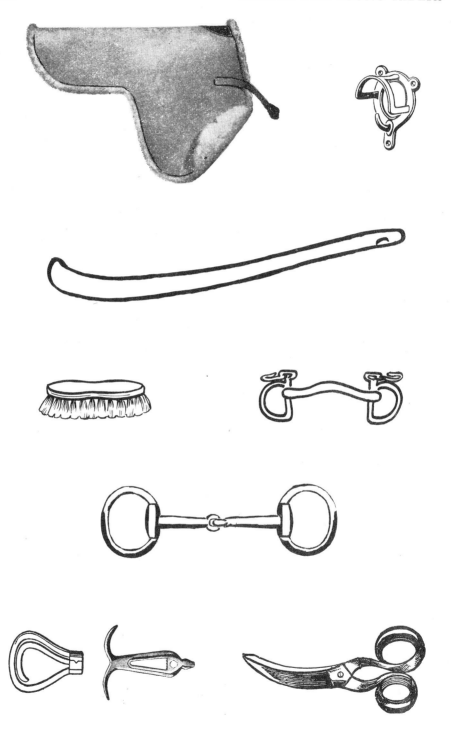

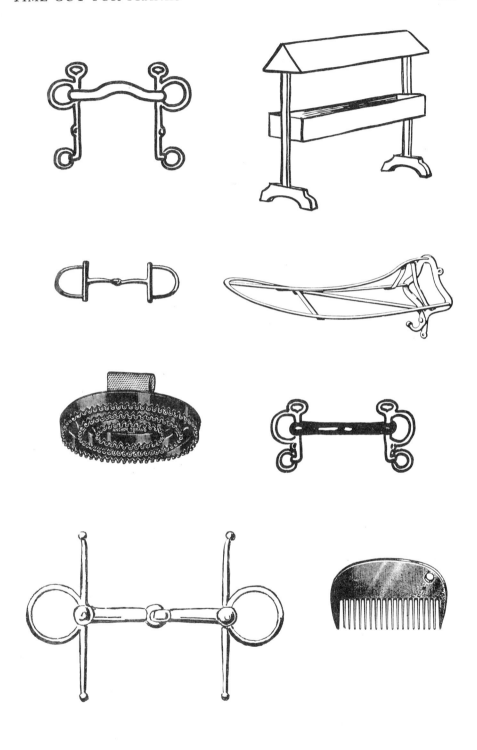

CHAPTER XIII

We Widen Our Knowledge

Mid-August. What an intensive course I had had for the past six months! It hardly seems possible that the figure you met in that first horse show such a short time ago, had been I. You may wonder if riders should be expected to progress as fast as we did. I hope I won't sound conceited if I say that most of the classes did not come on as fast. This isn't because our particular group was smarter, but we were the "avid" ones. At that stage of our lives, we had no other interests.

Another thing that helped our group was the fact that the parents of the members of our class (all excepting mine) were tremendously interested in this sport too. Sophie's and Sally's mothers were instructors; Fred Compton's mother was our school secretary. Greta's parents were closely associated with the school in many ways. Christine was another who we knew would improve rapidly because of her family's love of the sport. My family weren't interested in horses, but they thought it was fine for me, and would help me all they could. I suppose I was accepted in this inner circle because I was one of the especially keen ones.

The last time we discussed work in the ring on the flat (as opposed to jumping) we were working on contact, and using contact in transitions, halts, and wide turns. Before the summer was over we must add to this a working knowledge of the following: extending the walk; two speeds at the trot and canter; canter departure on the designated lead; backing; turns; circular movements used in schooling; turns on the forehand.

In order to do these things properly you should know the five standard rein aids and three standard leg aids. In one of our quizzes, this summer, we were required to list them. We were expected to be completely familiar with them, properly termed, in addition to being able to execute them.

I am sure that I cannot improve on the way that is put in Captain Vladimir Littauer's COMMONSENSE HORSEMANSHIP * so I am quoting directly from that source.

* Littauer, Vladimir S., *Commonsense Horsemanship*, pp. 112, 113, 114.

LEG ACTIONS

Leg action #1: Both legs acting just behind the girth, simultaneously and with equal strength. Used when urging horse forward.

Leg action #2: One leg acts just behind the girth. Used, for instance (inside leg), when making a turn in motion to prevent horse from cutting it.

Leg action #3: One leg acts farther behind the girth to range the hindquarters. Used, for instance, at the turn on the forehand to rotate the hindquarters.

REIN ACTIONS

Rein action #1 (sketch): TWO REINS OF DIRECT OPPOSITION. Both hands being fixed or producing tension to the rear, normally keeping the neck and head straight. Used to slow down, halt or back the horse.

Rein action #2 (sketch): ONE REIN OF DIRECT OPPOSITION. The active hand (the right one in this case) carried slightly outward and then increasing the tension to the rear. Used, for instance, when making a sharp turn to right. This action tends to diminish the speed of the gait. The passive hand must give as much as the active one has taken, unless a certain correction in the attitude of the horse's neck is required.

Rein action #3 (sketch): THE LEADING REIN. The active hand (the right one in this case) is carried outwardly and acts to the right and slightly forward. Used, for instance, when turning the horse on a wide curve. This action doesn't impede the speed. Unless a certain correction in the attitude of the horse's neck is required, the passive hand gives as much as the active has taken.

Rein action #4 (sketch): THE REIN OF INDIRECT OPPOSITION IN FRONT OF THE WITHERS. The active hand (the right one in this case) is carried to left across horse's neck, just in front of the withers, and tension is to left rear. The left rein often assists with leading effect (remaining parallel to the right rein) or as a rein of direct opposition. This action is used, for instance, to keep the horse flat against the wall of the ring.

Rein action #5 (sketch): THE REIN OF INDIRECT OPPOSITION IN REAR OF THE WITHERS. The active hand (the right one in this case) is carried somewhat to the left (but doesn't cross the neck) and produces tension to rear and left, toward horse's left hip. The passive hand normally gives. Used, for instance, to move the horse to the side, while advancing forward (to the left in this case). *In my method this rein is used only to combat resistance.*

There is one more standard rein effect which you will find in most textbooks on riding—that is the "bearing" or "neck" rein. It is used to

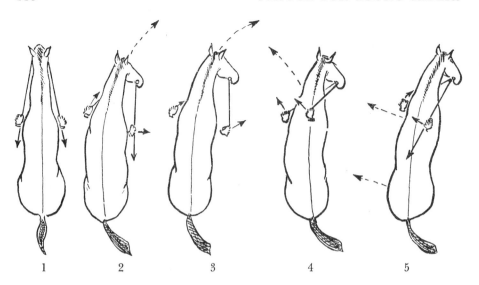

turn the horse with one hand. This hand is moved forward and upward and then presses one of the reins against the *upper half* of the horse's neck. This type of rein action is used primarily in western riding and in polo.

So much for the leg and rein actions, which you will need to memorize. And now for a discussion of the ring movements in which you will use all of these leg and hand signals.

To try to explain each of these movements even briefly will make a long chapter. Furthermore, it can hardly avoid being a "textbook" chapter. You may want to skim over it until such time as you are getting ready for a Pony Club Rally, or a U.S.E.T. (United States Equestrian Team, Jr. Division) Class. Then you will need to come back, and study it carefully, movement by movement.

In any case, don't try to absorb it at a single reading. In fact, you may easily spend a week or so practicing each exercise described just to begin to get the "feel."

To make the chapter easier to follow, and also to make it easier to find the particular section you may want to review, I have divided it into sections under large headings.

EXTENDING THE WALK

Suppose we start with a discussion of extending the walk. First of all, you must consider that in improving your horse's walk you want him to take *longer* strides rather than short fast ones. Each time he pushes off with a longer swing of the leg, he will cover the ground faster and will pass the poor walker. He won't be "chopping" or shuffling along, but will move faster while seeming relaxed and unhurried. How shall we teach him to do this?

Let's review the mechanics of this gait. In walking, counting off from the right hind, the next leg to move will be the right front; next the left hind and then the left front. Now the only time you can stimulate your horse into moving a certain leg more energetically is at the instant that it *prepares* to push off and swing through the air. Once it is in the air, you are too late; there is nothing he can do in response to your urging. So you must use your own legs to urge—right, left, right, left and so on—as your horse *prepares to push off* with the right hind, left hind, etc. (Remember his "motor" is in his quarters.) Now, which leg comes forward just ahead of the right hind? Left front, of course. So if you are going to catch him before he pushes off with the right hind you had best use your own right leg as his *left front* leg hits the ground or you will be too late. This is the simplest way to do it. Watch the shoulder. As it moves forward, the leg is in the air. As the left front hoof grounds, tap with your right leg; as the right front grounds, tap with your left. By the time you attempt this exercise, your horse should, of course, have been taught to move more energetically in response to the rider's legs.

So now, watching his shoulders to get the exact second, you close your own legs alternately, right, left, tap, tap. You should do this for no more than twelve or fifteen strides at a time at first, and as soon as your horse responds by lengthening his stride for a few steps, drop the reins and pat him.

I have failed to say that this exercise almost has to be done on contact, although schooled horses will answer the request of riders' legs to lengthen stride even on loose reins. However, in teaching your horse, you will always *practice* it on contact, and under all normal circumstancs you will be riding on contact when you use it as an exercise. Incidentally, it is a wonderful feeling, as you ride, to have your horse respond and the walk lengthen. This is done first as an exercise; the *result* of the exercise should be a better walk. You will find, too, in the show ring, it helps catch the judge's eye in that first part of a hack class when everybody is walking.

TWO SPEEDS AT THE TROT AND CANTER

Two speeds at the trot and canter are terribly important exercises for your horse for all sorts of reasons. They, and any other exercises that make your horse more flexible the *long way*, are called exercises in "longitudinal flexibility." I know that this term is a mouthful, but if you consider for a minute what it says, it won't seem hard. Longitudinal—think of it as *long*itudinal (long way), and flexibility, of course, means just what you think—suppleness.

Everything you teach your horse, after his first elementary training, is aimed at making him more pleasant to ride. Among other things, you want him to be light in your hands, agile in his movement, and able to adjust his stride to the situation—such as to a jump coming up for which he must lengthen or shorten his stride to put himself in a position for a comfortable take-off. Young horses, and many mature horses who have not had proper schooling, have not developed this ability, and most colts are extremely awkward in their first efforts.

Let's start with the trot in discussing two speeds. The class will have established a "good ordinary trot" on contact. This is normally about eight miles an hour. You probably can't figure out how many miles an hour you are riding, but you try to get a good energetic trot without pushing the horse hard. It should be a comfortable though alert trot, and you would be posting to it. Then the command comes, "slow trot, sitting." You cease posting, let your weight drift slightly back from the position it has at the faster trot, and your fingers close on the reins (possibly vibrate the bit, possibly wrists create "give and take") in an effort to get a soft slowing-down. As you go from ordinary to slow trot your horse may want to come to a walk, and your legs must urge sufficiently to prevent this. Now as you sit, you will find that you have to keep quite a lot of weight down in the stirrups, and a good frictional grip with your legs to prevent your seat from going "bump, bump, bump." At the same time, you have to keep the main springs of the body (ankles, knees, and hips) soft and springy. This sitting at the slow trot takes quite a bit of practice to do comfortably, but is very pleasant once you have acquired the knack.

In the slow trot, not only does the horse cover the ground more slowly but his stride is shortened. (You say that his legs do not "engage" as much, which means that they do not swing as far under the body and back as they do at a good ordinary trot.) From the slow trot, again you hear the command, "ordinary trot, posting." Now you close your legs on your horse, increase the forward leaning of your body, and *only after he has increased the speed of his gait* (this is called "accomplishing the transition") do you resume posting.

After we grew to understand how to get two speeds at a trot, this exercise became part of warming up in almost every class we had in the ring for quite a while. I said it had many purposes, and mentioned that it helped your horse to become more agile and flexible and developed in him the ability to lengthen and shorten his stride as necessary. The slowing down is also considered an important "coming back" exercise—that is, an exercise to teach the horse to respond to the increased feel of the bit on the bars of the mouth. Some horses move too heavily on their forehands, and this exercise in slowing down (particularly when done more abruptly, as you might in later stages of schooling or of your riding) is good to "lighten the forehand." Since in slowing down (especially in abrupt slowing down) the horse's weight comes back somewhat toward his quarters and off his forehand, it helps teach him to distribute his weight a little differently as he travels.

The moving forward and lengthening the stride in response to legs is, among other things, a lesson in the development of "impulse." Impulse means an *energetic forward movement* on the part of the horse. He should respond energetically though calmly to the legs, and they should not have to be used hard to get this energetic movement. In fact, if a horse responds sluggishly to your legs, when you use them softly, don't use them more and more strenuously. (This is a form of nagging, such as we discussed in Chapter V.) Instead, use a whip *emphatically* back of your own leg, which calls attention to the *soft* signal you have given. It puts teeth into your argument, and is part of the whole theory of schooling and handling we have discussed before: be reasonable in everything you say, and don't say something that is too difficult for your horse or that you can't back up with action. Having given the command, be emphatic and get obedience.

Two speeds at a canter is another exercise in longitudinal flexibility— that is, in stretching out longer and moving faster and then coming back together and moving more slowly. You might think of the horse as an accordion. This is an exaggerated figure of speech, but maybe it helps put across the idea.

Let's say you are cantering on contact, and hear the command "Gallop." Your legs close to urge your horse to move on faster and at the same second your hands and arms give to allow for the increased stretching forward of his neck. As you move from canter to gallop you get up in gallop position and *remain that way* while galloping. As the command "Canter" comes, your hands check and slow the horse down, and the rider resumes the cantering position. Remember, when you go from galloping to cantering position, you merely sink down over your feet, you do not sit back. This exercise is important for the same reasons as two speeds at a trot, but it is a more powerful method of gaining the same results.

CANTER DEPARTURE ON A DESIGNATED LEAD

We all had known when the horse is on the correct "lead" since our elementary riding. But now we were to consider *good canter departures* on a specific lead.

When you say that the horse is on the right (meaning correct) lead, you mean that it looks as if his inside legs are coming forward ahead of his outside legs. Normally you want him to "lead" with his inside legs around curves, and I always think of that inside front leg coming forward and acting as a prop as he rounds a corner. When he is on the track to the left (his left legs on the inside) you normally expect him to lead with the left leg. In Chapter 8 we discussed putting the horse into a canter, but without regard to lead. Now we will use the same signals to the horse, except that the final signal to move forward with cantering stride will be given by the rider's outside leg used behind the girth, instead of both legs together.

Let's review the aids for the canter departure and add the signal for commencing it on a designated lead:

1. Close both legs on the horse to tell him to move more energetically.
2. Check with your hands on the reins so that he will not respond by trotting faster.
3. Use your outside leg behind the girth (at first at a corner or turn) in a final signal to the horse to move forward in a canter and to lead with the inside leg. On the first cantering stride hands immediately give and begin to follow the gestures of head and neck. When this is done well the aids will not be visible to any but the keenest eye.

At first, to make it simple for the horse to understand what you are telling him, give him the signal to canter at a bend or corner. It is his natural tendency to throw forward that inside leg in such a situation. When he has done this numerous times at the same moment that the rider's outside leg is used behind the girth, he will begin to put the two things together; the rider's outside leg used in conjunction with the other aids described will become the signal to pick up the canter, leading with his inside leg.

It is important that you keep the horse's head and neck straight on the canter departure. The horse may "look in" ever so slightly. He should *not* have his head pulled to the outside and start the canter crooked, with inside shoulder popping.

BACKING

Backing is one of those tricky matters that looks simple when well done, but in which all sorts of things can, and often do, go wrong. There are all sorts of things which are part of bad backing that perhaps you have

Photos by Marler

"When the horse backs calmly and well his legs move in diagonal pairs."

never even noticed until they are pointed out and contrasted with good backing. Have you ever noticed, for instance, that when a horse backs calmly and well, that it is as if he is *trotting* backwards, as far as the way his legs work? He should not move as fast as he does when he trots, but just as in trotting, his legs will move in *diagonal pairs*. Only with stiff, bad backing does the horse move each leg separately.

There is more to consider in contrasting good backing with bad back-·ing than the way the legs move. When the horse backs well, not only will the legs move in diagonal pairs, his head and neck will stay somewhat extended, and his mouth closed. The movement will be relaxed, unhurried, smooth, and straight back.

Bad backing can take many forms. The head may be raised, poll and jaw set or mouth opened. Along with any of these head positions probably you will see, if you look closely, that the legs move stiffly, one at a time. The backing will almost certainly be crooked, too, rather than the forehand following the same path that the quarters took. Bad backing may take another form: the horse may tuck his chin in, drop the bit, and plunge backwards.

Now, how does the rider persuade the horse to back? To begin with, when we were having our first lessons in backing, we were put on horses that would back decently—anything else would have been the blind leading the blind. Our instructions went about this way:

Halt your horse (the halt in these first backing lessons always came from a walk). Wait until he is perfectly calm and relaxed—we don't want to give him a command when he is fidgeting. Now, when he is standing quietly, but is attentive to your commands, *gently* pull straight back with even reins. If he does not respond immediately, vibrate the bit ever so slightly, but do *not* tug or "haul" him back. As he commences the first step backwards, *immediately* relax the pull on the reins and as soon as he completes that step, ask for another. (This is another form of "give and take," which, you will remember, was explained in Chapter IX.) When you have gotten about four good steps, pat your horse and walk him quietly forward.

There are several places you may run into difficulties, even on a horse that generally backs pretty well. He may begin to back crookedly. If instead of backing straight, he swings his quarters to one side, do as your commonsense tells you; use your leg behind the girth on the side where he has begun to "bulge out" to urge him to move his quarters over until he is straight again (leg action #3). Help by increasing the tension of the rein on the same side. Should he begin to rush back, stop him between each step by legs closing on him, and hands completely relaxing the tension on the reins. Of course, if you overdo this procedure, he may take it as a signal to move forward, in which case you have to check him. Again, it is the same old business of synchronizing leg and hand signals.

Please remember this: you do not need to use your legs in commencing to back your horse, unless he has become so relaxed after the halt that he is standing on three legs, half asleep. This happens sometimes, and when it does, you must wake him up. Get his attention by closing in your legs, saying in effect, "pay attention, horse, you are going to be asked to move." Then your hands tell him *where* he is to move.

One other point in connection with backing might be explained here, even though we did not learn it at this particular time. I said we were never to pull hard or *haul* the horse backwards. Someone might ask, "What are you going to do if the horse is stubborn and resists?" As in so many instances where you want to get your way with a horse, you sneak up on him from another angle. You will create a situation in which it is simpler and more comfortable for the horse to obey than disobey.

Stand beside him with the reins over his head as they would be if you were riding. Taking them in your hand about eight inches from the bit, pull gently backwards (toward the hands of an imaginary rider) and use the voice command at the same time. If he ignores your *polite* request, use a crop on his front legs, just above the hooves. He almost certainly will move backwards to avoid this punishment; as he completes several steps pat him and praise him to the skies, and give him a tidbit. It won't take him long to learn what you want, and how to earn a reward.

When he seems to understand this method, try it mounted, but have someone on the ground with a crop in hand if there is any doubt that he has learned the lesson completely. When he does *this* readily and quietly, you will no longer need the assistant. The final step will be to abandon the use of voice.

That is the story on backing, although not all of it even yet. I'll bet you never imagined there was so much to it! We didn't either, or to a lot of other techniques we were learning, until we got into them.

TURNS

We talked about turns at gaits earlier, but discussed only wide turns. However, there is no great difference in the way a shorter turn is made (that is, until we get to the really short turn at speed) except that the rein on the side to which one is turning is not carried out so far. It is carried only slightly out, and also pulls back a little. The opposite hand gives as much as the one hand takes. The other instructions hold good—inside leg on the girth; outside leg behind the girth if necessary to keep the horse's hind legs following the same path as the front legs. In addition to using your inside leg on the girth to prevent the horse from "falling in" to the arc of the curve you ride, and to maintain the correct design of his body, neck and head, you may need to use the rein of indirect opposition. Remember these rein aids may be used to straighten the forehand when necessary, or to assist in bending, or to require the horse to look slightly in, so that head, neck and body all conform to the path the horse travels. The rider must use both his legs sufficiently to maintain the desired speed. The rider steps down in his inside stirrup enough to stay in balance with his horse.

CIRCULAR MOVEMENTS USED IN SCHOOLING

Thus far, we haven't talked schooling exercises that involve bending, other than in the description of turns.

All exercises that include riding along curved lines rather than along straight lines are called exercises in "lateral flexibility" and develop the horse's ability to handle himself with ease and agility as he makes turns. This ability to handle his legs and body effortlessly and comfortably as he shifts the direction in which he is moving is tremendously important. When you hunt, and find yourself galloping down a twisting woods trail, it's awfully nice to feel that your horse knows exactly how to handle his legs and isn't going to topple over on his nose! Again, if you are going to ride your horse in horse shows over jump courses, he will have to be able to change his direction quickly and smoothly.

The main ring exercises to develop the horse in this way are: circle, half circle, half circle in reverse, zigzag, serpentine, and figure eight.

In making circles, we were always cautioned not to attempt a circle of such small size that we would cramp the horse's gait. The aids used are just the same as for an ordinary turn, except that you continue riding along the curved path until you are back at your starting place.

The half circle begins the same way, but, as you see from the diagram, when you are facing in the direction from which you came, you take a straight line obliquely back to the track. This exercise requires the use of aids in a little different combination, as you commence with a circular movement, then change to a straight movement, and at the last, as you reach the track, once again you have a bend.

We used to do these exercises in long columns along the track. They also provided lessons to the horses in "advanced stabilization." Horses *must* hold even gaits, both on the straightaway and throughout the movement, or the whole class will become snarled. Riders had to think of the other people on the track as well as about themselves and their own horses.

When the whole class of horses and riders are working together smoothly
and with precision it becomes a "fun" class, as well as a valuable one.

There isn't much to tell about riding zigzags and serpentines. The aids
are no different than for any other circular movement, and you just have
to be sure you understand the movement you are riding and ride it with
precision. The half circle in reverse is ridden just as the diagram indicates,
too.

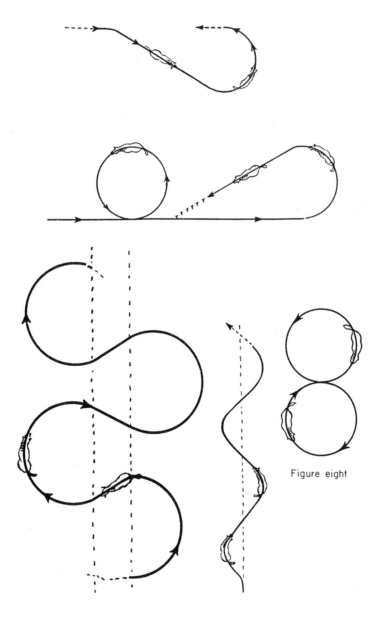

Figure eight

In all of these movements it was stressed that we must require the horse to maintain even speeds and that we must not make the curves too small for him to execute comfortably. Ideally, the horse's spine curves ever so slightly to follow the path of the curve you ride, and he should look *in* just a little—about enough for you to see the corner of his eye.

Figure eights are used quite often in horsemanship classes at shows, and are usually ridden at a canter. At this stage of the game, we were taught to bring the horse down to a trot through the center and to pick up the canter on the opposite lead after crossing the center line.

TURN ON THE FOREHAND

One other movement was taken up that first summer that I was a pupil at Gaymeadows. That was the half turn on the forehand. This is fun to teach your horse, and *so* useful. It is really teaching him to move his quarters over in response to your leg used behind the girth. You make use of this understanding in other movements, in addition to its having very practical usages in field riding. For example, in hunting you often find a line of horses strung out along a narrow little woods trail. The staff (more will be explained about this in the chapters on foxhunting) may have to double back and you must move your horse quickly out of the way; the members of the staff do *not* want to gallop past a group of excited horses with heels ready to fly at them! If your horse knows the turn on the forehand, it is simple to move his quarters out of the way so that his head faces the group galloping by. Again, when you are opening a gate, it's nice not to have to struggle with your horse, but have him rotate his quarters politely around for you, so that you don't have to hang head down in an effort to reach the latch.

This is what we were told to do: Halt somewhere along the fence, but not so close to it that the horse will hook his head over it as he makes the turn. Move your outside leg (the leg nearest the rail) behind the girth, and tap, tap, tap with it until the horse moves his quarters away from it. Hands must be ready to check if horse tries to move forward. Legs must be ready to urge if horse tries to back. If the horse is not entirely familiar with the movement, you may need to use a dull spur to make what you are saying more emphatic. As soon as he moves his hind legs around, making one step, stop him, pat him, praise him and tell him what a fine horse he is! Then you ask for another step in the same way. When he has completed four steps he should be facing back in the opposite direction, and his quarters have made a circle around his front legs. His front legs will have made a tiny circle, the inside front making the smallest of all; in fact, it should have *almost* marked time in place.

As in everything we were taught, there were all sorts of pitfalls, even though the instructors considered this one of the simplest of all movements. For example, in our concentration on the hindquarters—getting them to move around as they were supposed to—we often pulled the head

Photo by Marler   *Photo by Marler*

The photo shows excellent crossing over of the legs, and we would have a first class turn but for the crooked line of head and neck.

Here you see the horse making the third step. Notice the straight body, head and neck, and the relaxed attitude of the horse throughout.

and neck crooked. That is all wrong—the head and neck must remain straight throughout the movement. Again, it is easy to overdo the use of reins, and start your horse backing. This is wrong, too—it is important that you keep the feeling of *forwardness* throughout the movement. The legs are supposed to cross as the horse makes each step, and the moving leg must cross in *front of the one* that hasn't moved, never behind. So the horse must be urged forward enough with both the rider's legs to prevent any backing up. The third pitfall is that the forehand may try to wander around, instead of acting as a pivot. The hands must check just sufficiently to prevent this.

So there you have the movements that were part of class work that summer. In reading this chapter over, I realize that it includes enough material to keep one working for a whole season. (In fact, it did!) Also, in reading, I wonder if it sounds dry to someone who has not had the fun of experimenting with each technique as we did? Actually, as you feel your horse respond and begin to work with you, each step achieved is a real thrill. Try it, step by step, and you will find out.

QUIZ FOR CHAPTER XIII

To be scored as three (3) separate quizzes.

SECTION 1—To be scored as full value quiz of eight (8) parts.
LIST THE THREE (3) LEG ACTIONS AND THE FIVE (5) REIN ACTIONS AND EXPLAIN HOW EACH IS USED.

SECTIONS 2 AND 3—To be scored as two (2) quizzes of sixteen (16) parts each. Mark *TRUE* if all parts of the statement are true; *FALSE* if any part is false.

1. In extending the walk the rider aims to teach the horse to take shorter and faster strides.
2. In extending the walk, the rider's own legs are used to tap to induce the horse to move more energetically. As the horse prepares to "push off" with his left hind leg the rider uses his own left leg to stimulate a more energetic movement; his right as the horse prepares to swing his right hind forward. The rider can determine the correct instant to use his own legs by watching the horse's shoulders, as the left hind will push off immediately after the horse's right front foot has grounded.
3. Exercises that tend to make your horse more flexible the *long way* (i.e., exercises in lengthening and shortening strides) are called exercises in "lateral flexibility."
4. Exercises that tend to make your horse more flexible the *long way* (i.e., exercises in lengthening and shortening strides) are called exercises in "longitudinal flexibility."
5. In order to negotiate a jump course efficiently, it is important for the horse to be able to lengthen and shorten strides on the approach to a fence, for a comfortable take-off.
6. An ordinary trot covers the ground at about fourteen (14) miles an hour.
7. In the slow trot, not only does the horse cover the ground more slowly, but his stride is shortened.
8. In the slow trot the horse's legs do not swing as far under the body and back as they do at an ordinary trot; that is, they do not "engage" as much.
9. In going from the slow to the ordinary trot the rider resumes posting first and then accomplishes his transition (change of speed) secondly

10. Developing the ability in your horse to go from faster to slower speeds is valuable as a "coming back exercise."

11. Abrupt slowing down and halting, such as you might do in the later stages of your horse's schooling or your own riding, is good for the horse who is inclined to move too heavily on the forehand.

12. "Impulse forward" means a calm but energetic forward movement in response to rider's legs.

13. If the horse responds sluggishly to the use of the rider's legs, he should use them more and more strenuously, persisting until the horse obeys.

14. In riding at a gallop the rider should *sit* in the saddle.

15. When you say the horse is on the correct lead you mean that his inside legs seem to move forward in advance of his outside legs.

16. When you say that the horse is on the track to the left, you mean that his left legs are on the inside.

17. When on the track to the left, you normally expect the horse to lead with his right legs.

18. In a good canter departure, the rider collapses to the inside, pulls the horse's head to the rail so that the horse's inside shoulder "pops" and commences the canter departure with the horse crooked.

19. When the horse backs calmly and well, his legs will move in diagonal pairs.

20. When the horse backs well, he will either raise his head and open his mouth, or tuck his chin in and rush back.

21. If the horse begins to back crookedly, the rider uses his leg behind the girth on the side where the horse's quarters are swinging out.

22. If the horse does not respond to the gentle use of the reins asking him to back, it is well to give him backing lessons dismounted, using a whip on his forelegs to enforce the request of the reins. Backing should never be taught by continuing to pull harder and harder on the reins.

23. In making a turn to the right, the right rein is carried very slightly out and slightly back; the left hand gives as much as the right takes, unless a correction to head and neck is required. The rider's right leg remains at the girth; the left is generally carried somewhat behind the girth to induce the horse to allow his quarters to follow the path which his forehand takes. The rider steps down on his inside stirrup.

24. All exercises that involve riding along curved lines are termed lessons in "lateral flexibility."

25. It is important in riding your circular movements that you teach the horse to maintain even speeds, and that you do not attempt a circular movement that is too small for the horse to make comfortably.

26. In a figure eight at a canter on the change of direction the horse is generally expected to canter on the wrong lead for that loop, rather than to come to a trot and pick up the correct lead.

27. In teaching the horse the turn on the forehand you are, among other

things, teaching him obedience in moving his quarters over in response to the rider's leg used behind the girth.

28. In the turn on the forehand the horse's outside hind leg should cross over *behind* the other hind leg, and the horse should back slightly throughout the movement.

29. In the turn on the forehand, correctly executed, the horse's inside front leg will *almost* mark time in place.

30. The turn on the forehand should be executed in about four (4) distinct steps, with the horse's body remaining straight from poll to croup.

31. Draw diagrams of:
    a. a circle
    b. a half circle
    c. a half circle in reverse

32. Draw diagrams of:
    a. a zigzag
    b. a serpentine
    c. a figure eight

CHAPTER XIV

Stable Duty

Bzzzzzzzzz! *Trigger's* legs froze under him, and he refused to move. I was in an agony of embarrassment. Even more awful, it seemed to me, than being "tooted" out of the ring, a gong continued to sound telling me to get out, and I couldn't get my pony to move a peg. Bzzzzzzzzzz! Still it continued. I shot bolt upright in bed—I wasn't in a horse show at all—I was in bed and the alarm was going off. It was five o'clock, and today I was to take Sunday stable duty, together with my friend Jimmy Hudson.

On Sunday, when there was no class, the regular stablemen were off. We riders who had horses or ponies of our own alternated in taking stable duty. Personally, I loved it, and the fact that we got paid made it even nicer.

I pulled on my old blue jeans and sneakers and crept down stairs to gobble down several bowls of cereal with bananas and milk, and if I had time, to flip an egg in the pan and make myself a fried egg sandwich. My agreement with my parents was that if I took Sunday stable duty I would fix myself what my mother called a "decent breakfast," and leave the house quietly. So now I threw together the things Mother had fixed for my lunch and stole out on the front porch to wait for Jimmy. Jimmy had gotten his driver's license this summer, so he and I had the inside track on stable duty, because we now had our own transportation. Or rather Jimmy had transportation, and lived right in our neighborhood, which simplified things for me.

As we drove down to the farm we planned that by getting such an early start we would have our feeding done and stalls cleaned by noon and would have from then until afternoon feeding time to do what we wanted.

Most of the "school string" (horses owned by DSH as opposed to the boarders) were turned out at night in summer, and as we approached the stable, they came crowding around, plainly saying, "Is breakfast about ready?" We had to tell them to be patient. First we start with the boarders who stayed up at night. (I don't mean that they "stayed up" at night in the sense that they didn't go to bed. They "stayed up" in the stalls instead of being turned out at night.)

The first thing we do on stable duty is to water all the horses who are in overnight. Jimmy took the long hose and started in the front stable; I did the same thing in the main stable. Each horse has his own water bucket in his stall, and as nearly as possible you try to see that it is never empty. Horses should have good clean water at all times. During the week, the stablemen take the buckets out once a day to wash them, but on Sundays we were told that we need do just the absolutely essential things.

If you have never had their care, you will want to know what horses get to eat and why the feeding is done in a certain way. Hay and grain are the main elements of their diet. Hay is their bulk food and grain their

Courtesy of Lt. Col. Franklin Hickman

"We put the hay in each horse's hay rick."

energy food. They are always fed in this order: 1. *Water*. 2. *Hay*. 3. *Grain*. The water is supposed to be there all the time and buckets must always be refilled before they eat. If they bolt their food and then gulp down a lot of water it can cause the grain to swell and give them colic. Hay comes before the grain to take the edge off their first hunger so that they won't eat their grain too fast. Also, if it were done the other way (grain before hay) the bulky hay can actually push the grain through before it is digested, and the value of the grain lost. I always think of the hay making a nice soft bed for the grain to lie on, to be digested.

After we watered all around we put the hay in each horse's hay bin. Our school used the best grade of timothy mixed with a little clover. Mrs. D. held that it never does to economize on a poor grade of hay, or any other feed, for that matter. Jimmy threw the bales down from the hayloft, and I began breaking them open. These were big bales, about 70 pounds each, and we split them six ways for the big horses; about seven or eight ways for large ponies, and eight or ten ways for the small ones. Then when all the ricks were filled, we let the school horses, who had been waiting impatiently at the doors, come in to their stalls to breakfast.

Next we start measuring out the grain (we use straight oats in summer; a mixed feed that is more heating in winter), and while this is going on, all the horses and ponies really kick up a rumpus. They are funny, but their table manners are dreadful. The ponies are the worst; *Sauce Box* and *Little Red* actually stand up with their hooves in their grain boxes, pawing and nickering. The horses manage to restrain themselves a little better, although they too keep up a soft nickering to attract the attention of the person carrying the grain bucket. They are cute about it. You know that they are saying "Don't forget me. I've done lots of favors for you and the other riders—please come over this way next. Really, I am starving to death; can't you hurry?" And then when you have completed your rounds, the most blessed peace settles over the stable. At this point Jimmy and I used to take a breather for a few minutes. We'd sit down with a coke or an orange and listen to the munching and enjoy the nice sweet smell of the hay.

"Today was pleasant, so out they went."

When the horses finished their morning feed, I checked them over to make sure no one had a scraped cannon or a banged knee. I did find a scrape on *Storm Cloud's* gaskin—it wasn't deep or bad looking, so I used scarlet oil on it. This is a disinfectant and at the same time has healing value. Then there were a couple of the ponies who had skinned places on their necks; for that we were using vaseline so the hair will come in smoothly. The ponies are such rascals that they are forever playing and nibbling on one another and keeping each other skinned up.

While I was doing this, Jimmy was spraying. This has to be done every day in summer, and even then it is hard to keep the flies down. It's sort of tricky business, too, because you don't want to get the spray on the hay, and have to be careful just to do the walls and floors of the stall.

Stable duty was a snap in summer. Unless the day was too awfully hot and sunny, or unless it was pouring rain, we could turn the school string out again right after they finished their morning feed and were checked over. That meant that cleaning their stalls took practically no time. Today was pleasant, so out they went. Then we started putting the boarders out, separately or two good friends together, in the different paddocks, so they would get a little exercise. Each would stay out about an hour, and as the day got hotter, we would put all the boarders in. There wasn't as much

Fork

Rake

Broom

Wheelbarrow

Sketches in Chapter Courtesy
of Mrs. Richard Ruffner

"Each stall must be cleaned thoroughly
every day."

shade in the paddocks as out in the fields, where the school string goes. Not only are horses more comfortable in their stalls than out in hot sun, but too much hot sun will bleach their coats and destroy the gloss.

After the horses are put out, we start on our stalls. Jimmy and I divide the stable in half, and to make it more interesting the person who finishes last has to treat the other to a cold drink. Each stall is thoroughly cleaned every day. Every bit of soiled bedding must be taken out and what clean straw is left banked up against the sides of the stall. They are left bare during the day, so that the clay floor will dry out before the stall is bedded for the next night. When the stalls are done this way every day, and the horses are out so much, it only takes about three minutes for each straight stall. The boxes take about fifteen minutes each. In all, we have thirty-nine stalls of which twenty-two are regular box stalls, four pony size boxes, five tiny boxes for the little ponies, and eight straight stalls.

As usual, Jimmy finished his stalls first, even though he had been chivalrous and taken the one odd stall. Then he helped me finish, although I wasn't too far behind him. We were through about 12:00 right on schedule, just in time to refill water buckets for the horses who were in their stalls before giving them their noon feed. In the middle of the day, they get

"I managed to hold his head up so he couldn't spit out the medicine."

Dose syringe.

hay only, unless they are on a special schedule. The school string didn't get anything in the middle of the day on Sunday, as they were out eating grass anyway.

Whee! 1:00 o'clock and all our work was up. Now Jimmy and I would sit down and enjoy our lunches and then could lark around until time to start the afternoon work about 4:00 or 4:30. We could, huh? Just as we started out of the stable we saw something that stopped us dead in our tracks. *Demon's Bliss* was in a cold sweat, getting up and getting down, nipping at his sides. No doubt about it—a bad colic. While Jimmy ran to the tack room to get a blanket to put on him, I stayed down in his stall to keep him from rolling. I had dried him off some with the sweat scraper and was rubbing him with a towel when Jimmy came back with a blanket and the colic medicine. Horses are not too cooperative about taking colic medicine out of a syringe (I can't blame them!) but *Demon* was a pretty good patient. I managed to hold his head up so he couldn't spit out the medicine while Jimmy poured the two ounces down him. Then we stayed down in his stall to watch him for a while. If he didn't show signs of relief within 45 minutes or an hour we would call the veterinarian.

As I write this, it occurs to me that I sound as though I am suggesting to my readers to go ahead and dose their sick horses with any old colic medicine. This is not the case at all. In fact, it was quite a long time before Mrs. Douglas was willing to agree to any "home doctoring" for colic. Our veterinarian finally persuaded her to let him leave a colic medicine which, he assured us, in the majority of cases would straighten out colic due to gas. If the colic is of another type, it could do no harm. And of course unless the horse got pretty prompt relief, we were to call the veterinarian anyway.

We had very careful classes, at first under the direction of Dr. Kiger, our vet, in learning to recognize colic symptoms and then in learning to use the dose syringe. No one was ever to give medicine of any kind unless on official stable duty, and they must first be coached in its use as well as the treatment of other minor ailments. No one could take stable duty until fifteen years old, unless on as a junior assistant, which I was today. At thirteen, I was the youngest member of the stable duty crew, and could take the job only with Jimmy, who was now sixteen, and considered very trustworthy.

Sick horses always scare me. Today the Douglases and most of the other families were away at a horse show and we felt an awful load of responsibility. If ever there was any question as to whether or not we needed the vet, we were supposed to call him. However, Dr. Kiger wasn't too keen on being called on Sunday afternoon unless it was a real emergency. The colic medicine was on hand at all times, and the rule was if the horse continued to have a lot of discomfort for as long as an hour after taking a dose, we were to call him. So we hung around *Demon's* stall for about a half an hour and he did seem to feel lots better. He wasn't sweating now, and only got down and up once in the half hour. And now he was just giving his side an occasional distressed look, instead of nipping at it the way he had been. We decided we could go on up to the club room and have our lunch, and check him again in about fifteen minutes.

Just as I got Jimmy the coke I owed him and we sat down to have our lunch (it was now almost 2:00 P.M.) a car drew up and a man and his daughter got out. Part of our Sunday job was to act as hosts to anyone who came down to the stable, so taking one big gulp of my coke to save myself from starvation, I went out to see them.

They wanted to see *Funny Boy,* whose owner, Paula Julian, was going to college in the fall, and had put him up for sale. Paula had told them to come on down to the stable and ask me to ride and show *Funny* to them. Now I never remember being too tired or hungry to ride, and I thought it was fun to show off someone else's horse. So I quickly ran the brush over him, tacked him and brought him out. *Funny* was a cute little bay, about fifteen hands, an excellent and very willing jumper although still a little green. First I took him up to the ring and hacked him around for a while. Then we put up a little course, and he went on just as nicely and willingly as you please. Next, they wanted to see him over the outside course, and here he became a little too bold and put in several "monster" fences that I could barely stay with. Somehow, we managed without their noticing anything wrong (or were they just polite?), and they seemed to like his jumping very much.

The young girl who was interested, Mary Atkinson, was ready to try him now. I held my breath, as *Funny* could get "buzzed up" very easily by rough hands. But this girl really rode well, and they hit it off right away. He turned in even nicer fences for her than he had for me, and was quieter out on the hunter course. I was sure that he was just the horse for her, but she seemed a little dubious. Apparently she was looking for a little conformation and *Funny* wasn't handsome. He was an excellent performer under tactful hands, and I was crazy about the way this girl rode. They left saying that they would get in touch with Paula. It turned out that she liked him more than she indicated, and she did buy him. Incidently, she is still hunting the little horse with the Orange County hounds, and he is said to be one of the best hunters who ever followed hounds in their territory.

Paula was so delighted that the sale went through that she insisted on getting me a new hunting snaffle for *Trigger*. She seemed to feel that I had made the sale for her, although actually *Funny* had sold himself.

But to get back to the day's stable duty, and to lunch—it was now three o'clock and I decided to make another try at eating. In case you are feeling too sorry for me, I will reassure you by admitting that Jimmy and I had stopped for a mid-morning snack, at which time I had eaten two hard boiled eggs, three apples, a Hershey bar, and drunk the pint of milk out of my thermos, so I wasn't in as bad shape as you probably imagine. About all that was left for my official lunch, anyway, was a ham sandwich and a banana, except for the carrots I had brought to the horses. However, I was so hungry by now that I ate the horses' carrots too, except for one that I saved for *Trigger*. I couldn't be so base as to eat his!

Jimmy had given *Demon* a second dose of the colic medicine, and he seemed to feel just about all right now. However, Jimmy and I were worried, because we felt that it was our fault that he had gotten colic.

He had been a little thin when he arrived at Gaymeadows, and was one of the horses on three grain feeds a day. But what we had forgotten when we grained that morning was that his owner, Trudy May, was away on vacation, and he wasn't getting half as much exercise as usual. Therefore, his grain order was supposed to be cut way down, and we had neglected to check his stall card with this note on it. He had started getting sick before he finished his noon grain, and of course we had taken what was left out of his box. Now, he should have no grain at the evening feed and this little upset would probably slow down his gaining weight for about a week. But I could hardly believe that getting overgrained that one feed could bring on colic so fast—I wondered if the stablemen hadn't been pushing him a little too much, too. Or was I just trying to alibi for my own mistake? Well, it was too late to worry now, and thank goodness he had straightened out. Jimmy and I would be more careful after this.

We were just going to get out horses for ourselves when a long impressive-looking limousine drew up. Somehow, it looked very funny to us to see a liveried chauffeur alighting and holding the door for a lady and two children at such an informal spot as our stable. We choked back our impulse to laugh and came out to greet the visitors. They were from one of the South American embassies, and their English was equally as bad as my Spanish. Jimmy could talk a little French, and they got along in that tongue better than either of the other two. I decided that he might as well take them around, and that I would go on and ride. As I was getting *Cornflakes* out, I heard Jimmy saying about *Jumping Giraffe,* who was his favorite mount, "Ce cheval est le meilleur cheval dans l'écurie." What a fraud!

The little girls were crazy about the small ponies (who had started coming up to the stable, with supper on their minds) and after nearly an hour could hardly be torn away from them. By the time the visitors left, it was too late for poor Jimmy to ride at all. Time to start bedding the horses who stayed in for the night, then to water, then to put the hay in all around and lastly to grain. Then when the school string finished, they would be put out again for the night.

Did I say stable duty was a snap in summer? However, we agreed, as we drove home, that even when our free time seemed to evaporate as it had today, there was something terribly satisfying about "horse keeping" thirty-nine horses and ponies. And every Sunday's stable duty brought my new saddle closer!

QUIZ FOR CHAPTER XIV

To be scored as one (1) quiz of ten (10) parts.
Mark as correct *one statement only.*

1. Horses should always be fed in this order:
    a. grain, water, hay
    b. water, hay, grain
    c. grain, hay, water
2. The usual way to take care of a minor scrape on a horse's leg would be to:
    a. call a veterinarian immediately so he can administer a tetanus shot
    b. leave it to heal itself; scratches are never serious
    c. apply scarlet oil or some similar disinfectant
3. During the hot summer days, horses should be turned out:
    a. only for short periods, unless there is plenty of shade in their field
    b. as much as possible, so they can enjoy the sun
4. The symptoms of colic can generally be recognized by the fact that the horse will:
    a. continually get up and down and nip at his sides
    b. stand with his head in the corner and breathe heavily
    c. neigh loudly and have a ravenous appetite
5. The stalls should be bedded down every afternoon with:
    a. plenty of hay so the horse can eat while he lies down at night
    b. clean straw
6. In summer, fly spray is used every day around the stable to:
    a. keep bugs out of the hay
    b. keep the stable as free as possible of flies
7. Stalls are left bare during the day so that:
    a. the clay floors will dry out
    b. the horses will really appreciate their bedding at night
8. When a horse is getting less than his normal exercise you should:
    a. increase his feed to give him something to do and relieve his boredom
    b. cut down his grain
9. Colic medicine is normally:
    a. rubbed on the horse's abdomen
    b. administered by mouth with a dose syringe
10. An average sized horse doing a normal amount of work would get approximately:
    a. 60 or 70 pounds of hay at a feed
    b. 6 or 7 pounds of hay at a feed
    c. 11 or 12 pounds of hay at a feed

CHAPTER XV

Schooling to Hunt

Summer was almost over. The gloom that came over us at the prospect of school opening, keeping us away from our horses until afternoon of every day, was lessened by one thing only. Mrs. D. had said that our group could start foxhunting this fall. The most delicious shivers of excitement would run up and down our spines at the prospect, and somehow it changed our entire attitudes about seeing September roll around.

We hung on every word of our lecture on foxhunting, and took avid notes. From these, I have tried to rewrite the lecture, and here it is:

Books are written on the history and art of foxhunting. We have less than two hours to cover the essential things you must know before you go into the hunt field.

We will start with the organization of the hunt. The head of all hunting activities is the Master of Foxhounds—generally spoken of as the MFH. It is up to the MFH to decide over what country the hunt will move each week. This decision is governed by conditions of weather, ground, habits of the foxes, size of the field and many other factors. The position of MFH is an honorary one (done for love of the sport and not for reimbursement) but none the less the Master is the hardest working individual in the hunt. He tries to see that every member of the field enjoys the best possible sport; that no damage is done to fields, fences or crops; that no undue risk to rider, horse or hound is taken. The Master is your host and should be accorded every possible courtesy.

Directly in charge of the hounds is the huntsman. Usually he is a paid employee of the hunt. He has full charge of hounds, in the kennels as well as in the field. He is said to "hunt the hounds." He carries a horn on which he blows various calls. This is one of the ways in which he controls his hounds, as each call has a specific meaning. He can also communicate with the other members of the staff through its use. In addition to using the horn, the huntsman uses his voice in various ways to control and encourage the pack.

Assisting in the management of the hounds are the whippers in, or "whips" as they are called. They may be either honorary or professional;

in our hunt they are honorary. These officials of the hunt are known as the staff. The members, other than the staff, are known as the field. Some hunts also have a field master, who is directly in charge of the field. It is the duty of the field master to lead the field. It is his job to see that the field does not ride so close that they interfere with hunting the hounds. Under no circumstances may a member of the field pass the field master.

In some hunts the master "hunts his own hounds"; that means that there is no professional huntsman in the field. In our hunt, we have a professional huntsman to hunt the hounds, and our MFH acts as field master.

Now, let's think about your manners and the manners of your horses in the hunt field. In the first place, it is a courtesy to the MFH and the

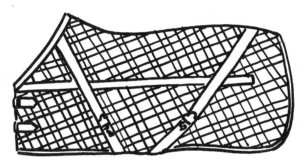

Horse blanket

other members of the hunt to arrive looking well turned out—both you and your horse. If your horse gets a heavy winter coat, he should be clipped, or he will look like a shaggy goat. Furthermore, if you hunt a horse with a heavy winter coat, you are flirting with pneumonia. He will get hot and wet and can become chilled before the long coat dries out. Naturally, after your horse is clipped you will want to keep him blanketed in his stall, and you won't turn him out for exercise on very cold, windy days. If you did this, and he just stood around, he could get pneumonia that way too.

That he should be thoroughly clean goes without saying, and here too, clipping makes your job easier. You want to be sure that his shoes are all right—you certainly don't want to start out with your mount's feet all grown out over his shoes, or with loose shoes. It is equally important that your tack should be in good shape. A weak bridle rein or stirrup leather can cause a serious accident. And of course your tack should be clean and well oiled, bits and stirrup irons shining.

As far as your own attire goes, your first season of hunting, you really

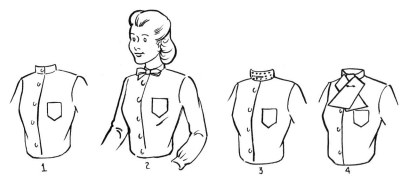

This is what the standard ratcatcher shirt looks like. As you see, it has no collar, only a little band. Sketch 2 shows it with its own little detachable tie. Sketch 3 shows it worn with a silk neck band. Sketch 4 shows it with a white stock. (For your white stock, you need a white shirt.)

Silk polka dot stock

Velvet hunt cap, Tweed coat, Breeches and Boots —all correct "ratcatcher" hunt attire. But for hunting, the wearer should substitute a silk print or polka dot stock for the turtle neck sweater.

Velvet hunt cap

Bowler or Derby

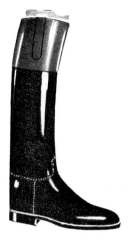

Yellow vest—with this you wear your white stock and black coat

Men or boys' black boot, tan topped

Ladies or girls' plain boot

Jodhpur shoe

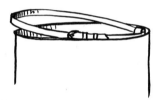

This is what boot garters look like. The buckle actually should be directly over your shin bone.

Prince of Wales Spurs. The leather strap that goes through the loop end and holds the spur on is not shown.

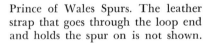

are supposed to wear what are called "ratcatcher" clothes—this means tweed coat, with breeches or jodhpurs in any of the tan or brick tones (naturally you know that you would never appear in black or green breeches or jodhpurs); plain shirt with colored polka-dot or silk print stock. Turtleneck sweaters or silk neckbands are *not* satisfactory substitutes for stocks. With the tweed jacket, you wear brown boots with boot garters; or if you are wearing jodhpurs, brown jodhpur shoes. Now,

I know that most of you have only one presentable riding jacket and that it probably is black. It is perfectly all right to wear the black coat, even though traditionally the tweed is considered more correct for the first season. But if you wear a black coat, then you must wear white stock, fawn or brick breeches, and black boots with boot garters. Yellow vest is correct but not obligatory.

Of course no one will be allowed in the hunt field without his hunt cap. By the way, you juniors will wear the velvet hunt cap, until you are

Officers of the Fairfax Junior Hunt, properly "turned out." Notice that three of the girls have won their buttons, as you can tell by their collars. The boy in the center shows the correct attire for a junior (boy) who wears the colors of his hunt.

eighteen. After that you will have to wear bowlers (also called derbies)—unless you are honorary hunt staff members by that time! In that case you would still wear your velvet hunt cap. And if you are a boy, you would wear a scarlet coat with your hunt cap.

Which brings me to another custom I should explain briefly. If you are a member of a hunt, after several seasons you are generally invited to wear the official buttons of the hunt together with the hunt colors—that is, if you have been a pleasant, capable, and thoughtful addition to the hunt. Each hunt has its own buttons and colors, and girls or ladies have the collars of their hunt coats faced with this color. At the same time, they should wear the official hunt buttons—each hunt has buttons with its own crest. Boys and men look very dazzling when they win *their* colors—they then wear scarlet coats with the hunt buttons and collars in their hunt's colors. These scarlet coats are never referred to as red—they may be called scarlet, but, oddly enough, are generally termed "pink." With the scarlet coat, one wears white breeches.

If you are an *adult* male member of the field, wearing scarlet, you would wear a high silk hat. But if you are an adult male member of the field who is also an honorary staff member, then you could still elect to wear your velvet hunt cap with your scarlet coat. Either men or boys may have their black boots "topped" with tan calfskin; with the scarlet coat you *always* would wear "topped" boots.

Girls or ladies may have their black boots "topped" also, but their boots are topped with black patent leather. This is optional on a lady's boot, whether or not she has won her buttons and colors. Boot garters are also considered a necessary accessory on boys', girls', men's· or women's boots.

However, pink coats or even hunt colors are so far in the future for you children that you needn't worry about saving up for them just yet! Just worry about having your tweed or black coat clean and pressed, your breeches fitting correctly, your boots shining, and your stock properly tied (I'll do it for you the first few times) with the gold stock pin straight across. There are reasons for, or history connected with, all the small details of hunt attire. Someday, we will go into it all more carefully, but for the time being you need only know what to wear yourselves, and how it is that some of the people out hunting will be dressed differently from you.

There are quite a few "do's and don't's" in connection with foxhunting, and to save time, I will list the most essential ones.

Be punctual. Arrive before the moment when hounds are to move off.

Greet the Master on your arrival. Boys or men tip their hats to him. If he does not know you, introduce yourself, and remind him of the arrangements that were made for you to hunt.

Give your name to the hunt secretary.

Walk your horse around to accustom him to the other horses. As the hunt moves off, prepare to drop in towards the back of the field, unless specifically invited by the Master or your host to ride further forward.

Remember to stay off the heels of the horse in front of you. There is nothing more annoying to people than to have a horse sitting on their tails. Also, it can be quite dangerous.

If you find yourself behind a horse with a red ribbon tied on his tail, be very sure that you give him a wide berth. The ribbon means that he kicks.

You will probably ride slowly until the hounds "find" (get up a fox)—

if they do! Then all of a sudden you may find yourself riding like the wind. And this is when you have to start using your head, and *really* riding.

When you come to a fence, *you must take your turn and be careful not to cut off another rider.* Before committing his horse to a fence, one usually glances around, to be sure that he is next. If the fence has several jumpable panels, put your horse straight at the panel you have indicated you will take, and do not "cross panels"—you may run into someone else and cause a serious accident.

Have I explained what we mean by panels? Panels are sections—either chicken coops or straight rails—set in a wire fence to make jumping feasible. In an all-rail fence, the sections between posts are panels. (The photo on page 157, Chapter XVI, shows such a "chicken coop" panel, set in the wire fence.)

If you get a refusal, go to the back immediately—do not take a second try at the fence, holding up others.

Don't race your horse at fences. There are too many situations in which a fence or a coop is set in such a way as to be very "trappy." Perhaps there is a stream or hard surfaced road close to the landing side of the jump; perhaps you are jumping into a seeded or grass field, in which case you must turn sharply right or left immediately after landing in order to avoid damaging the field. If your horse forms the habit of racing over his jumps you will be in for trouble. Teach him to approach quietly. In most instances, you can perfectly well trot up to the jump and permit only a few cantering strides before the take off. In this way, you are pretty certain to be able to control your horse promptly on the landing side.

Make your horse walk through bogs and across streams wherever possible. Otherwise, you may find him with a strained tendon.

When you hear the Master call back, "Hold hard," *freeze* in your tracks. Try to keep your horse from pawing, rattling his bit or rustling leaves. The staff must be able to listen to hounds, and will not appreciate any distraction from you and your horse.

Often when you have galloped up a woods trail, there may be a check (a halt) after which you may hear someone calling "Staff, please," or " 'Ware staff," or " 'Ware huntsman." That means that the staff plans to double back down the trail over which you have just ridden, and no matter how dense the wood, you *must pull off the trail, with your horse's head facing* in, *quarters and heels away from the passing horses.*

One of the big responsibilities of the hunt is to see that no gates are left open, letting stock out, no fences broken down or wire snipped and left unrepaired. I'll see to it that none of you are in a position to have to get off and close a gate for some time, by being sure that you aren't at the *very* back of the field. However, *be sure to pass the word back, "gate please" to the last man,* to indicate that it is to be closed. But if your horse breaks a rail in jumping a fence, we *will* have to stop right then and there, repair it as best we can and then report the mishap to the hunt secretary or the MFH at the earliest opportunity.

You often hear that you must be careful never to cross a seeded field or a grass field when it is wet. This is true, but you children won't have to worry about such decisions for quite a while, as of course I will keep you behind me; naturally I won't do either thing. The staff may, but that is their privilege, and the hunt will pay for any damage to crops or pasture. The field *must skirt* the edge.

You may hear someone call out " 'Ware hound." This will mean that a hound is coming up from behind, and it is up to you to see that your horse doesn't step on him or, crime of crimes, kick at him. If that should happen, just dig a little hole and crawl into it, pulling the earth over you!

Just as we do when we are out hacking, if the person in front of you notices any hazard such as wire or a hole, he will say " 'Ware wire" or " 'Ware hole." You must be sure to point out the danger and to pass the warning back.

If yours should be the bright eyes that sight the fox when no one else has, no doubt you will be so excited that you will want to shout out, "OOOOh! Look! There he goes!" However, restrain yourself; in spite of the traditional idea that one shouts "Tally-ho" on viewing the fox, your best bet is to remain silent. The chances are that if *you* have viewed him, the staff, who, after all, are up front watching very carefully, have done likewise. A great babble of "tally-ho's" can completely upset the hound work. If the whips should view the fox when the huntsman doesn't, they don't shout out. They remain perfectly silent and point with hunt cap to the line which the fox took. Point, if you wish, but don't shout!

Never pull out and leave the hunt without first gaining permission from the MFH or FM (field master). There are two reasons for this: in the first place the MFH or FM is accountable for every person in the field. In the second place, in hacking home you may cross the line the fox has taken, turn him, or in some other way, upset hound work. I'm pretty sure that this won't apply to any of you kids, as I imagine it would take an earthquake to persuade you to pull out; and in any case, you will be with me, and I will be watching out for you, and responsible for you.

While I think of it, I should also mention that in hacking to the hunt meet, you should go by the roads rather than cross country. Can you think of the reason? Naturally, you don't want to spoil the chances of a chase by getting up foxes before the hunt starts, do you?

At the end of the day, when you hack back to the hunt club, or if you leave the hunt and hack directly home, be sure you go up to the MFH and thank him for the day.

You cannot possibly be expected to acquire any appreciable knowledge of hound work in your first season of hunting, particularly as you will be required to stay in the back of the field this year. But I would like you to understand enough hunting terms to be able to follow a description of a hunt, or to know how to describe what happened on a day when you were out. I will use some of the more common expressions you will hear in sentences. This may make it easier to remember their meaning than to ask you to memorize them "cold."

The huntsman will probably keep the hounds closely packed around him until the first *cast*. (*Cast* is spreading out in search of the fox's scent.)

The place where the hounds are *cast* is the *covert* (*covert*—pronounced *cover*—is a heavily wooded area or thicket where the fox finds shelter).

As the fox leaves the *covert*, if you actually see him leave, you say that he is *viewed away*.

Hounds follow the fox (their *quarry*) by *scent* (*scent* is the odor given off by the fox) rather than by sight.

You would say that *"Jester* was the first to *challenge* on *finding the line."* (That means that *Jester* was the first hound to *speak*, when they found the *scent*. This scent trail which they follow is called the *line*.) You say that a hound *speaks*, or *gives tongue*, or *cries*. (He *never* "barks!") You speak of these *cries* as *hound music*.

As the hounds *"settle to the line,"* if the scent is very good or strong you might say it is *screaming* or *burning*.

If the huntsman blows the "gone away" at this moment it means that fox and hounds are moving off at speed, and to get ready for a fast chase. In this connection you may hear someone say that they had "quite a burst" for the first few minutes.

Then you might say that the hounds *carried* or *worked the line* on down across Sidwell's meadow, let's say, to Difficult, where they *lost*. (This means lost the scent.) After a brief *check* (interruption to the run as a result of losing the scent) the field thought that hounds had *found* (recovered the scent) about twenty feet downstream, when *Jill*, who was *flighty* (or a *babbler*, or *mouthy*, or inclined to *fling her tongue*—all meaning that she might *speak* falsely) *spoke* first and the others *owned* to it ("spoke" also in agreement).

The pack was off again, but the huntsman was almost sure that they were *rioting* (to riot is to run any game but their legitimate quarry) on deer, and it so happened that he was right.

With the help of the whips he got them back, and *rated* (punished) them.

Then he *lifted* them (lifted means to take the hounds from a lost scent to another point, with a view to hitting the line somewhere else or may be used simply to indicate taking hounds from one point to another) to a point upstream where once again they *found*.

This time, the hounds ran for an hour and a half with only two brief *checks,* until the fox finally went to *ground* (or *earth*—any underground passage, or hole into which the fox escapes) over in, let's say, Darrel's wood.

The huntsman didn't try to dig him out, even though he had hoped for a kill that day, as some of the *young entry* (hound puppies) had never been *blooded* (had never been in on a kill).

That covers quite a few of the more common terms, and to them I should add a few I couldn't quite weave into such an account.

If a *covert* is empty, you say it is *blank,* or *drawn blank.* If hounds do not *find* on a particular day, you say that it was a *blank* day.

When the quarry is killed or run to ground, you say it is *accounted for.* His tail is called the *brush;* his head is called the *mask.*

A male fox is known as a *dog fox;* a female as a *vixen.* Their young are *cubs;* their home is called a *den.*

Hounds are always referred to as *couples;* thus fourteen hounds are called seven couples. This term is derived from the custom, dating back hundreds of years, of "coupling" two hounds together. There are many reasons for doing this. In our own hunt a hound puppy is coupled to an older hound so that the youngster will learn how he is expected to behave. The hound's tail is called his *stern.* You say that a hound is *feathering* when he moves his *stern* from side to side; this usually indicates that he is on the edge of recognizing the *scent,* but possibly isn't sure enough to *speak.*

You say that the huntsman *cheers* his hounds—this is any hunting cry to encourage them. You say that hounds are in *full cry,* when, as they run at speed, you hear the joyous *"hound music."*

This covers most of the things you should understand and the terms you should know before you start out on a hunt. Actually, you could "get by" without knowing the terms that relate to the actual hunting of hounds, but it is nice not to have to feel a complete greenhorn when hunting is discussed. It is *absolutely essential* that you understand thoroughly matters relating to hunt etiquette before you appear in the field, and that your horse is schooled in such a way that he will not cause embarrassment. For the rest of the semester, we will concentrate on actual work to improve your horses' manners and behavior in the hunt field.

And so the lecture ended. This was probably the most difficult lecture we had been given, and certainly it contained more new terms. But it didn't matter—we were so eager to hunt that we almost memorized the lecture, word for word.

According to plan, almost every day for the rest of the semester we were asked to report for class out on the hunter course.

Everything we had been learning in the ring should contribute to our horses' good performance in the hunt field: the *habit of obedience* to hand and leg signals; *confidence* that the rider will never ask him to try what is too difficult for him to perform; *dexterity* in handling himself— the ability to lengthen and shorten strides and to turn with ease. We felt that our mounts had absorbed these lessons well, but now they would find themselves in more stimulating situations—situations in which complete calmness is almost too much to expect. This calm attitude and frame of mind must now be taught in field and woods.

When we were assembled on the outside course, we would count off, so that half of us would have odd numbers, half even. We would form a column and "fall in" two or three horses' lengths apart. After our horses were warmed up at a walk (this would be interspersed with halts during which horses must stand quietly) we would commence a trot, and our horses must maintain even speeds and distances, up and down the slopes of the hunter course.

Then we would be given all sorts of commands which our horses must perform individually. The last horse in the column might be asked to canter past the group of trotting horses and then to take up first position. Then the next and the next would do the same, and so on throughout the line. Then perhaps, with the whole group cantering, the odd numbers would be asked to gallop past the even numbers, and then come back to a canter when they are in front. This puts a real test of manners on both groups—if there is no bucking and playing during this maneuver, everybody should have carrots! Or perhaps we are all cantering and the "odds" are asked to come to a walk; "evens" to canter on past. Then the process is reversed, and the "evens" must now walk, while the "odds" canter past them. All these exercises are designed to make the horses understand that they must pay attention to what we, the riders, say. Hard as they may find it at first, they gradually learn that they can't let themselves be carried away by the fact that they are galloping in a field with a group of other horses. By building up to the faster work from lots of slow preparation, it will become just a part of the day's work.

When this part of the class goes smoothly it is time to include work over fences in your hunter exercises. Here again the horse must be convinced that he is never to head into a jump like a bat, or to take a particular fence just because the horse in front of him took it. He must listen to the rider. So we drilled in the same way to achieve calmness and attentiveness to the rider's commands. Now we would form our column and have the "odds" take the fence; the "evens" bypass it; then this procedure would be reversed, so the horse will never develop the notion that a jump in front of him means, "Whoops, kids! Hold your hats. Here we go!" You might be surprised at how many horses entertain exactly that thought.

As the horses became accustomed to this field work and behaved well, classes were made progressively more difficult. We started doing some of the same exercises out on cross country rides, with all sorts of variations. Sometimes several horses would be sent on ahead and out of sight at a good gallop. They would wait for the rest around a bend and others would have to proceed at a quiet walk. Sometimes one or two would have to stay back, and be asked to close a gate, while all the others cantered on off. Again, one of us would trot briskly up to sliding bars that we ordinarily jumped, and halt. Then the rider would reach down and drop the top bar, rein back a few feet and "pop" the fence. Each rider following should also trot and "pop" the jump and the last rider must replace the bar.

We took our "hounds" with us on these junkets—our "pack" was most colorful. It was composed of a Gordon Setter, an Irish Setter, a Dalmatian, a Great Dane, a French Poodle and a mutt. Our "hounds" were encouraged to stay close around us, so that the horses would get used to having them brush against their legs and run almost under their feet. This is good training, as we certainly didn't want to be guilty of that most dreadful crime in hunting—having our horses kick a hound.

Besides trying to teach our horses to take their orders from us rather than from herd instinct, we spent as much time as we could conditioning. To get and keep a horse fit for hunting, he must have plenty of slow work over hilly terrain, and in addition must have some galloping to develop wind.

By Labor Day our horses were plenty fit, knew what they were supposed to do, and all in all, were quite good about doing it in the field and cross country. Would it all carry over when the weather was nippy, hounds running, large fields of strange horses galloping? We would find out in October.

CHAPTER XVI

Tally-ho!

This time, as the alarm went off at 5:30 A.M. it was as if we had been waiting for it. I was spending the night with Sally Hilton, and we were so excited that we hardly slept at all. This was the day of which we had dreamed for months—the opening meet of the Fairfax Hunt!

We had made great and elaborate preparations for this long awaited event. We had exercised our mounts bareback and in borrowed bridles the day before. Thursday night (two days before the hunt) we had spent hours oiling, soaping and polishing our tack, and couldn't bear to get it dirty again Friday.

At this moment, saddles, bridles and breastplates were hanging over chairs in Sally's room, and I went over to feel the leather—it was wonderfully soft and smelled heavenly. My new hunting snaffle with its nice heavy laced reins looked very impressive, I thought. Sally and I had "blown ourselves" to new breastplates, and had carefully darkened the leather with neat's-foot oil the past week to get rid of the glaringly new look. All in all, we felt that our tack looked quite workmanlike.

I looked over my own attire with a less approving eye. My only "good" coat was black. I had bought it at the school's "Out Grown" shop, when, unfortunately, it was almost outgrown for me too! My breeches were okay—they had been the spring's big investment, and were good ones and an excellent fit. My boots were "outgrowns" also, and they didn't quite achieve that look of tall slender elegance that boots should have. Another inch and a half in height would have made all the difference. But at least they were immaculate and looked as handsome as saddle soap and boot polish could make them. Beside them were my Prince of Wales spurs, also newly purchased for hunting, and they would "dress up" the boots somewhat. I had gotten my "hardtop" (black velvet hunt cap) for my birthday in the summer, so I was all set on that score. For the first time in my life I would wear a hair net, as the point had been stressed that hair straggling out from under the hunt cap was messy and unworkmanlike in appearance. (Sally, with her pigtails, didn't need a net.) My finances would not stretch to include the yellow vest that should be worn with the black coat, but I did have a new white stock and gold stock pin, and new pigskin gloves.

Sally was wearing "ratcatchers" as her good jacket was a tweed. With it she was wearing good looking tan "jods," light blue shirt and a blue polka dot stock. Her jodhpur boots were the high laced shoe type that looked very smart.

After we were dressed, we looked one another over carefully. No one ever dressed for their first dance with greater thought for every detail. All in all, we decided that we looked reasonably well turned out, although each of us would like to have changed one or two items of our attire.

We raced down to breakfast, carrying our stocks and stock pins in our hands—Mrs. D. would put these on us at Gaymeadows.

Sally's mother was almost as excited over the first hunt as we were. She had gotten up even before we had, and now breakfast was on the table. We were too excited to eat, but she made us drink some milk and tried to persuade us to choke down eggs, but it was just impossible. So she finally let us off after we managed to eat grapefruit, and some toast and jelly.

We drove up to the stable before seven, with several other cars right behind us. Our horses had been fed when we arrived, but we must clean and polish them, and then tack up. While we did this, we wore old rain coats over our good clothes, so we wouldn't get dirty. Then when our horses were all ready, we dashed to the Douglas's house for a final slicking up—we ran a rag over boots once more, washed our hands, and got Mrs. Douglas to tie our stocks.

Now it was seven-thirty, and we were mounting. Today we were to hack to the hunt club, some six miles away, as all of our mounts were very fit, and Mrs. D. felt that the hack would help settle them down.

I shall never forget a minute of that first hunt—the wonderful early morning feeling; the sun beginning to come out through a slight haze and the morning air quite nippy; the woods all in color; our horses apparently sensing our excitement, feeling very keen; our own spirits soaring to the skies!

The opening hunt is always a gala affair. What a blood stirring sight awaited us as we hacked up to the club house grounds! Vans and trailers were pulling up, and shining mounts were being led off. Quite a few were braided for the opener, although for the regular hunts one seldom braids. Many of the members were already mounted and warming up in the ring; others were hacking around on the club's hunter course.

The scene was made more colorful by the gentlemen in their scarlet coats. The ladies looked very elegant in black. Riders were greeting one another in high spirits; some were riding up to the entrance of the club for coffee and doughnuts. Non-riding husbands or wives were on hand to see the hunt move off, and to take pictures. Newspaper photographers were snapping the MFH and the rest of the staff. The huntsman had just come into the ring with our beautiful tri-colored hounds closely packed around him, and the photographers were trying to photograph the scene.

Mrs. Douglas was waiting for a chance to say "Good morning" to Mr. Greene, our MFH, and to introduce us. Mr. Greene, a tall, impressive looking man, mounted on a seventeen hand bay, looked as if he might

Courtesy of Gertrude and Walker Ridgely

Hacking over to the hunt club.

have stepped right out of a hunting print, and we suddenly felt very shy as we were taken up to meet him. However, he seemed delighted to see us, and said that he was sure that any of Mrs. Douglas's riders would know how to behave in the hunt field.

In just a few more minutes we heard the thrilling notes that meant we were to move off. We went out across the club grounds, across a little hard surfaced road, then into an open field with a wooded area towards one end. Suddenly before those of us at the back knew what had happened we heard the wonderful deep throated chorus that meant that hounds had "found" and everybody was galloping. Now it seemed to me that I had never known the meaning of galloping before—*Trigger's* short legs had to take about twice as many strides as the horses' to stay with them. I was directly behind Mrs. Douglas; old *Wireless* on my right was covering the ground in an effortless manner; *Penny Ante,* behind me, also had a nice style of galloping. Greta, on *Tango,* was having a little trouble keeping the mare from passing Mrs. Douglas, and Greta was making an all out effort to keep her where she wanted her. *Trigger* felt like a small locomotive, ears pinned back in the wind and legs pounding the ground.

I saw someone's hand raised in front and then everyone was slowing down for a minute. Now we could see why—we were to take a chicken coop

Courtesy of Gertrude and Walker Ridgely

"The opening meet is always a very gala affair." Here the hunt prepares to move off. In the foreground is Mr. Greene, our MFH.

Courtesy of Frances and Homer Heller

"Across the field and over a coop we pelted."

jump on the left that led out of this field, and the horses up front were cutting up as they waited their turn. But everything was happening so fast, that no one waited long. It was zip, zip, zip and everyone was disappearing down a woods trail. None of our horses or ponies had any trouble at the jump and we found ourselves tearing down a rutty, rocky woods trail, still at a full gallop. We wouldn't have believed that horses or ponies *could* be galloped in such conditions, but here we all were doing it, with no difficulty at all. We tried to pull down for a little stream (hadn't our lecture said "walk across stream crossings and bogs"?) but no one else was doing it. Mrs. Douglas looked back with a grin after she let *Pied Piper* leap the little stream in order to stay up with the rest of the field, so we did likewise. Up the hill, and in front of us we heard the crackle of a rail splitting, so we knew that a fence was coming up—and also that it was coming down! We were right—the top rail of a very solid looking fence had been broken, but I couldn't see anyone standing beside it "to repair it as best he could." (What had actually happened was that a staff member's horse had broken it, and he would come back later on that day to see about it. We discovered that there are few things you stop for when "on a run.") We weren't a bit sorry to see that top rail down either, as the fence had been close to four feet before the mishap; now it looked just a nice jumpable size.

Over the fence, and we were still galloping in another open field, but in front of us we could see that the staff was pulling up outside someone's barnyard. The fox apparently had run through this lot, and very neatly managed to lose his pursuers amongst the pigs, chickens and cows.

We were just looking around to see how each of the others had fared during this mad gallop (I had lost my net, Mrs. Douglas had a blob of mud on her forehead, and a little branch had left a long scratch across Greta's cheek) when we saw a farmer excitedly pointing out across the open fields again. Hounds picked up the line after only a four or five minute check, and away we went again. Back into the woods we were now on a rougher trail—in fact, it could hardly be called a trail at all. We were still galloping, although not quite as fast, when we heard a gasp and a "plop" behind us, and then saw *Wayward* coming on behind, riderless. Our group pulled up, and there was Sophie running up the trail laughing —she had been pulled right off her horse by a branch across her chest. By the time we had caught *Wayward* and Sophie was back in the saddle, the hunt had disappeared. We could hear the hounds quite far away, and we weren't sure where the rest of the hunt had gone.

We made our way, more slowly now, on up this trail that almost wasn't a trail, and continued to listen and look. Not a sign of anyone! So we kept on going, and obviously took some wrong turns, as for the next hour we were riding around hunting the hunt.

Then we began to hear the hounds coming closer to us—we turned in the direction we thought they must be running, and just as we came out into the open again we saw a brilliant red streak come out from a section of the woods some hundred yards away from us straight across the open field. Oh! Oh! Oh! *Look!* We found ourselves babbling—Fred was the first to recover sufficiently to say "Tally-ho!" Then some distance behind came the hounds, in full cry. Still no sign of the hunt, and I could see that Mrs. Douglas was debating what to do, when the huntsman, staff and members began to pour out of the woods.

We controlled ourselves with great effort until we could drop in towards the back, and once again we were off. Across the field, and over a coop we pelted. Greta was in front of me now, and just as she put *Tango,* who was bouncing up and down and giving little rears, at the jump, a hound puppy appeared out of nowhere and started scrambling over the coop. I saw Greta's face freeze with horror as it looked almost impossible to avoid landing on the puppy. Somehow, she managed to check *Tango* and turn her away from the jump just in time (thank goodness for the hunter exercises we had practiced!) and the puppy was over and out of the way. On the other side of this fence there was another brief check. The fox had run through a herd of cattle and hounds were having a little difficulty finding the line again. Now they found, and again we were off, but at this point we couldn't quite stay with huntsman and hounds. There was a high wire fence separating this field from the next, and the huntsman had picked up a loose board he had found lying on the ground, woven it through the top strands of wire, and gone on. One whip had followed, but the MFH, who was also field master, was galloping down the fence line to show the field where they could take a panel at the far end. By the time we were over and in the next field, the hunt was over. The fox, after leading us all a glorious chase, had gone to ground in a hole along the bank of a stream. How nice that after giving us such a wonderful day, he was safe and sound, and undoubtedly would give us many more!

The hunt that I described is one of the most exciting I remember. Hunting isn't always galloping; sometimes you walk and walk for hours before hounds find. And sometimes when they do find, they manage to get into country where you can't follow. Sometimes you may have a few short runs, and lots of long, long, checks. And occasionally, you have a blank day, with no runs at all.

On this memorable opening hunt, fortune had smiled on all of us. The fox had been viewed at close range twice; he had been sporting enough to run across open fields as well as in woods, and we had had a fast chase for about two hours, with only a few brief checks. Of course, we had spent a little while trying to find the hunt after Sophie's fall, but then we had ended up practically on top of the fox, so we couldn't complain.

When we had thanked Mr. Greene for the day and started to hack on home, we were filled with such a sense of elation and well being that it cannot be described. You can only understand if you go foxhunting too!

QUIZ FOR CHAPTERS XV AND XVI

To be scored as three (3) quizzes. In Sections I and II you have twenty-seven (27) statements which must be marked "FALSE" or "TRUE." The third Section, supplying the correct foxhunting terms, is probably the most difficult, and gives "bonus points" for a score above ninety. Details in back of book on page 225 along with other "scoring" directions.

SECTIONS I AND II—Mark *TRUE* if all parts of the statement are true; *FALSE* if any part is false.

1. The head of all hunting activities is the president of the hunt club.
2. Directly in charge of the hounds, both in the field and in the kennels, is the huntsman.
3. The purpose of having whips in the field is to stay at the back of the field and help whip any horses over fences who refuse.
4. It is important that your horse have a good heavy coat in winter to keep him warm when out hunting.
5. It is correct for a junior to wear white shirt and white pique stock, tan breeches, black boots, brown tweed jacket his first season of hunting.
6. It is permissible for the junior who can afford to buy them to wear the black coat with the hunt's colors and buttons his first season of hunting.
7. If you are a girl wearing black coat and black boots, you would wear black breeches.
8. If you are a seventeen year old boy who has won his buttons and colors you would be entitled to wear a scarlet coat, with which you would wear white breeches, black boots topped with tan calfskin and your velvet hunt cap.
9. It is permissible to substitute a silk print, polka dot or solid colored neck band for the white stock with black coat, fawn breeches and black boots.
10. You are a fifteen year old girl, hunting your first year. It is correct for you to wear a tan tweed riding jacket, white or colored shirt, polka dot or silk print stock, brick or tan breeches, brown boots and black velvet hunt cap.
11. It is correct to wear green breeches, white turtle neck sweater and green tweed jacket your first season of hunting.
12. You are a fifteen year old girl, hunting your first year. It is permissible for you to wear your black jacket, with white shirt and white stock, yellow vest, fawn or brick breeches or jodhpurs, black boots (with boot garters),

or jodhpur shoes, and your velvet hunt cap. You would not wear the official buttons or colors of the hunt.

13. When you arrive at the hunt meet it would be very fresh for you to go up and greet the master.

14. As the hunt moves off, you should try to get in front of the grown people and move your horse in directly behind the field master.

15. You should stay off the heels of the horse in front of you. Allow at least one horse's length; more distance if riding faster.

16. A horse with a red ribbon on his tail indicates that the owner takes the trouble to spruce up his mount for the holiday season.

17. When you come to a fence, you must be quick and try to beat other riders to the particular panel at which you set your horse.

18. The rider with a real sense of humor will "cross panels" (take the panel adjacent to the one he indicates he will take) and jostle the horse and rider coming into that panel; this also shows whether the other rider is on his toes and able to get his horse out of the way.

19. You should not race your horse at fences. Teach him to approach quietly and under control.

20. When you hear the words "Hold hard," you should freeze in your tracks.

21. When you hear the words " 'Ware staff" it means that the staff plans to pass and you should get out of the way.

22. When you move your horse off the trail to let the staff pass, you should turn your horse with his heels towards the passing horses.

23. When you hear the words "Gate please" passed back it means that people are asking permission to jump a gate.

24. As a member of the field, you should not cut across a seeded field.

25. When you hear the words " 'Ware hound" it means that an angry hound is sneaking up on your horse from behind; get out your hunt whip to be ready to strike him.

26. If you catch sight of the fox before anyone else does, you should call out as loudly as possible, "There goes the critter."

27. At the end of the day, you should go up to the MFH and give him your candid opinion of the day's hunt, good or bad. He will appreciate your honesty.

*   *   *

SECTION III—In the following account, many terms are used which would not be so worded by a person who hunts and is familiar with foxhunting terms. These wrongly used terms are underscored. Rewrite the account and supply the foxhunting term in each instance. (Examples: The huntsman kept the hounds closely packed around him until they first spread out in search of the fox's scent. This should be: until the first cast.)

(1)   (2)   (3)

The first thicket didn't have a fox in it, so the man who managed the hounds

(4)
lifted his hounds through a field to another heavily wooded area where the
(5)   (6)   (7)
hounds did discover a fox. The fox, a large male fox was seen getting away by
(8)   (9)
all members. *Jester* was the first to start barking on smelling the scent of the fox.
(10)
The hounds were off in hot pursuit with a glorious burst of hounds barking.
(11)
They ran along following the scent all the way over to the river where they
(12)   (13)
lost track of the scent. After about a ten minute interruption to the run the
(14)
field thought that once again the hounds must have recovered the scent when
(15)   (16)
Jill barked first and the other hounds all started barking in agreement. It
(17)
just happened that *Jill* was inclined to bark without due cause.
(18)
It turned out that the pack was off chasing a rabbit, so the huntsman got
(19)
them back and punished them.
(20)
When hounds once again did discover the fox's scent they ran for nearly an
(21)
hour until he finally ran down in a hole over by Johnson's creek. As the hunt
was hacking home the hounds jumped another fox and this time after a fast
(22)
chase of about 40 minutes they polished off their quarry. The huntsman was
(23)
particularly glad to have a kill that day as some of the young hounds had
never been blooded.
(24)   (25)
The tail was given to the first lady to ride in at the kill; the head to the
first gentleman.

CHAPTER XVII

We Will Be Exhibitors

The winter passed. We got out to hunt some eight or ten times during the season. A few of the hunts were disappointing, but for the most part those Saturdays were glorious days. Recounting our hunting experiences kept us in conversation all week—there was the day the hunt was out five hours and we chased two red foxes all over Fairfax County, until first one and then the other went to ground. There was the day Frances Fell got rolled off in a stream, but everybody was having too good a time to go in, including Frances—so she finished out the day looking like a drowned rat. There was the day we all had to take a four foot fence during a fast run and even the ponies sailed over. There was the day that we scrambled up a wooded ridge so steep that Fred slid off over his horse's tail, and then he and *Wireless* were barely able to clamber up the rest of the way even with Fred on foot. There was the Thursday when we had a holiday and went out with only the huntsman and Mrs. Douglas, and the huntsman let Sally and me act as whips!

All during this time we were becoming stronger riders, and developing our sense of timing and ability to manage our horses under all sorts of conditions. At the beginning of the season, we were grabbing mane over fences. Without having thought much about it, our seats were beginning to be strong enough so that we didn't need this support any more. We had begun to make the transition to "following hands and arms" over fences, just naturally.

Now spring was here again, and the horse show season would be starting in a few weeks. This year, we would take our horses and ponies around to the big shows. None of us had expensive horses, so we must develop them and our own riding in such a way that they would out-perform the higher priced horses. We liked the challenge. In fact, we all felt that this made showing twice the fun. If we simply got on the expensive pony which the dealer had made and the trainer kept schooled, and rode over a course of jumps in the show ring, what fun would that be? Through hard work, carefully developing our horses to the peak of their ability, we hoped to do creditably.

I knew that I was almost too big for *Trigger* but I was light, and I did want this one season on him. He was jumping so well now that I was almost sure he would provide real competition in pony jumper classes in any company. I could never put him in pony hunter classes in which conformation counted, and even in working hunter, where performance only counts, his *style* of galloping and jumping would always set him back. Again, although his manners in the ring were perfect now, his movement

"Sally had done so well with her own little mare." Note the excellent line from bit to elbow and *contrast* the style with that demonstrated in the photo on page 167. There Sally, riding over a big fence, accepts the advice to "go on and grab mane."

was poor, and I could never hope to place in hack classes. So I knew that about all we could do would be to compete in pony jumper classes, where style of jumping and galloping doesn't count. In this division, penalties are scored only on loss of forward motion, ticks, knock downs, run-outs or refusals, going "off course" or fall of horse and/or rider.

Sally Hilton had a real break this spring. Mrs. Douglas felt that she had done so well with her own little mare, *Penny,* that she put her on *April Dawn* for the season. Since *Dawn* was a horse rather than a pony, that meant that Sally would compete in the junior division (the division for riders eighteen and under mounted on horses rather than on ponies) which automatically would put her in a good deal stiffer competition. Sally, coming fourteen, was pretty young and inexperienced to be in this situation, but it worked out awfully well. Sally rode *April Dawn* for five years thereafter and together they won almost every honor of which a young rider could dream.

Sophie had done quite a job on *Wayward,* and the pony was performing brilliantly this spring. Greta would ride *Cornflakes* this season; Sarah Shelly was to take over *Tango.* Fred Compton would retire his wonderful old mare, *Wireless,* this summer, and would start showing *Pied Piper.* Frances Fell, of course, would ride *Glennwood.* Ridgely Slater would try *Dark Knight* in a few local shows, and if he did anything, she would take him around to some of the bigger shows. Little Meg Hanover was beginning to do quite a job on *Sauce Box,* and they would be going to the shows this year. Another combination I don't believe I have mentioned was Roberta Adams and *Nutmeg. Nutmeg* was quite a remarkable pony jumper; he had nice style over fences too, but was a temperamental little customer. Berta had been able to hunt him during the season, and now would give showing a try. This was the main group of us who would go around to shows this particular season. There was another group coming on, who probably would start the following year, but this year they would go to the shows as spectators and to "groom" for those of us who would exhibit.

During the winter, our main interest, of course, had been hunting, and we had very few classes in the ring. And so now, "back to the salt mines" for a real working over.

We were put back in the ring and settled down to serious work. We had to start with a recheck of position, and have it polished up after the season of happy-go-lucky riding. At all times, we were to try to get the *best* performance possible from our mounts. We must consider whether transitions were smooth and without loss of contact. We must watch canter departures and be sure that they were prompt, calm, and straight. We must try to get good energetic forward movement from our horses, and soft slowing downs. We must review our mounts on their stabilization lessons.

Naturally, the part everyone likes the best was, and ever is, jumping. You will remember in Chapter III we talked about "jumping on the intermediate level." This, you recall, means that the rider can retain the correct design of body on the approach, over the fence, and on the landing, without needing to catch the mane to steady himself. We were now expected to ride over fences in this way, and if we needed any support from the horse's neck to slide our hands forward and along the sides of the neck. *We should try to keep a straight line from bit to elbow.*

We didn't talk about "following through the air" yet; none of us were ready for jumping on an advanced level. In fact, it was just in hunter classes that we could maintain this nice design of intermediate jumping. In open jumper classes, where one will find trickier and more difficult courses, and where the fences may be raised for jump-offs (more will be explained about this later) we were advised to *go on and grab the mane* at the expense of style, if there was any chance that we might get "left"

This photo illustrates a young rider "jumping on an intermediate level," with almost everything exactly right. Notice that the stirrup leathers hang approximately vertical, that the rider keeps her heels down and steps on the inside of her stirrups. Her head is up, shoulders open and seat out of the saddle. Notice particularly the nice line from bit to elbow, although she is taking a slight support from the sides of the neck. The only criticism would be of the open fingers. This is a risky practice. The pony is able to jump calmly and freely, with extended head and neck.

otherwise. Actually, Mrs. D. was never too keen on having us go in open jumper classes until our style was better and stronger than it could be this year. However, she appreciated the fact that the only place I could show my pony was in jumper classes and knew how much I wanted to take him around. In fact, when there is one jumper class in a division (here, I mean division in the sense of the small pony division, large pony division, junior division) counting towards championship, we all wanted to enter it.

Our horses and ponies jumped so well and so willingly as a result of the methods by which they were schooled that it seemed a shame not to put them in these classes, particularly since they couldn't compete under as favorable circumstances where conformation counted. So generally

We didn't talk about following through the air yet. This picture, taken several years later of Sally Hilton on her mare *Shadow Patch,* demonstrates jumping on an advanced level and shows excellent following through the air.

"We were advised to go on and grab mane at the expense of style."

Mrs. D. agreed, although she always reminded us that we really should be jumping better and better over lower fences rather than grabbing mane over higher fences.

We now kept courses set up in the ring almost all the time, and drilled and drilled on every aspect (within our ability range) of riding a course. It was pointed out and noted that the approach is quite as important as the jump itself. Many times you can see that a run-out started a long way

Photo by Marler

"When we saw a horse round a bend and approach a fence with a popping shoulder we could see trouble starting." Here Sally demonstrates on *Penny Ante* so you can see the fault.

from the jump, as a result of the rider not thinking ahead and putting his mount *straight* at the middle of the jump. We were expected to ride on contact between fences, remembering to follow at all times, except when checking or slowing down. We noted how important it is to keep the horse's body straight from poll to croup—when we saw a horse round a turn and approach a fence with a "popping shoulder" (see photo) we could see trouble starting right then and there. We realized more and more that a good performance *over fences* usually can be traced back to intelligent work on the flat.

We were taught to interfere with our horses as little as possible when riding a jump course. In our schooling, we had tried to teach the horse to lengthen and shorten his stride as he needed to get in right, to judge his take-offs properly, to make turns comfortably and smoothly, and to remain calm so that he could function efficiently. If he had learned these lessons well, he would need very little placing by us. If too bold by nature, he might need a little steadying; if slightly lethargic, he might need a little stimulating—but mostly we should try to ride in a non-disturbing way, letting the horse use himself freely.

Naturally, we practiced many hours on just the technique of beginning to follow, sliding our hands along the sides of the horse's neck. We practiced, too, maintaining correct position out of the saddle with hands not touching the neck at all but on either side of it, keeping the reins looping throughout the jump, just in case we might snap back. This exercise, perfected, is the step before "following through the air."

In the show ring, we would still take a little support from the horse's neck and let our hands and arms slide forward. Our design was beginning to be nice over hunter type fences, and in general most of us could ride creditable rounds over outside courses as well as in the ring.

As we made plans for the season, one point was stressed over and over to us. We weren't to go to shows to win ribbons. We were to go for the fun, the stimulation, the chance to see what careful schooling could accomplish. But if there was one sour look from any disappointed rider on a DSH horse, that rider could stay home from then on. Showing is for sport, not for blood. The thing that really counted, in the school's opinion, was turning in the best performance one could, and accepting the decision of the judge gracefully.

It is hard for kids just entering horse show competition not to place too much emphasis on winning ribbons, but the opinion of everyone at DSH as to the *real fun* of horse shows helped us to develop the same attitude. And I'm pretty sure that our whole group had ever so much more fun as a result of absorbing this outlook.

CHAPTER XVIII

Show Day Tomorrow!

Life with horses is just one climax after another. We thought nothing could ever match the thrill of hunting, and now we were in just as much of a tizzy over the prospect of our first big show. Tomorrow, we would take some eight or ten horses and ponies to the Bailey's Cross Roads Horse Show. The occasion had special significance for me. It was just a year ago that I had ridden out of that very ring feeling completely disgraced. At that time, I had been too crushed ever to plan a return trip, but tomorrow I would be back in that same ring, on the same pony.

Most of us had wangled excused absences from our afternoon classes at school, so that we could get out to the stable for an early start on our braiding. We could all do a pretty decent braid job on the manes if we had plenty of time. Tails are harder. Tails are done in French braids and only a few of us had mastered this art. Bettina McCoy was the recognized "tail artist" and generally had about six customers. She could put up a beautiful tail, and it seemed well worth the fifty cents she charged to have a really professional looking job.

I often think about all this braiding. In a way, it's too bad such a style ever started. It's true, it does show off the horse's neck and the quarters to greater advantage but it takes a lot of time. So it means that if you are going to show in hunter and hack classes, you can't just pick up and go to a show on the spur of the moment—you have to braid. Braiding a mane takes the expert about a half an hour or forty minutes. It took us kids who weren't so expert about two hours just for the mane. Tina could do a tail up in about twenty minutes or half an hour; it took the rest of us nearly an hour.

If you aren't going to show in hunter or hack, but only in open jumper classes, it isn't necessary to braid. I usually did anyway, just for practice, and also because I thought it made *Trigger* (whose show name had become *Small Wonder*) look neater. But he had the most awful coarse, bushy mane, and it was a nightmare to put up. On this particular afternoon, I decided that if I was going to braid, it might help to pull and thin it first. So I pulled and thinned and pulled and thinned. Unfortunately, I overdid this pulling and thinning; by the time I started to braid, there wasn't

Courtesy of Mrs. Alfred Sieminski

"When horses are vanned, you generally bandage their legs, from hooves to knees or hocks, to be sure that they don't nick themselves in loading or travelling. You also need a fifth bandage for the tail."

Courtesy of Dr. Ruth White

Enticing your horse on the van may require a little time and patience.

enough mane left. It stood up in a little ruffle along the neck, and braiding was impossible. I consoled myself that he was only going in jumper classes anyway, and decided that the time I had left should go on trimming whiskers, grooming and polishing.

The day before the show is a fun time at the stable. Everyone is running around braiding or admiring someone else's braid job; collecting their fetlock scissors or borrowing someone else's; holding someone's horse while they trim out ears; spilling their baby oil in the manger (we used a tiny bit of baby oil to put a final sheen on our horses' coats). Sometimes you will hear an outraged shout that "the person who borrowed my hoof dressing used the last of it." Or you may hear someone else moan that one of their new bandages is torn.

About leg bandages—when horses are vanned, you generally bandage their legs, from hoofs to knees or hocks, to be sure that they don't nick

Leg bandage   Light weight sheet

themselves in loading or traveling. You wrap the legs first in great sheets of cotton and then around them you wrap the bandages, good and tight, so they will stay in place during the trip. You also need a fifth bandage for the tail, so that it won't get rubbed and fuzzy in traveling. Some of us thought that white bandages were the best looking, and they do show up better on dark horses. But most of our group used red bandages and sheets to match, red and white being our stable colors.

In winter you use blankets on your horses. This time of year, you generally substitute a sheet for the blanket. Actually, I don't think sheets have a lot of practical value (they are such light versions of blankets), but most people ship their horses to and from shows in them. To be honest, I expect the real reason is that it makes them look snappier. If it is a little cool, I suppose you might say that the blanket is too warm, but that the horse needs some light protection, and so the sheet is a good idea. There *is* some advantage to having an *old* stable sheet to put on your horse in his stall the night before a show. If he lies down, he won't get as dirty, and your job in the early morning hours won't be as hard.

We reluctantly leave the stable that evening after last minute repairs to a braid that won't stay in; or a little more last minute polishing; or putting additional straw in the stall for a knee deep bed—this, too, helps to keep your horse clean overnight.

As usual on the night before a show, it was seven o'clock when Mrs. Hilton managed to drag us away from the stable, by the hair of our heads! Berta and I were both spending the night at Sally's—Mrs. Hilton was so wonderful about getting up early with us that we did this a lot. On the way home, we studied the prize list once more.

Here is the list of classes, with their conditions described.

LIST OF CLASSES

CLASS 1—Model Ponies (under 13 hands). To be judged on conformation, quality, substance and soundness. (Outside Ring.)

Trophy—4 ribbons

CLASS 2—Model Ponies (13 to 14.2). To be judged on conformation, quality, substance and soundness. (Outside Ring.)

Trophy—4 ribbons

CLASS 3—Model Hunters (Horses). Conditions same as Classes 1 and 2.

Trophy—4 ribbons

CLASS 4—Large Ponies under saddle—over 13.0 hands and not to exceed 14.2. To be shown at a walk, trot and canter. To be judged on performance, manners and way of going 75%, conformation 25%.

Trophy—4 ribbons

CLASS 5—Small Ponies under saddle—not to exceed 13.0 hands. Conditions the same as Class 4.

Trophy—4 ribbons

CLASS 6—Junior Hacks (Horses Only). To be shown at a walk, trot, canter and hand gallop. May be asked to back, and to stand quietly while rider dismounts and remounts. Performance, manners, and way of going 75%, conformation 25%.

Trophy—4 ribbons

CLASS 7—Small Pony Working Hunter—not to exceed 13.0 hands. (In the ring.) Fences not to exceed 2½ feet. Conformation will not be considered, hunting soundness only required. To be judged on performance, manners and way of going.

$10.00 $5.00 $3.00 $2.00

CLASS 8—Large Pony Working Hunter—over 13.0 and not exceeding 14.2 hands. (In the ring.) Fences not to exceed 3 feet. Conditions the same as Class 7.

$10.00 $5.00 $3.00 $2.00

CLASS 9—Junior Working Hunter (Horses Only). (Outside Course.) Fences not to exceed 3½ feet. Conditions the same as Class 7.

$10.00 $5.00 $3.00 $2.00

CLASS 10—Small Pony Knock Down and Out—Ponies under 13.0. Jumps to be set at 2½ feet. Winner to be the pony clearing the most obstacles without a knockdown or comparable fault. To be raised and/or spread in case of a tie.

$10.00 $5.00 $3.00 $2.00

CLASS 11—Large Pony Knock Down and Out—Ponies over 13.0 and not exceeding 14.2 hands. Jumps to be set at 3 feet. Conditions the same as Class 10.

$10.00 $5.00 $3.00 $2.00

CLASS 12—Junior Knock Down and Out (Horses Only). Jumps to be set at 3 feet 6 inches. Conditions the same as Class 10.

$10.00 $5.00 $3.00 $2.00

CLASS 13—Novice Horsemanship—Open to riders who have not won 3 first ribbons in Horsemanship classes at recognized shows. To walk, trot and canter both ways of the ring. To be judged on seat, hands, guidance and control and general appearance of rider, non-abuse of mount and general knowledge. Judges may ask riders to change mounts if they so desire. Martingales not permitted.

Challenge Trophy—6 ribbons

CLASS 14—Small Pony Hunting Attire—Ponies 13.0 and under. Fences not to exceed 2½ feet. To be ridden in full hunting attire. Performance, manners and way of going with emphasis on brilliancy 70%, conformation 15%, appointments 15%.

Challenge Trophy $5.00 $3.00 $2.00

CLASS 15—Large Pony Hunting Attire—Ponies over 13.0 and not exceeding 14.2 hands. Fences not to exceed 3 feet. Conditions same as Class 14.

Challenge Trophy $5.00 $3.00 $2.00

CLASS 16—Junior Hunting Attire (Horses Only). Fences not to exceed 3 feet 6 inches. Conditions same as Class 14.

Challenge Trophy $5.00 $3.00 $2.00

CLASS 17—Virginia Horse Shows Association Equitation Class—The contestant to ride either a horse or pony and first jump eight fences. Ponies to jump 3 feet and horses to jump 3 feet 6 inches. The Judges will then select as many of the riders as they wish, but not less than one-fourth of the entrants in the class to show at a walk, trot and canter. Class to be judged on seat and hands, guidance and control throughout. Jumping faults of mount not to count. Fall of horse or rider or three disobediences shall eliminate a contender. Judges may require riders to change horses, mount, dismount or exhibit any other individual requirement of equitation they may deem necessary. No horse or pony may be withdrawn after start of class without permission of Judges.

Medal—Ribbons

CLASS 18—Pony Hunt Teams—Teams must consist of 3 ponies from the same size group. Performance, manners and way of going as a team 75%, conformation and similarity 25%.

Trophies—Ribbons

CLASS 19—Junior Hunt Teams—Teams of 3 horses. Performance, manners and way of going as a team 75%, conformation and similarity 25%.

Trophies—Ribbons

SMALL PONY CHAMPIONSHIP—1*–5*–7–10–14

LARGE PONY CHAMPIONSHIP—2*–4*–8–11–15

JUNIOR CHAMPIONSHIP—3*–6*–9–12–16

* Denotes half value class.

As you see, I had only one bona fide class for *Trigger* (pardon me, I mean *Small Wonder*) but I would also ride him in the Novice Horsemanship, and the VHSA Equitation Class. In addition, I had been asked to ride a large pony throughout that division for a rider who had just started taking lessons at DSH. *Gingercake,* the pony, wasn't much of a show prospect either, but at least I would have the fun of going in the whole large pony division.

Sally was beside herself with excitement; it would be her first show on *April Dawn,* and she was torn between elation and goose pimples.

Dawn was such a terrific performer that she was afraid she might not do the mare justice, and felt that she could never hold up her head again if she didn't handle her well. Roberta was also having her first try in a recognized show with *Nutmeg,* and she too was in a twit. And the same thing with Meg and *Saucy.* Fred would show his own *Wireless* in this one show, and the rest of the season he would be on *Pied,* so we knew how much he must want her to go well.

After we had supper we got busy on tack cleaning and preparing our clothes for the next day. We spread newspapers over the recreation room

Button type leggings

Jodhpur strap. These, worn below the knee, improve the fit and appearance of your jodhpurs.

floor in the Hilton's basement, and began to go over every item of our equipment. There are quite a few special things to arrange in the way of tack when entering the "Hunting Attire" class (see Class 14). This class is also termed "Corinthian" or an "appointments" class, and there are very definite rules as to what horse (or pony) and rider must wear.

Perhaps this would be a good time to talk about clothes suitable for the show ring. I will start with the most casual type permissible and work up to Corinthian, or more formal attire. The following description of clothes applies to hunter and jumper classes. Correct attire for riding three- or five-gaited saddle horses is altogether different.

A tweed jacket may be worn with breeches or jodhpurs (the breeches or jods in the shade called "brick" or any of the tan tones. I don't suppose I need to add that black or green breeches or jodhpurs are considered impossibly bad taste!) in any class but the appointments class—and one year that rule was modified in Virginia to permit tweeds in this class, although very few people took advantage of the fact. (I'll explain more about that in a minute.) As in hunting, with tweeds, boots or jodhpur shoes should be brown. But here again, as in most matters, I can think of one exception—if your jacket is blueish grey or grey tweed, you might wear black boots. Another substitution in costume that is popular now is the use of breeches with brown laced jodhpur boots (sometimes called paddock boots or just riding shoes), and then leggings (see illustration). We all

Photo by Marler

This picture shows one rider in light-weight tweed coat, silk neck band, laced riding shoes and leggings. The other wears silk neck band, salt sack jacket, jodhpurs (the jodhpurs should fit in a little tighter around the leg) with jodhpur garters worn below the knees, and jodhpur shoes.

thought these leggings terribly smart, particularly the ones with the suède cuffs, and had mentally added these items to the others we would get when we could afford them. With the clothes I have just described, one can wear a "ratcatcher" shirt, with either a silk stock in solid print, or polka dot, or a neck band (see illustration). Neck bands were just beginning to come in when we started showing, and everyone was crazy about them. Or you can wear the ratcatcher shirt's own little bow tie. Or, you can wear a regular shirt (like a man's) with a bow tie or a regular long tie.

As the weather gets warmer, you may substitute a white or cream "salt sack" or linen, or other tropical weight coat—possibly a glen plaid, in a soft shade, or some other of the new fabrics, for the tweed coat. So much for more casual horse show clothes.

Most juniors (riders eighteen or under in our state) show in black coats, with black boots, canaries (yellow breeches), white shirt, white stock,

Lady in formal hunt attire. This is called a "shad-belly" coat and corresponds to a gentleman's scarlet coat. Needless to say, only girls and ladies who have won their buttons and colors may wear them. The coat is black and the collar is faced with the hunt's colors. With this coat, only the high silk hat is permissable, never a derby or hunt cap. This attire is suitable for gala hunt meets or Corinthian classes in horse shows. (The lady depicted should have her stock pin straight across, rather than slanted.)

yellow vest, black velvet hard top. This is more or less standard horse show attire for children.

These are the clothes you wear in the "Hunt Attire" class, too, with accessories that must be exactly *so*. You must wear pigskin or other leather gloves, and must carry, fastened under the billet straps of your saddle, white string gloves, thumbs up. Stock pin (a plain gold safety pin is in the best taste) must be fastened straight across. You must have garters on your boots. You must wear hunting spurs. You carry a hunt crop. In this class, your neat workmanlike appearance counts a specified percentage.

There is another type of formal hunt attire which you will see in Corinthian classes or at the more festive holiday hunt meets from time to time. This is the "shad belly" hunt coat (see sketch) for girls and ladies. It creates a very "dressed up" effect. The coat, as you see from the illustration, is cut straight across in front, and has tails, coming almost to the wearer's knees. With this coat, one always wears a high silk hat.

Not only must the rider wear prescribed clothes, and these clothes be neat and well fitting, but the horse or pony must also have specified equipment. These specifications sometimes change from year to year, and a few seem to be as much precedent as rule. For example, the year we started showing, it was required that bits and reins be sewn in. This was amended later, but most of us still abide by the old rule, just in case the judge considers "sewn in" bits and reins preferable. Also, the year we started showing in hunt attire, or Corinthian classes, mounts had to be shown in breastplates. Later, this too was made optional. Other items, such as laced or braided reins, seem to be preferred, or at least customary. Most people would hesitate to go into the appointments class with smooth leather reins.

There are a few items, however, that have been, and still are definitely required in these classes. The sandwich case is one of them. (See illustration.) Likwise, hunting crop and spurs; the rider in pigskin or other suitable leather gloves, and carrying string gloves—these requirements seem permanent.

The real idea of this class is to require correct and workmanlike equipment, such as the rider would have and wear in actual hunting, *when correctly turned out in every detail.* Therefore, the ruling was sensible that children might wear tweed (although almost none did, as it just didn't seem "Corinthian" attire to anybody), since that is really correct attire for the first year of hunting. Children might also wear jodhpurs with the black coat and with the other items all the same as described; there were quite a few who did this.

Riders who have won their hunt buttons and colors should wear them on their hunt coats. Naturally, boys who have earned the right to wear scarlet coats, would wear their white hunt breeches with the "pink" coat.

I am sure this seems to be a long discussion of clothes, but let's face it, for most of us, clothes and equipment for riding and showing are one of the big problems to solve.

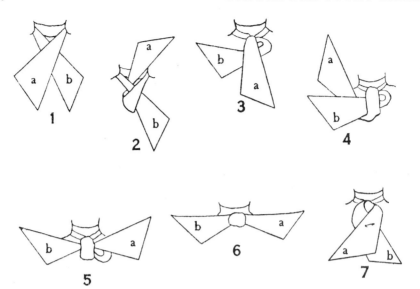

A properly made stock is wrapped around neck twice before starting Operation 1. Pull knot up snugly. Small pin fastened to shirt at (a) and (b) as in 7 will keep stock from riding up. (If you find this too baffling, buy yourself a ready tied stock.)

Laced bridle reins. Suitable for your snaffle bridle, either hunting or in Corinthian class.

Sandwich case

Plaited bridle reins. Suitable as the snaffle rein for your Pelham bridle, either hunting or in Corinthian class. These reins are more satisfactory than smooth leather that slips through your fingers.

Huntcrop or whip

Generally, the problem *can* be solved. An "outgrown" system, such as we had at our school is a great help, and one can also canvass other "outgrown" shops. Once Sally (this happened later, but I will mention it here) picked up the most luscious pair of heavy canaries, handmade, of the type that cost at least $85.00 custom made, for $6.00! And they were in perfect condition and fitted her as if they had been made for her, too! Our families all check these shops for us. Of course one has to be lucky to hit what one needs in the right size, but we *were* lucky a lot of times!

Rider correctly turned out for the "Corinthian" class. The sandwich case does not show as it is attached to dees on the off (right) side. Note the tips of the string gloves just showing.

A little ingenuity helps a lot. We found someone who would make the yellow vest worn with the black coat for about one-third of the cost at most riding shops. One of the mothers took orders for the little silk neck bands that are so snappy with ratcatcher shirts, and found she could sell them for less than half of the retail sales price. All of us saved our money for the riding clothes and tack we needed. Birthdays and Christmas we usually managed to build up our equipment too. Almost no one in our school ever had the works presented to them all in one swoop!

On the evening before this show, most of us were equipped with the things we really needed for the next day, with the exception of sandwich cases. Only one or two of our whole group had managed to acquire this particular item. They are expensive; they are used in this one type of class only (of course they are nice, but not essential to have when you hunt) and they just never turn up "outgrown." However, Mrs. D. had two to lend around, and by canny planning and borrowing, we had it figured out so that all of us who wanted to go in the appointments class would be able to borrow what we needed.

With the Hiltons' recreation room littered with saddles, bridles, breast-plates, boots, spurs, halters, lead shanks, etc., we worked and talked. Mrs. Hilton had given us until 10:00 o'clock only to finish cleaning our tack and boots, and have our clothes all laid out for the morning. Now at five minutes before the deadline we were pleading for a few more minutes. Berta still had to iron her stock, and I hadn't cleaned my spurs and spur straps. Mrs. Hilton was firm about our getting to bed, and ended by doing the last minute ironing herself for Berta as well as for Sally.

We crawled into our respective beds, on our honor not to lie awake and talk. So we must all shiver and shake in delicious anticipation of the morning in complete silence, until we finally fall asleep.

CHAPTER XIX

In the Show Ring

Here I was, once again, back in the same show ring where you first saw me. The green jodhpurs and western bridle were gone. No one would recognize *Small Wonder* as the shaggy pony who was tooted out of the ring a year ago. And now I was a member of the group I had admired so much last season.

There was no time for dreaming, however. The large "model" ponies were in the ring when we arrived, and we should have our entries ready for their first classes in a very few minutes.

In a model class the horse or pony is stripped and led into the ring to be "stood up" and judged on *conformation, quality, substance* and *soundness.* (When you say a horse is "stripped" you mean that he is led in and shown in bridle only. This class is also called a "strip" class.) When you speak of conformation you mean body build of ideally functional beauty. Quality is fineness and the look of breeding. Substance indicates sufficiently heavy bone, sufficient depth of chest, sufficient *sturdiness* to indicate that the fineness is balanced with strength and "staying power." Soundness is physical well being and freedom from weaknesses, injuries or illness which render the horse anything but completely fit physically.

There is quite a bit of art connected with "standing up" a horse or pony for conformation. He should stand alertly and reach out with his head and neck and of course flick his ears forward.

We would have loved to watch the models, but there was no time at the moment—horses must be unbandaged as soon as led off the vans, and then tacked. When you first reach the show, everyone runs around in a great flurry, trying to locate their equipment and get themselves and their mounts organized. And always, there is a tail that has gotten rubbed and fuzzy on the van, or a braid that has come loose, and the rider's agitation is great until these mishaps have been repaired.

As soon as you have your mount all ready, you must go over to the entry desk to make your entries and pick up your number—or get your mother or a companion who is "grooming" for you to do it. During the first part of the morning at a post entry show (a show in which entries are taken on the grounds, rather than having been accepted by mail prior to the date of the show) there will be a mob at the entry stand, and the poor entry clerks will be going slightly mad. Everybody is anxious to get their entries in at the same time and fearful that they may miss their first class. Somehow, it all straightens out, and by mid morning, the entry clerks can take a deep breath and get their first glimpse of the show.

The first class in which we had entries was the large pony hack (under saddle) class. (See prize list, page 173, Chapter XVIII, in order to follow

Courtesy of Vaudine Herbster

Here you see some of the best quality large ponies in the state of Virginia. As in this case, mounts are frequently "stood up" and judged on conformation outside the show ring.

the classes as they are described.) *Wayward* and *Gingercake* were the only entries we had to uphold the honor of our school. *Gingercake* didn't place, but Sophie did manage to score on *Wayward* with a white (fourth place) ribbon, and was happy as a lark about it. *Wayward* went awfully well, but was inclined to carry her head a little too high, which generally put her back somewhat.

In the small pony hack class, we thought both *Saucy* and *Nutmeg* performed quite well, and both were at least left in when "the sheep were separated from the goats." In most hack classes, the judges first excuse the horses or ponies who either misbehave, make mistakes or obviously are not of show quality. Then they can get a closer look at the entries left in the ring, and find it easier to make their final decision. So we were pleased that *Saucy* and *Nutmeg* were at least "sheep" rather than goats. To be honest, *Nutmeg* moved a little sluggishly in a hack class, and while *Saucy* had plenty of impulse and was very obedient and knowledgeable, he didn't move too well or have the *quality* to win a hack where conformation counts. *Nutmeg* was lined up fifth and *Saucy* sixth, and both Berta and Meg were delighted, even though there were no fifth or sixth place ribbons.

Junior hacks followed, and here our school had five entries in the ring, (*Dawn, Dark Knight, Cornflakes, Tango* and *Glennwood*) all attractive looking, and all having excellent manners. I knew Mrs. Douglas considered *Dark Knight* the best mover in the group. *Dawn,* because of her conformation, lacked that long lovely way of moving that one looks for, but her manners were flawless, and many judges liked her style. *Glennwood* and *Cornflakes* are always flashy in the ring, and each had a look of style and quality. *Tango's* ring manners were outstanding, and some judges liked the vertical face and rocking chair canter.

While there was plenty of good competition in this class, we were pretty sure that our group would hold their own here, and sure enough, we almost made a clean sweep. *April Dawn* placed second; *Dark Knight* placed third (Mrs. Douglas said she would have pinned them in the reverse order) and *Glennwood,* fourth. The class was won by a lovely big chestnut gelding, *Seron.*

Small pony working hunters went in next, and little *Saucy* turned in his usual steady, consistent round for a third (yellow) ribbon, and *Nutmeg* managed to annex the fourth place ribbon.

When the large ponies went in the ring for their hunter class, they seemed to be jinxed. There was an in-and-out, composed of two movable rustics, at the end of the ring that spelled disaster for pony after pony. We decided that it must be set at an awkward angle, as almost every pony refused the second if not the first element, or knocked one or the other down, or twisted, or scrambled over. Finally, a beautiful liver chestnut pony had a good round throughout, and seemed the certain winner, as the entries following had every bit as much trouble as the ones who preceded him. I had ridden down the rail on the outside of the ring to take a good look at the troublesome fences. The jump was set too close to the turn for the ponies to manage comfortably, unless the rider pulled down somewhat after taking the two fences on the long rail, and then went deep into the corner to get the best possible approach.

I had little idea that my somewhat green and also somewhat common entry would have a chance, but resolved to give her the best and most strategic ride I could. While evenness of pace counts in a hunter class, I felt pretty sure that the way things were going if I could just get *Gingercake* around the course without a refusal or knockdown, she would automatically be in the ribbons. She took the first two fences quite decently and now I checked her a little, but still used my legs, so she wouldn't die away on me, and lose all impulse (the rustics were fair-sized fences for the ponies) and made the deepest corner I could. Actually, it was a bit of a struggle to do this, as she wasn't the best-schooled animal in the world. It took a really strong indirect rein behind the withers and inside spur rolled into her to put her where I wanted her. But what do you know? My much out-classed pony actually made it through the in-and-out with no difficulty, and a cheer went up as she went on out over the last two fences boldly and in stride. What a lark! Her owner, Marion Smith, was beside herself as we were called back in the ring and lined up over top flight show ponies. *Gingercake* was pinned second, and I know that red ribbon meant more to Marion than a win at Madison Square would to "veteran" exhibitors!

Junior Working Hunters over the outside course, in which we had all six of our horses entered, came next. *Teeny*, a wonderful little bay mare, was the first horse to go. This mare had an almost flawless style over fences and in addition was one of the best natural jumpers in the country. Fence by fence she turned in perfectly steady, capable jumps, and galloped easily and quietly between them. Whee! That would be some round to beat! Next we watched a horse that looked as if he was out to win the Grand National. He galloped so fast that his jumps become long and flat and we felt that he hurled himself over them. Then followed a very green round, with the horse slowing down to look at each fence, and then climbing over in a manner that almost unseated his rider. The next good round was turned in by *Show Circuit,* a big, good-looking chestnut. *Show Circuit* was perhaps a little rapid, but his pace was even and every jump the same, so that you didn't have the feeling that it was a chancy round.

When you speak of "chancy" fences, you generally mean that the pace is too rapid for the horse's ability to handle himself comfortably, safely, and in stride, and you have the feeling that it is only by good luck that he gets over. At the other extreme, you speak of a "sticky" round, or "sticky" fences. Here the pace is generally too slow, or the horse puts in short strides before the jumps, and seems to "climb" over. Of course, there can be many variations of chancy or sticky fences. A jump might look chancy, even though the horse hadn't been going awfully fast, if it looked unsafe, and as if he didn't know what he was doing. Or a horse might race between fences and still slow down and put in sticky jumps. But most of the time, chancy fences are unsafe fences taken at too great speed; sticky fences are uncomfortable fences taken too slowly with the free forward movement interrupted.

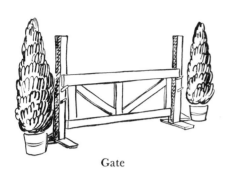

Gate

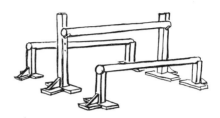

Hog's back

Rustic

Brush

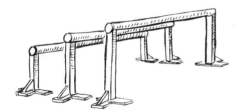

Triple

Painted panel and poles

Chicken coop

Post and rail

Courtesy of Mrs. Richard Ruffner

Our first horse to go was *Tango,* and while her round looked safe, she got in close on two of her fences. Sarah Shelly rode out trying hard not to look disappointed. Now *Glennwood* commenced his round in very nice style. His first four fences were lovely, but as he started down the hill and over the fences leading back into the ring he picked up speed, became too bold and spoiled his nice even pace. The first of our horses to turn in a really good round throughout was *Wireless.* The game old mare, now almost twenty, no longer looked the show ring hunter, but she sailed around the course as if she was galloping to hounds. Fred jumped off and threw his arms around her when he had finished, he was so delighted with her performance.

Now *Dark Knight* commenced his trip, and started out over the course galloping and jumping effortlessly, making beautiful fences, but jumping too big over each. At the in-and-out on the top of the hill his first fence was so big that he couldn't get a decent take-off for the second element. He twisted badly and just managed to get over it, so we knew his goose was cooked as far as placing in that class.

Greta brought *Cornflakes* in and started out over the course. We knew that Greta was not quite sure how she should try to ride it. *Cornflakes* was still inclined to be too rapid and overly bold if allowed to set her own pace on an outside course. But she would get fussed up and resist if you tried to slow her down. Greta managed her better than anyone else, and gained her results more by psychology and tact than by open battle. In this case, psychology and tact didn't work and *Cornflakes* went blazing around the course brilliantly, but, we were pretty sure, *much* too boldly for a junior horse in a "working" class. In a Corinthian class, where brilliance is demanded, most judges expect and allow more speed than they want to see in the children's working hunter. So we all were laughing, even Greta, when *Cornflakes* came back into the ring in record time. We all thought *Cornflakes* looked very pleased with herself.

And now, last, it was Sally's turn on *Dawn.* We knew how eager she was for a good performance. It's pretty hard to ride a horse that is *expected* to do well! *Dawn* went around the course like a bird, but again—were her jumps too big and brilliant? She wasn't nearly as rapid as *Cornflakes,* but her leaps had been huge. We just didn't know—it would all boil down to the taste of these particular judges, we felt.

As the judges studied their cards at the end of the class, we debated amongst ourselves. We were pretty sure that the class was *Teeny's*—her round had been absolutely steady, safe and even, with every fence in stride and jumps neither too bold nor too slow. How would the judges rate the others? *Show Circuit* had had an excellent round, but was it too fast? *Cornflakes'* pretty definitely had been, we all agreed. *Dawn's* certainly was sparkling, but her jumps had looked awfully big. And how about old *Wireless?* She had looked the true field hunter, and as if she knew exactly what she was doing.

Mrs. Douglas joined us in this railside judging. She felt that it was important for us to be able to evaluate every round carefully and impartially, but she always warned us that the official judge might see the results a little differently from the way we did. For example, one judge might place heavier emphasis on *style of galloping* between fences than the judge at the next show. One judge might feel that the prime requirement for a child's hunter was complete safety, and so might not fault slightly sticky fences as heavily as he would too rapid a pace. These individual differences between judges make showing all the more fun. But if *no judge ever likes your horse,* you might as well face it—there must be quite a lot wrong with the way he performs, and you had better get busy and find out what it is. Or get yourself a different horse, if you can't correct his failings!

In any event, none of us felt that we had any real complaints when the horses were called back and pinned in this order: First, *Teeny;* second, *Show Circuit;* third, *April Dawn;* fourth, *Wireless.*

We had been watching and judging so closely that the small pony jumper class was on us before we knew it. Meg, Berta and I were entered, and we decided to go last to have more time to warm up our ponies. This class was a Knock Down and Out jumper, which, as the name indicates, means that you are out if your pony rolls a pole or commits a comparable error, such as a refusal or run-out. When we finally put our numbers in at the gate with the announcer, we were feeling pretty tense. (The announcer takes the number of each entry in the order in which he, or she, wants to go in the class. Riders are then called in that order.) Meg said afterwards she got numb, and the course seemed to "do" itself. As for me, while I get tense in such situations, everything seems to clarify and come into sharper focus, and I seem to be able to think more clearly.

Little *Saucy* was the first of our group to go in and had a clean round. As he went through the out gate, a general chuckle went up along the rail, Meg and *Saucy* looked so little. Actually, *Saucy* was the smallest pony at the show today, and the spectators always got a big bang out of watching him go around. Now Berta went in, but that wretch of a *Nutmeg* went into a bucking spree before the first fence, took it while bucking and managed to pull the top rail. I know Berta could have murdered him as this was nothing in the world but temperament; the pony could and did jump four feet.

Courtesy of J. D. Baxter

Meg warming up *Saucy* in the hacking ring.

Courtesy of J. D. Baxter

"Fence by fence, *Saucy* continued to negotiate jumps about as big as he was." (Note Meg's rounded back. However, she was both numb and tired by this jump-off.)

Now I came in on *Trigger,* and I believe I stopped breathing as we went around the course. Only very bad luck could put us out at this level (two and a half feet) but he *could* slip or get in wrong. He didn't, and I breathed again as we went out of the ring. Now the jumps were raised. The six small ponies who had clean rounds, amongst them *Saucy* and *Trigger,* were called back for the jump off. *Saucy* was the fifth to come in,

Photo by Thomas Neil Darling

Trigger over the triple. This is the first trip around, when jumps were only 2½ feet.

and thus far, none had gotten all the way around the course in the jump off without a knock down. Meg's jaw was set as she circled and prepared to set *Saucy* at the first fence. She needn't have worried. *Saucy* looked like a wound-up toy performing steadily and economically, never jumping higher than he needed, and never bothered or upset by anything. Jump by jump he continued, until over the last, a little triple bar, he was still clean, and Meg rode out of the ring with everyone clapping madly. *Trigger* and I were the last in the jump off, and again I held my breath. *Trigger's* style was altogether different from *Saucy's.* He generally jumped 'way up over his fences, and his jumps were never pretty. Pretty or not, he too was over the last fence clean, and that meant that Meg and I were still tied and must jump off for first place.

This time the jumps were raised three inches only, as this is the legal limit in Virginia for small ponies (3′3″) and should there still be a tie, additional jumps are introduced, as there can be no further raises.

This time as Meg went in, I knew she was scared, and somehow I felt guilty. *Saucy* was smaller than *Trigger,* and Meg a lot younger than I. I had never expected to be jumping off against the "wind-up toy." But for first place the rule book says you must jump to decide the point; you may not toss.

Meg was already heading into the first fence, and this time the crowd held their collective breaths, I think. Fence by fence *Saucy* continued to negotiate jumps about as big as he was, and Meg to ride a quiet and non-disturbing ride. On the last fence, he trailed his toes and pulled the top rail. A loud "Ah!" of disappointment went up from the crowd.

As *Trigger* came back into the ring, I wanted him to win the class—for himself and for doing so poorly last year; and I didn't want him to win it, for Meg and *Saucy.* But I suppose I didn't "not want him to win it" enough not to ride my very best, and as he cleared the last fence, I drew a deep breath of relief. When ponies were lined up and pinned, and *Trigger* trotted out of the ring with the blue rosette on his bridle, a dream had come true. Yes, the plow pony was a real show pony at last, and all the world could see it!

And now the class which probably holds the keenest spectator appeal— the Junior Knock Down and Out! All of our horses were entered in this, although we felt that *Dawn* was the only one who had much of a chance of doing anything, if the fences got high. However, in a Knock Down and Out class, you always have a sporting chance, and sometimes odd things happen. Everybody but you just *might* have bad luck, and your horse just might win the class without having to jump very high. Mrs. Douglas had already told us that all of our horses but *Dawn* would have to pull out and concede at the four foot level if we were still in the competition at that height. With six horses in the ring, this class was terribly exciting for us, and became more so when all six did go clean in the first round. But at the raise to four feet, rails began to fall right and left. *Glennwood, Tango,* and *Cornflakes* each had a knock down or refusal at this level. To everybody's surprise, old *Dark Knight* went soaring over everything, with some six inches to spare at each fence. *Wireless* was in great form too, and was still clean. Likewise *Dawn.* But Mrs. Douglas made Ridgely concede at this point, as she felt neither horse nor rider knew enough to tackle the course on the next raise, which would put the fences at 4′6″. In fact, she hadn't quite expected *Wireless* to get around at this height either. We knew that the mare was a very able jumper, but we hadn't been sure how she would feel about the funny looking obstacles in this class.

Fred wanted to go back in even though he had never jumped a course this high. Well, it was *Wireless'* last show, and neither his mother nor Mrs. Douglas had the heart to say no. Two other horses had been clean at the four foot level, the wonderful little bay mare *Teeny,* who had won the Junior Working Hunter, and a bouncy grey, named *Manic.*

With Ridgely and *Dark Knight* conceding, it meant that since there were now only four horses to go in the jump off, each would have a ribbon in any case.

Manic, rearing and leaping in the air, went in first. She got over the first fence, but at the next jump, a panel with a striped pole over it, she got in too close, and just sat down and stopped. It was Fred's turn next, and we crossed our fingers—*Wireless* somehow looked terribly gallant to all of us. She was such a sweet old mare, and performed so willingly—Fred didn't even carry a crop. It was just a matter of putting her straight at her fence, and she would do her best. Over the first, over the second, over the third, coming into the fourth (cross bars) very nicely—a groan from her rooting section—when we thought she was over the fence, the rail fell. She had twisted just enough for her hind legs to knock down the cross pole. But this would still give Fred and *Wireless* at least a third, since they had gotten further than *Manic.*

And now little *April Dawn,* with the sun lighting up her golden coat, came trotting in. As usual, she looked both calm and perky, and as she circled and prepared for her go, there was no rearing and charging around —she was cool as a cucumber. You could hear a pin drop as she headed into the first fence and was over, jumping with complete ease. And so on around the course, as if it had been three feet instead of four and a half, never getting in wrong, galloping, picking up and sailing over obstacles like a bird. The last fence was the triple bar, and we knew Sally felt a little afraid of it; it did look monstrous. As they came down to it, Sally pushed her a little; *Dawn* seemed to say, "Oh, Fie for this!" She increased her speed, stood back a full stride and commenced to sail through the air. The huge leap quite naturally caught Sally off guard and she snapped back on the reins, pulling *Dawn's* hind legs into the top element of the triple bar. Down it went. Sally rode out, so mad at herself that she was almost in tears. We tried to console her—it had been the sort of jump that really is awfully hard to stay with, but Sally knew that it was her own fault for pushing *Dawn* too fast those last strides and then getting left. Mrs. D. told her just to chalk it up to experience, and to stop worrying— this was part of learning to ride a course over big fences, and all in all, she had given the mare an excellent ride.

Now *Teeny* was in the ring, and commenced her round in her business-like and capable way. Fence by fence she went clean, and now she was over the triple bar and was the winner.

By the time this class was over, people were beginning to check points for championship. These points are posted by the sound truck. Have I explained the point system? It goes like this: For each first (blue) ribbon

Courtesy Mrs. B. H. McElhinney, Jr.

Teeny, a wonderful little bay mare.

five points on championship are scored; for second (red) three; for third (yellow) two; and for fourth (white) one point. In classes indicated in the prize list as "half value" naturally you get just one half of this point value. The horses and ponies who win the most points in their respective divisions are awarded championships and reserve championships (reserve is runner-up) for the show. In Virginia, points are accumulated from all shows that are members of Virginia Horse Shows Association until at the end of the season each horse's total points are tallied, and annual championships awarded in each division.

Anyway, at this point, *Teeny* was leading by quite a margin for Junior Champion of the show, with her two wins in full value classes giving her ten points. *April Dawn* had six and a half. Her second place in the hack (a half value class) gave her only one and a half points; third in working hunter two more; second in the Knock Down and Out, three more to total six and a half. *Dawn* had won six straight championships last season, under Snowden Mills, and we knew that Sally had dreamed last night of chalking up one more today. Well, after all, it was her first show on the mare, and she was pretty inexperienced for show ring competition of this type. We told her that she shouldn't feel badly—she had been in the ribbons in all three of her classes. There would be only one more class (the hunting attire) to count towards junior championship and we felt that *Teeny* had it in the bag. She was almost bound to place, at least, and she already had a three and a half point lead over *Dawn*. Sally was trying to act very casual. Of course she was pleased over the way *Dawn* had performed but I knew she had a lump in her throat, thinking of the way the Knock Down and Out class had been thrown away. Well, that is showing, and it's all in the day!

In the next class, the Novice Horsemanship, we were delighted to see Greta, whose smooth, quiet style and pretty design were always pleasing, the eventual winner. The only other member of our school to place was Sarah Shelly, on *Tango,* who took second. *Tango* was a wonderful equitation mount on the flat, and we were awfully glad for Sarah, as *Tango* kept missing out in her own classes—I mean the classes judged on the performance of the horse. I suppose this would be a good place to call attention to the point that in horsemanship classes, presumably, the performance of the horse is not considered at all; the rider only is being judged. In spite of this, certain horses definitely help show the rider off to advantage; others make it practically impossible for the rider to look attractive. So when you go in your horsemanship (or equitation class— the two terms mean the same thing) you should try to ride an animal that will show off your riding to the best possible advantage.

In all classes but horsemanship classes, only the performance of the horse counts. While a skillful rider makes it possible for the horse to perform at his best, it is *the horse that is being judged.*

Following this, the ponies and riders must be gotten ready for their appointments class. This was fairly easy, as we had only two entries in each.

In the small pony division, *Nutmeg* wound up third; little *Saucy* was moved back on conformation from forth to fifth which put him out of the ribbons.

In the large pony division, Sophie and *Wayward* again scored a second.

And now another class with all six of our horses in it—the Junior Hunting Attire. Such a time we had, rounding up equipment for all six! Sandwich cases that had been loaned for the pony Corinthians were recalled; people from outside our school who had promised the loan of sandwich cases were tracked down. Sandwich boxes were filled with the traditional "white meat of turkey" sandwiches. Flasks were filled with lemonade or other fruit drinks. The judge may actually check all this. Everybody's daddy or mother or groom was polishing tack or boots that had gotten dusty during the day. People were wrestling with the string gloves that must be inserted under the billets of the saddle in such a way that the tips just show. Someone had lost her spurs and was trying to borrow a pair for the class. Somebody else's stock had gotten chocolate ice cream on it during the course of the day, and it had to be taken off and turned inside-out to look fresh. Someone else found that one of his buckle guards (I forgot to mention that this is part of required equipment for Corinthian classes) was mysteriously gone and he was in an absolute frenzy trying to borrow a pair. By the time we were all assembled and at the in gate, parents and grooms were panting and perspiring. But here we were—all six, miraculously equipped with all necessary trappings—waiting at the gate before the first number was called!

Again, tension was high. Our group decided to go last. *Teeny* was the big competition, we all felt. After her round, we looked at one another, a little puzzled as to how to rate it in a Corinthian class. All her jumps were good and her pace was even; you couldn't really say there was anything *wrong* with it, but on the other hand, it wasn't exactly brilliant.

Now DSH entries commenced their tries. *Cornflakes* was the first of our group to go, and by this time she had settled down quite a lot. Her round was excellent for a Corinthian, retaining its brilliance but looking more relaxed than the first trip. Next, *Tango* came in and Sarah Shelly tried to push her on a little too much in an effort to gain brilliance. She rapped the in-and-out hard, and that settled that round. Now *Dark Knight,* and this time he figured the in-and-out perfectly, and as he came back into the ring, Mrs. Douglas whistled and told Ridgely his round was one to re-member. *Wireless* breezed over the course next, but somehow she man-aged to get into the jump coming down the hill wrong, and twisted over it. "Tough luck, Fred," we agreed, but undoubtedly the mare had been tired after that Knock Down and Out class. After all, she wasn't a spring chicken! Now *Glennwood* commenced his trip and fenced well the whole way around, until the last coop, coming back into the ring. Here, he be-came too confident and stood back so far to clear it that a gasp went up from the crowd.

And now it was *Dawn's* turn. The day's work apparently had agreed with her, as this time, her manners, pace and jumps all were quite lovely the whole way around. "Was it as good as it felt?" Sally whispered to me, as she came through the gate. "It looked awfully good, Sally," I answered, "but there were quite a few good trips right in our own group this time—it's sort of hard to figure."

At this point, horses were called back in the ring to have appointments checked. This takes forever. The judges walk slowly from horse to horse. We see them point out a boot garter that is on backwards. Now one judge opens Greta's sandwich case, and tries a bite of her sandwich. The other judge is talking to Sally and smiling—has she forgotten something? Finally, the judges pull out about eight horses and tell them to form a separate line. Surely these are the winners? Don't count on anything yet—they may get moved backwards or forwards on conformation. And when they are jogged out for soundness (this is done at the end of each hunter class) it's always possible that a horse may have stepped on a stone and may look lame momentarily. Anything can happen until the judges sign their cards and send them to the announcer's stand.

Ah! that *must* be the final line up—there go the cards! Yes, that's it— *April Dawn* is first, *Cornflakes* second, *Dark Knight* third and *Teeny* fourth!

When Sally rode out of the ring, her face was positively comical. She was so happy that it was all she could do to control herself—we had been taught that you don't jump up and down and crow when you win any more than you pout when you lose. Greta and Ridgely were in happy hazes, too. It seemed too good to be true! Our horses had scored first, second and third in this class.

As we left the ring, Barbee Dardiner, *Teeny's* rider, came up to Sally, smiling. Barbee was the riding marvel of our section—she had ridden in her first class over fences at the age of three; she had made her debut at Madison Square when she was five. She could and would ride any horse for any person, at any time, and could be counted on to do a top flight job. Furthermore, the Dardiners were ever ready to lend a Pelham bridle, or to van your horse, or to help a young rider school his pony over a fence.

Barbee now said in a completely ungrudging manner, "Congratulations, Sally. You are doing a swell job on the little mare. I guess that class gives you championship, doesn't it?" This was almost too much. Sally was not only thrilled by such flattering words, but the fine spirit of sportsmanship made even more of an impression. She later commented to me that she knew that while she might not have *shown* disappointment if the situation were reversed, she couldn't have been as genuinely warm and friendly. I suppose we all began learning many such lessons in this way.

Barbee was right about the championship. *April Dawn* had won it,

by one half point! The five points added to her original six and a half gave
her a total of eleven and a half points. *Teeny* had added one more to the
ten she had before the class started, and wound up with eleven, for reserve championship.

From that point on, we were so happy we hardly knew what we were
doing. Fred placed second in the VHSA Equitation Class, and Sally fourth,

Fred, on his grand old mare, *Wireless*. "Fred placed second in the VHSA class." Note
the excellent form of rider and horse.

which of course was gratifying. But Sally was feeling positively slap happy
by this time, and hardly knew if she placed or didn't—she had to be
punched to ride up and accept her ribbon when her equitation number
was called. (You see, you have a different number for horsemanship classes,
in which *you* are being judged.)

Sally and Greta would have liked to scratch (cancel their entries) in the
last class of the day, the hunt teams. They felt that their horses had done
enough for one day, but Frances had had very little luck so far, and they
had planned to go with her. So go they went, for another win. Competition is never quite as keen in the hunt teams, as generally by the end of
the day, people and horses are tired, and the class winds up with only
four or five teams. This was the case today, but it was nice, as it gave
Frances and *Glennwood* one blue to take home. Likewise, the hunt teams

class gave Sarah Shelly one ribbon to add to *Tango's* collection—her team scored third.

And so the day ended. As anyone can imagine, it was one happy bunch of children who rebandaged their horses and led them on the van. We were exhausted, we were dirty, we were starving, but we were absolutely jubilant. Every station wagon sported a collection of ribbons fluttering over its windshield.

It could be done—it could be done—it could be done—we could take our two- and three-hundred dollar horses and ponies to shows and join the winners' circle!

QUIZ FOR CHAPTERS XVII, XVIII AND XIX

To be scored as two (2) quizzes, one (1) of twelve (12) parts, one (1) of thirteen (13) parts.

Mark *TRUE* if all parts of the statement are true; *FALSE* if any part is false.

1. Horses are generally shown with flowing manes and tails in hunter classes.
2. Horses are generally bandaged from hooves to hocks or knees when vanned any distance, to protect their legs from nicks or scrapes.
3. In a "model class" the horse is judged on conformation, quality, substance and soundness.
4. In "standing up" a horse you try to get him to tuck his chin in and show his spirit by laying back his ears.
5. An "under saddle" class is a class in which horse or pony is shown at gaits only—that is, at walk, trot, canter and sometimes gallop—rather than over fences.
6. A hack class is also termed an "under saddle" class.
7. A working hunter class is a class in which the horse or pony's style of galloping and performance over fences, manners, safety and soundness are the factors to be considered.
8. In a class which reads "performance, manners and way of going 75 percent; conformation 25 percent" the horse will be judged not only on the way he performs but on his body build.
9. A horsemanship class is also termed an equitation class.
10. In a horsemanship class the horse, rather than the rider, is being judged.
11. In jumper, as opposed to hunter classes, the horse is scored on a straight numerical basis for specific jumping faults (i.e., knock downs, refusals, etc.) and the manners and style of jumping are not considered in determining the winners.
12. In the event of a tie between horses having clean rounds the jumps are raised in a jumper class.

13. Ribbons are awarded in the United States in the following order: for first place, red; for second, blue; for third, white; for fourth, yellow.

14. The "Corinthian" class is also termed the "hunt attire" or "appointments" class.

15. In your hunter class you may wear either a tweed with appropriate accessories or a black coat with its appropriate accessories.

16. Under no circumstances is it correct to wear black or green breeches or jodhpurs in a hunter show.

17. You might hear people speak of their "canaries." This refers to the yellow vests which are worn with black coats.

18. "Shad belly" refers to the traditional fare served at exhibitors' suppers held after most horse shows.

19. In an appointments class one tries to get the fanciest stock pin he can find; stock pins set with rhinestones are considered very smart.

20. The rider (boy) who can afford to purchase a scarlet coat should wear it, with the buttons and colors of the nearest hunt in Corinthian classes, whether or not he is a member of a hunt.

21. Two equally honest and capable judges might judge the same hunter class a little differently—for example, one might place heavier emphasis on style of galloping and jumping than the other; the second might consider safe jumping in a child's hunter the prime requisite.

22. The sole purpose of taking horses to horse shows is to win ribbons. The rider can hardly be expected to be pleasant and cheerful if his horse is beaten by better horses.

23. In a Corinthian class "brilliance" counts a certain percentage.

24. In hunter or jumper classes the horse is being judged, not the rider. However, a skillful rider makes it possible for the horse to perform at his best.

25. In Corinthian classes, the rider carries hunting crop and extra string gloves under the billet straps of his saddle; he wears pigskin or other leather gloves and hunt spurs; he also has a sandwich case attached to his saddle, filled with a sandwich, and something to drink in the flask.

CHAPTER XX

Riding Clinic

Most of that spring and summer we went to shows two or three times each month. Of course, we didn't always have as much good fortune as we did at the show I described, but generally our horses and ponies were in the ribbons.

During August in Virginia, we almost always have a drought and the ground becomes hard baked. This year was no exception, so during August we didn't go to many shows. Mrs. D. was never too keen to have her horses jump on hard ground. However, we were to have a most exciting event right at home.

Captain Vladimir Littauer, whose books on riding and schooling were used as textbooks at our school, would conduct a clinic at DSH the latter part of the month. (We called any get together in which the performance of horse and rider was studied, a clinic. Evolving from these studies, various schooling techniques, new to us, would be presented.) We boned up like mad on Captain Littauer's books. For days before his visit, we went around mumbling definitions of such terms as lateral flexibility, engagement, connected trot, direct flexions, or quizzing one another on them.

Some twelve of us were to ride, and it was indeed a high day at our school when Captain L. walked into the ring. I think we had expected a very formal approach and were immediately charmed by the friendly manner in which we were greeted.

It turned out that we needn't have worried about involved definitions—the points that were covered in this clinic were explained in the simplest possible way, although Captain Littauer was pleased that we possessed some knowledge of terms.

The first day, our positions were checked, and in general found to be correct. For the rest of that day, Captain L. worked with us on our "following," which he considered rather poor. So we worked, with a few short rest periods for horse and rider, the better part of the morning and again in the afternoon. Most of us could maintain a straight line from bit to elbow, but our hands were inclined to be too set. It seemed that our

201

hands stayed still, even though our bodies moved with the movement of the horses.

We were told to pick up the reins between thumb and forefinger in what we later called a "gingerly" fashion, and let the other three fingers simply wave in the air; we were to do anything to *soften* our feel on the reins so that we would permit the horse to move our hands forward and back freely. Of course, we all thought we had been doing this, and Mrs. Douglas said she must have developed a blind spot as far as our hands were concerned, as she hadn't noticed how "wooden" they were.

Part of the time, we were divided into two sections and told to watch and coach one another, and each to tell his pupil when he was managing *really* to follow. Our following was beginning to become softer and better by the end of the afternoon session. Captain Littauer had an inspired trick of injecting *drama* and competition into what might have been just a long hard day's work, so we wound up the session in high spirits.

Bright and early the next morning we were warming up our horses in the ring, ready for the next class. First of all we were reviewed on the contact work we had done the day before, and everybody was definitely better after the concentrated effort of the last day. Now we worked for a while on following hands and arms while galloping and maintaining a correct galloping position. This takes a really strong seat as it is impossible to follow the gestures of the horse's head and neck unless you can keep your legs completely steady, with seat out of the saddle, and arms and hands free to work independently. Actually, most of us had fairly strong seats, undoubtedly developed by our cross-country riding and hunting, so we did better at this than might have been expected.

In the afternoon, several new movements were introduced. The first was the *turn on the haunches,* which Mrs. D. had felt we were not quite ready for, up until this time. We discovered that when Captain Littauer came we could learn all sorts of things we had not dared tackle before.

The turn on the haunches (or quarters) is just the reverse of the turn on the forehand (see Chapter XIII, page 128). To put it as I *think* it, in the turn on the forehand, you want to swing the horse's rear end (his quarters) around his front end (his forehand). So, your hands hold the front end in place, and your legs move the rear end around—or rather, they ask the horse to move the rear end around.

In the turn on the haunches, you want to swing the front end around the rear end, which must stay in place. So your legs hold, and your hands move the front end around—or rather ask the horse to move it around.

This is not a correct technical explanation, but it was only when I thought of it this way that I could understand what I wanted to do.

When we were on the track to the right and were to make the turn to the right, our instructions went something like this:

Halt the horse along the rail. Close your legs sufficiently to say, "Horse, pay attention." Carry both hands to the right, so that the horse is between two straight reins, which act as traces. Your legs will need to urge sufficiently to persuade the horse to make a step, and your hands tell the horse the direction in which the step is to be made. But your hands also

Photo by Marler

Turn on the quarters. "As he makes each step, his outside front leg (left here) should cross *in front of* his inside (right) leg, maintaining the forward impulse."

check just enough to tell him that he is to move his forehand only—to the right, in this particular case. At the same time he must maintain the *forward* feeling. It is as if he would walk off, but hands indicate that he is to *rotate his forehand* instead. In learning this movement, the horse undoubtedly will want to swing his quarters around. This is easier for him physically since, when standing, he normally carries more of his weight on his forehand than on his quarters. To prevent this, the rider will need to keep his inside (right, here) leg on the girth to act as a "holder" or "steadier" and to use his outside (left, here) leg behind the girth to prevent the quarters from bulging out, or roaming around.

When the horse begins to do the turn correctly, he should make it in four distinct steps. The first two provide half of the turn, and the last two finish it, making it a 180° turn. As he makes each step, his outside front leg (left in this case) should cross *in front of* his inside (right) leg, main-taining the forward impulse. Outside hind (left, here) will make a little circle since the inside hind (right) ideally marks time in place. Through-out the turn, it is important that the horse is calm and relaxed, and re-mains straight from poll to croup.

This isn't an accurate quotation of how it was explained to us. I don't remember the exact words, but this is the explanation that makes sense to me. And it was only when I got that feeling of keeping the horse's forehand straight between two lines, the reins, and swinging it (to right or left, according to the direction in which the turn was to be made), with my own legs holding the quarters where I wanted them, that I could begin to ride this turn without *thinking out* each step as I worked. Of course, none of us reached a stage of performing it *without thinking* about each aid during that clinic. But we were surprised to discover that in an elementary way both riders and horses were beginning to get the idea of what to do that very morning. We discovered that the first one or two steps which carried the horse's forehand away from the rail were much easier for the horse than the last two that should bring it back to the rail, facing in the opposite direction. The horse who does not know this movement will try to complete it as a turn on the forehand—that is, by letting his quarters swing out and pivoting on his *front* legs. Here the rider must be quick to act with the inside (holding leg) and, taking his outside leg back, to tap a little with his spur, in order to prevent the quarters from swinging out.

April Dawn and Sally got the knack of all this very quickly, and before the end of the morning were making very decent turns. *Tango* was an apt pupil in one way—she was perfectly happy to shift her weight back to her quarters (she moved a little bit this way all the time) and to rotate her forehand, but it was her tendency to back and bring the moving leg across *behind* the other foreleg, which is all wrong. Captain Littauer worked with Sarah Shelly and *Tango* on this, and suggested that she try making the turn, without a complete halt, in order not to lose the forward impulse. This made it quite a lot easier in her particular case.

I was riding a very un-handsome brown gelding, *Cadeau*, part of the time that summer. He was not at all a brilliant animal, but was most co-operative and calm by nature. By the early part of the afternoon, *Cadeau*, in his unhurried fashion, was making turns second best to *April Dawn's*.

Logically, the sharp turn at the gallop followed the turn on the quarters. This, in a sense, *is* a turn on the quarters, done at speed, instead of stand-ing still.

Since in the sharp turn at a gallop you want to swing the horse's fore-hand quickly around, keeping the body straight, you use exactly the same aids that you use for your turn on the haunches. Naturally, we found it more fun, and more exciting, just because it is fast. We were told to gallop down the rail and at a designated point to swing the horse's forehand around in a right angle (90°) turn, keeping him straight from poll to croup. If making this turn to the right, naturally, the rider moves both hands to the right, right leg against the girth, left leg behind it. Just as in the turn on the haunches, the legs hold and the hands show the horse where and how much he is to turn. This sharp turn showed us the practical use of the turn on the haunches, as we all could see how helpful it would be on a jump course, particularly one in which time counted.

After we had practiced this turn on the flat, we set up two jumps at right angles to one another and put the technique to work. We used a fairly tight little turn, and in every instance where the horse got into the second jump crooked or ran out, it was easy to see that the trouble had started on the turn itself.

After practicing the sharp turn at speed as a quarter (90°) turn, we next rode it as a 180° turn, completely reversing the direction. Two markers were set up, between which we must quickly swing the horse around, keeping the body straight. It's really quite difficult to do this quickly and well, and to do it without resorting to roughness. But when the horse develops sufficient agility to do it comfortably, here again you have mastered an extremely useful movement, which you will use many times on your jumping courses.

The next morning two more new movements were introduced; the first was the counter gallop (or "false gallop"); the second was the change of leads on the straightaway.

First we tackled the counter gallop. This means that the horse, while on the track to the left, or on a large circle to the left, leads with his right, instead of with his left legs. This feels terribly queer at first, and of course we all wanted to know why we should teach the horse to canter in this way. Captain Littauer explained that it develops the horse's dexterity and balance, lengthens his stride, and in the case of a horse who is inclined to carry his head too high, induces him to reach out with head and neck. He also made the point that the horse, armed with the ability to use either the flying change or the counter gallop, is in an ideal position to handle himself efficiently when required to make a quick change of direction. Your horse will make use of this ability both in horse show jumper courses and out foxhunting.

I can't remember now exactly how we were told to teach the horse the counter gallop, so I'll just explain how I do it, and how it feels. Let's say we are on the track cantering to the right, and the horse is leading with his right legs. Now I commence a large half circle which reverses my direction, but as we complete it, at no point do I give my horse the signal for a change of leads. In fact, I do just the reverse, to discourage a change. Since normally the canter is *maintained* by the rider's inside leg (although *established* with the outside leg), which urges the horse's leading legs along, I would now urge slightly with my outside leg which, in this case, still urges the horse's "leading" legs along. If the rider makes

Photo by Marler

The counter gallop. "The horse . . . on a large circle to the left, leads with his right, instead of his left legs. One gains the impression that here is a horse who is *really* well balanced."

his first circles large—so large that the curve you ride is quite slight, most horses find this movement perfectly simple. It's fascinating to watch the horse at the counter gallop, calm and relaxed. One gains the impression that here is a horse that is *really* well balanced.

The last new movement which was presented to us during this clinic was the change of leads on the straightaway. Like everything else you teach your horse, the change of leads on the straightaway is based on movements learned earlier. Your horse already knows that the rider's outside leg behind the girth, used immediately after both legs have urged and hands momentarily checked, means, "horse, canter, leading with your opposite leg." Now you will give these signals moving down the straightaway and, using your right leg, you say in effect, "horse, pick up the canter, leading with your left legs." Then you will bring the horse back to a trot for a few strides and, now using your left leg behind the girth, you will say, "horse, pick up the canter with your right legs leading."

You will continue to practice this, cutting down the trotting strides, until finally, instead of actually coming to a trot, the hands simply check and the rider moves his opposite leg behind the girth to ask the horse to change his lead. When this is done without any trotting strides, it is called a "flying change." Only *Dawn* reached the point of doing this without being brought down to a trot between changes, during this clinic.

However, the emphasis was not so much on the *promptness* as on the *smoothness* with which the change could be accomplished. We were faulted on the horse's neck being pulled crooked or mouth opening, or haunches ranged to one side or the other. We were to concentrate on keeping the horse straight from poll to croup and on a calm performance with the horse's head and neck extended.

So here were four new movements (turn on the haunches, sharp turn at the gallop, change of leads on the straightaway, either with or without interruption, and the counter gallop) on which we had made at least a creditable start. I said earlier that when Captain Littauer came to conduct clinics we found that we could do all sorts of things that we had not been ready to attempt before. Somehow, he enabled us to ride "over our heads" and as if we were on the road to being real horsemen and horsewomen.

Now Captain Littauer said he wanted us to put together the different movements we understood in what is called a "program ride." This is the same sort of ride that is also called "an elementary dressage test" except, in the programs we rode, we used a large (preferably oval) ring in which the horse could move with long free strides. Jumping was part of this sort of program. Program rides, as we do them, provide an excellent test of the suppleness and agility, keenness and yet calmness which one wants from his hunter—or from his all-purpose mount.

This is a typical program of the type we rode. Our own ring, unfortunately is rectangular, not oval. However, it is of sufficient size (148′ by 252′) to allow the horse to really move out freely and to show three distinct speeds of gaits.

1. At E, enter ring at trot, halt in center, pause 5 seconds.
2. Fast walk to A.
3. At A, track right, ordinary trot.
4. At G half circle (large) returning to track.
5. At D change direction at trot over jump to H.
6. At A, fast trot.
7. At E, ordinary trot.
8. At F, slow trot.
9. At H, halt, half turn on haunches.

10. From H, pick up canter, turn down center E to A, changing leads with interruption.
11. At A, track to right at canter.
12. At B, change direction over jump, changing leads at F, if necessary for "true gallop."
13. At A, half circle, change lead returning to wall.
14. At E, down center of ring to A, changing leads in center with interruption.
15. At A, track to left, gallop (1½ rings).
16. At E, walk loose reins.
17. At D, establish contact, canter, turn sharply down center at A.
18. Halt in center, back 4 steps.
19. Leave ring at trot.

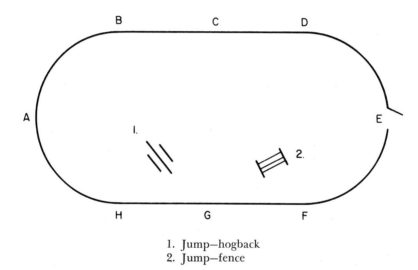

1. Jump—hogback
2. Jump—fence

On the last day of our first clinic with Captain Littauer, we rode this program as a little competition.

This type of ride is terrific fun. You have to be alert yourself, and to do it half way decently, your horse must be sensibly and carefully schooled. As an instructor at one of the nearby colleges used to say "There is *meat* to this sort of competition."

In addition to riding programs ourselves, we had to practice judging each other. This is almost as much fun as riding yourself, and helps one to develop a keen eye. Zero (which no one ever gets) is the perfect score. The rider is penalized minus one to minus three for mistakes on each of the eighteen or twenty movements. You score him minus one for a slight mistake (let's say the canter departure a tiny bit crooked, or very slight loss of contact on the departure, etc.); you will penalize him two for a more serious penalty, and minus three for a maximum fault—let's say, breaking into a canter on the fast trot, or picking up the wrong lead, or a mouth really roughly pulled open, or horse quite crooked on the line, or making his turn on the quarters as a turn on the forehand, etc. The winner, of course, is the horse and rider combination with the lowest score.

I neglected to say that you also penalize for bad position, or incorrectly used aids. These things generally show up in the poor results with the horse, and many times you don't have to give a separate penalty. Or you might give one numerical penalty on the whole program because the rider looked slightly down instead of between the horse's ears throughout the ride, or carried his hands too low the whole time, or had the reins too short. You wouldn't penalize him in each movement for this prevailing mistake.

We were all quite carried away with the fascination of this type of competition, and before Captain Littauer left, we had arranged to set up a challenge bowl event, to be composed of three phases. The first would be the sort of program ride we have described; the second would be a "cross country" phase; the third would be ring jumping, over varied fences, with *style* of horse and rider to count as well as performance. This sort of "combined test" for horses and riders since that time has become quite popular in our part of the country, except that most have the first phase in a very small arena, and the last phase is judged purely on the horse's ability to get over fences.

Captain Littauer left us all feeling inspired to ride more intelligently and with more finesse. We hoped to give him a pleasant surprise on his next visit!

QUIZ FOR CHAPTER XX

To be scored as one (1) quiz of thirteen (13) parts.
Mark *TRUE* if all parts of the statement are true; *FALSE* if any part is false.

1. In the turn on the haunches (or quarters) the horse is asked to rotate his quarters around his forehand.
2. In the finished turn, the horse will make the 180° turn, reversing his direction, in about four (4) distinct steps.
3. The moving (outside) foreleg should cross *in front of* the inside foreleg in making this turn.
4. It will be necessary to pull the head and neck crooked in order to persuade the horse to make the turn.

5. In the sharp turn at the gallop, you use just about the same combination of aids that you do in the turn on the forehand.
6. Ability to do the sharp turn correctly is very advantageous in riding a jump course in which the horse will have to change directions quickly, particularly when time counts.
7. In executing the sharp turn at a gallop, the rider should keep the horse straight from poll to croup.
8. In the counter gallop, also called the "false gallop" the horse leads with the outside legs instead of the inside.
9. The counter gallop is important to teach the horse balance and suppleness; it also aids in lengthening the stride and lowering the head and neck.
10. In the change of leads on a straightaway with interruption, the rider alternately gives the horse the signal to pick up the canter leading with one set of legs, then after one or more trotting strides, to pick up the canter with the other set of legs.
11. In a "flying change" there are no trotting strides between changes of lead.
12. The "program ride," as we ride it, is generally held in a tiny arena and aims primarily to teach the horse to handle himself in a small area with shortened strides.
13. Programs rides, as we ride them, are held in large, preferably oval rings of such size that the horses are able to move with long free strides. This type of ride, combining various schooling movements, provides an excellent test of the suppleness and agility, calmness and yet keenness which we want from our hunters or our all-purpose mounts.

CHAPTER XXI

The Years Pass

In the years that followed the ones that I have described, so much happened that it would take another book, much longer than this one, to tell the story.

Each year brought new events that were even more exciting than those of the year before. Time and again, we have said "nothing will ever match the thrill of . . ." But then another and another exciting episode would follow. So all I can do is to touch very briefly on a few of these more exciting incidents, and show you some of the pictures. Since I'm now just *mentioning* different things that happened over the next years, I won't necessarily present them in chronological order. Some day I'll write a real story of our horse show trips and our hunting experiences.

The fall that followed the summer clinic I described, we were invited to organize a junior hunt as a part of the regular Fairfax Hunt. We felt that we were really "somebody" now. We were members of a bona fide hunt!

We elected our own officials, both hunting (MFH and Whips) and business (Board of Directors, President, Vice President, Secretary, Treasurer). We held regular monthly meetings, conducted our business affairs, collected our dues and kept our books.

The Fairfax Hunt was (still is, for that matter) very generous with us, allowing us to use all facilities of the club house and kennels for a nominal membership fee.

We may hunt every week, if we wish, but three Saturdays a month we juniors are requested to stay in the back of the field. The fourth (Junior Day, it's called) we may have the front of the field directly behind Mr. Greene all to ourselves and the senior members hunt in the back.

During the Christmas holidays senior members give up one or two of their regular hunting days to us juniors, and we hold "all junior" meets. These are terrific fun, with our junior MFH and junior whips officiating. The huntsman to hunt the pack, Mrs. Douglas and Mr. Greene in the back of the field to watch out for any very young members, are the only adults out on these special junior hunts.

Following these holiday meets (one of which is always ·our "invitational," where we play host to any junior members of neighboring Virginia hunts) we have hunt breakfasts at the club house. While we pack away fantastic amounts of turkey and "trimmings" we hash over the amusing or exciting events of the day.

We ride all year around, bad weather as well as good. We have no inside arena at DSH and unless we want long interruptions to our riding programs, we must ignore rain and snow. So we get into riding raincoats and rubber boots and ride in all weather.

Members of the Fairfax Junior Hunt. Here you see three junior MFH's, past and present. Fred (far left), Sally (second from left) and I (extreme right) each have served in this capacity.

Snow riding is great sport. In a dry snow, landing over a jump is like landing on a cloud. Our horses snort and buck in high spirits and seem to like the fun just as much as we do.

Our fun with horses was not limited to hunting and schooling. That fall we made our first trip to the Pennsylvania National Show in Harrisburg. That first year, *Dawn* was our only entry, and Sally the sole member of our group to have the honor of competing in this competition. It seems almost too good to be true, doesn't it, that on this first trip *April Dawn* won the Children's Working Hunter Class at Harrisburg, placed third in the jumper and fourth in the hunter stake class? The next year we went to Harrisburg and New York both, and this time in Harrisburg *April Dawn* won the Children's Jumper Championship Class with jumps raised to four feet nine inches in the last jump off, and placed in both hunter classes. Home again and then to New York two weeks later, where *Dawn* really sort of stunned us all by winning the junior jumper class (this for

Courtesy of Frances and Homer Heller

Mary Lou Walters on *Little Mingo*. "In a dry snow, landing over a jump is like landing on a cloud."

"Since we have no inside arena at DSH we must ignore rain and snow."

the second time—she had won it on her only other trip to Madison Square the year Snowden Mills rode her) and—all in the same day—placing second in the working hunter, out of a field of eighty entries. *April Dawn* is really quite fantastic—in five years of trips to "National Shows" she has never been out of the ribbons! Some mare!

The rest of us never had as spectacular wins, but the several who made the annual trek to the big shows always returned with at least a ribbon or two to show for our efforts. Last fall when we were in Harrisburg, three of the six final ribbon winners (from seventy some entries) in the AHSA Hunter Seat Equitation Class were DSH pupils. Sally won it after a stiff ride-off over a changed course; I placed sixth. I don't mean to be bragging; I am trying to point out that hard work pays off with horses and riding!

While winning adds a very special zest to showing, and of course it is gratifying to take an inexpensive horse and win even at Harrisburg and Madison Square, we didn't make these trips to win ribbons. We simply love every minute at these big indoor shows. It's fun to visit around and watch the way the expensive stables turn out their conformation hunters. We listen avidly to the various theories expounded on schooling. We began to know all the grooms, and I often think how nice they are to us kids. I think of the years Dayton put up *Dawn's* tail for us and how he would never accept anything for doing it. I remember the time Wilton was up most of the night hosing the knee of the horse I was to ride in the open jumper class the next day. This horse had banged his knee in schooling, and we held our breaths until he actually went in, for a third in the senior jumper!

We visit the section where the Arabs are stabled, and make firm friendships there. We play with the little Shetland show ponies. We watch the five-gaited horses being prepared to go into the ring, tails being combed out, hair by hair. We watch the Olympic Team members schooling for their classes, and analyze the techniques of riders from different countries.

There is something about a big show, the variety of sights and sounds and smells; the confusion, the bustling, the willingness to help another exhibitor with the loan of a bridle or a stirrup leather; the wonderful feel of soft springy tanbark under your horse's hooves in the ring; the beautiful and elaborately worked-out jump courses under the lights; the tense anticipation of your own class and the almost suffocating happiness when your horse is called back into the winner's circle; the ceremony and pomp with which trophies are presented while cameras click—all of these factors and many others combine to make the big inside show a memorable event.

One year Mrs. Douglas got carried away and decided that it would be fun to go on up to the Royal Winter Fair at Toronto, Canada, a thousand mile trip from Vienna, Virginia. This, after we had returned from one more successful trip to Harrisburg and New York. She and two other ladies talked themselves into the trip, aided and abetted by some of us children.

Nora Durstfeld was one of the younger riders who had made amazing progress, and in the course of two years at DSH had become one of the top contenders. She had a wonderful pony, *Dum Dum,* who was a smooth, able jumping little animal. And she had a mother, who like Mrs. Hilton and Mrs. Douglas, was just as crazy about going around on such junkets as we kids were. So-oo, Mrs. Douglas, Mrs. Hilton and Mrs. Durstfeld, Sally and Nora, Tina McCoy and I (Tina and I had wangled grooming assignments for ourselves so we could go along), set forth, with *April Dawn* and *Dum Dum* in a trailer behind us, bound for Toronto, Canada! All the fathers had been full of dire warnings about our being caught up there in a snow storm, and trying to get out with horses and trailer. Mrs. Douglas gaily told everyone that if we didn't return in a week, to wait until snows melted and the spring thaw came, and then to look for a little rusted trailer. In that trailer, she said, people would find skeletal bones of horses and humans, huddled together for warmth. Yes, someone added, and in those skeletal fingers you would find clutched some scraps of faded red and blue ribbons! All these fears were unfounded, although we did get out of Canada with a snow storm right behind us—and we did have a few red and blue ribbons! We had a completely marvelous trip. Just the fact that we were going to show out of the United States seemed exciting to us. We loved the show itself. Our riders had never competed before such a responsive audience. Applause for good rounds would be quite deafening. Everybody was so interested in us, and so complimentary to Sally's and Nora's riding that we were quite bowled over. The warmth and friendliness in the attitude of show managers, announcers, ushers, and spectators gave you an awfully good feeling inside.

The show itself was beautifully run, and nowhere else have we seen such effective pageantry. I shall always remember the closing ceremonies. Since the show itself is only a part of a tremendous fair, the country fair flavor is preserved. In the background are wagons, heaped with the produce of the land, vegetables and flowers, piled high. They are drawn by teams of eight magnificent draft horses—a sight we rarely see at home.

The arena, in semi-darkness for this occasion, gives the feeling of a dramatic stage setting, with flags of all nations overhead, streamers from the ceiling, bands playing stirring music.

Champions are led through an archway, coats glowing like satin in the spotlight, to receive their awards. The international teams ride in, in the order in which they have finished the week's competition, to the strains of the national anthem of each country represented. The audience is tremendously enthusiastic, and seems to feel very much a part of the whole ceremony.

We left Canada not only much impressed with the way in which these people run their show, but equally with the wholehearted participation of the packed grandstands.

During the past two years I have found another fascinating aspect of riding. This is steeplechasing, and when I am doing this, I say, *"This is the most fun of all!"* Of course, part of the endless fascination of working with horses lies in the variety of exciting things you can do with them.

Courtesy of Marshall Hawkins

"I know the horse has a better chance to handle himself over a fence if I stay forward and allow him free use of head and neck." I am on the far side behind the other horse.

The steeplechase (or hunt race) season logically follows our foxhunting season in Virginia. During the fall and winter months, while you are hunting your horse, you are conditioning him for racing over timber. Then towards the end of the hunting season, people get together to see whose horse is the fittest, has the most speed and stamina and ability over fences, in various types of races.

Since I am riding other people's horses (not DSH horses in these races), I don't like to argue with the owners about how to ride their horses. Most of the race riders advocate sitting back over fences. But I can't make up my mind to ride that way, as I know the horse has a better chance to handle himself over a fence if I stay forward and allow him free use of his head and neck. And surely you should try to give your horse every break you can.

The photo on this page illustrates my point. This horse, as you can see, got into his fence all wrong and hit it above one knee, with a sickening thud. We were galloping at speed, and I really thought he was a goner. For once, I think I did just the right thing—I let the reins slide through my fingers so he could use his head and neck. And I know he could never have made it over that fence if I hadn't; just look at the way he is struggling! He managed, though, and we finished fourth.

Courtesy of Marshall Hawkins

"This horse got into his fence all wrong and hit it above the knees with a sickening thud. I let the reins slide through my fingers so he could use his head and neck."

After the hunt race season, the show season starts once again. Now that I am seventeen even my family recognizes the fact that riding will be my career. So I let it be known that I am happy to ride any horse for anybody. In this way, I feel that I am gaining the experience I need. In addition, by letting people know that I am *available,* I am beginning to get better and better horses to ride, both for racing and showing.

As I write this, I know that my attitude certainly isn't typical and shouldn't be recommended for many people. Mrs. Douglas, for example, would oppose this point of view on the part of any of her other pupils, but she knows that in my case, I am dead serious about it.

Last show season, I had several really good horses to ride. One, *Aniboo,* won the open jumper championship (senior) on Virginia's "Big Four" circuit—Staunton, Bath, Deep Run and Warrenton. *Aniboo* was a terrific individual though the most difficult horse to get along with I have ever known. But it all adds up to experience.

These last two years, while I have been riding a lot of open jumpers and 'chasers, Sally Hilton's riding has developed along slightly different lines. She has many times the finesse I'll ever have. In addition to riding *April Dawn* to three VHSA high score hunter championships, she has developed the mare's performance in program rides (called elementary

Courtesy of Marshall Hawkins

Here I am pivoting on my knees with my legs swinging back.

dressage tests) until she is always a challenge in this type of competition. For three years she has won the USET (United States Equestrian Team) medal class competition in our section, qualifying for the ride-off at Madison Square Garden, New York. This competition is composed of two phases: the first is dressage and, while we find this competition in its postage stamp arena not suited to the type of riding we do, still *Dawn's* schooling in program rides enables her, under Sally's skillful riding, to win here too. The second phase is stadium jumping, judged on the rider's skill and finesse as well as the horse's performance. This phase, horse and rider find more to their liking.

At the same time, Sally has developed a thoroughbred mare of her own, *Shadow Patch,* from a gawky three-year-old with nothing much to recommend her but a nice attitude, into a most versatile performer. *Shadow Patch* is one of the best and most pleasant hunting mares I have ever seen,

Courtesy of Allen Studio.

Here is Sally on *April Dawn*. This picture shows excellent following and very nice overall design. However, the left hand may have dropped a little low, judging from the appearance of the left rein.

Courtesy of Cary Jackson

Here I am on *Blenbes* in the picture I like best of myself. This mare is a magnificent jumper.

combining those qualities we consider ideal—keenness with obedience, light mouth with a willing nature. While *Bedo,* as she is called, is not a particularly able jumper by nature, Sally brought her along so slowly and carefully that now she jumps a four foot "modified Olympic" (open jumper) course with ease. She will go four and a half, but we feel that it is difficult for her. It's pleasant to watch the confidence this mare has in her rider, and to see how the *habit of obedience* and cooperation has been developed. And it is even pleasanter to watch her do a program ride. She has a lovely way of moving with long, low strides. This natural ability has been developed to its peak by Sally.

Now Sally has a new horse, *Blue Wasp,* whom we consider a terrific prospect. Here we seem to have the natural jumper, who combines courage with style, quality and excellent movement. It's too early to talk about *Blue Wasp,* but I think you will hear about him in the next few years.

So, as you see, Sally's path and mine have diverged in the past two years. While I have ridden dozens of horses, Sally was concentrating on doing a really finished job on *April Dawn* and *Shadow Patch.*

In spite of this, we see eye to eye on one point—the necessity of bettering our performances. Captain Littauer still comes once or twice a year to DSH (we hope he will come forever) and then we get back into the ring for a good working over—which we still need!

In our clinic last fall, the emphasis was on *style.* The point was not to have style because it looks pretty in itself, but because style generally produces the desired performance in the horse. In other words, if the rider can only learn to do things right, things generally work out right for the horse.

Page 219 shows our latest pictures. As can be seen, after all the years we have worked, there is still need for improvement. And that, no doubt, is the really *endless* fascination that horses offer us—we can keep on learning and working forever!

QUIZ AND SCORING DIRECTIONS FOR CHAPTER XXI

To be judged as two (2) full value quizzes, of nine (9) parts each.

Just as we often do at DSH, you are now to adopt the role of horse show judge. On the following pages you will find nine photos showing riders over fences. You are to line them up, first place through ninth, on the basis of horsemanship. You are to study their form: style, efficiency and non-abuse of mounts. This is a difficult job, and in this case, made more difficult by the fact that you see the rider on one jump only, and on one phase of the jump at that. Since you are judging an advanced horsemanship class, you are to place in first position the rider, *riding on an advanced level,* who demonstrates the

Photo 1

Photo 2

Photo 3

Photo 4

Photo 5

Photo 6

Photo 7

Photo 8

Photo 9
223

most nearly perfect form. The rider, jumping on an intermediate or elementary level, must of course place lower. There could be an exception to this rule, however, if a jump on the intermediate level is actually abusive, or is much poorer, than an outstandingly good jump on the beginner level. (We are using photos to show various faults, and the same person may appear in several pictures. Just pretend they are nine different riders!)

For the first section of your quiz, line up your contestants, 1 through 9. Even with members of our teaching staff at DSH there was some disagreement over the order in which these contestants should be "lined up," so, in order to bow to your opinion somewhat in this respect, deduct *four (4) points only* for each picture that is "out of place" according to the official answer.

For the second part of your quiz, evaluate—that is, tell what is good and what is bad, and give the reasons for your decisions. State whether the rider is jumping on an advanced, an intermediate or beginner level. For answers that are altogether wrong, according to our opinion, deduct ten points from 100 for each such wrong answer. If partly wrong, use your own judgment in determining the amount of penalty.

Enter your two scores in the spaces indicated on page 235.

Scoring Directions and Answers to Quizzes

Scoring directions and answers to initial quiz preceding Chapter I—To be scored as two (2) quizzes.

You will have identified sixty (60) parts of the horse and his equipment when you finish this quiz. Since it covers quite a lot of material, and so, of knowledge on your part, it will be scored as two (2) full value quizzes, of thirty (30) parts each. Also to give you a small advantage, you may count off three points from one hundred for each wrong answer, instead of three and one-third.

Check your answers against the diagrams of the horse and his equipment on page xvii and enter your two scores as the first parts of your overall scores on the spaces indicated on page 234.

Scoring directions and answers to quizzes for Chapters II and III—To be scored as two (2) quizzes.

If you are correct in your answers to all parts of this double value quiz, score yourself "100" on each of the two lines indicated on page 234. You receive a separate score for the first sixteen and the second seventeen parts. If you have any wrong, you must deduct six points from one hundred for each wrong answer. For example, let's say you have two wrong out of the first sixteen. You would then give yourself a grade of eighty-eight (twelve from one hundred) on the first section. Perhaps you have one wrong out the second group (six points from one hundred) of seventeen statements. You will score yourself ninety-four on this section. Enter your scores on the lines indicated on page 234.

ANSWERS:

1.–B; 2.–B; 3.–B; 4.–B; 5.–C; 6.–C; 7.–B; 8.–B; 9.–B; 10.–B; 11.–A; 12.–B; 13.–C; 14.–B; 15.–B; 16.–C;

*   *   *

17.–C; 18.–B; 19.–B; 20.–B; 21.–A; 22.–C; 23.–C; 24.–B; 25.–B; 26.–B; 27.–C; 28.–A; 29.–A; 30.–A; 31.–C; 32.–A; 33.–C.

Scoring directions and answers to quizzes for Chapters IV and V.

To be scored as two (2) quizzes of ten (10) parts each. Grade yourself one hundred (100) for each on the lines indicated if you have all correct answers. If you have any wrong answers, deduct ten points for each. Thus, if you have one wrong answer in the first ten, your score is ninety for that section. If you have two wrong answers in the second ten, you have a grade of eighty for that section. Enter your scores in the spaces indicated on page 234.

ANSWERS:

1.–B; 2.–A; 3.–A; 4.–A; 5.–A; 6.–B; 7.–B; 8.–C; 9.–B; 10.–A;

*   *   *

11.–B; 12.–A; 13.–B; 14.–B; 15.–A; 16.–C; 17.–B; 18.–B; 19.–A; 20.–B.

Scoring directions and answers to quiz for Chapters VI and VII.

To be scored as one (1) quiz of twelve (12) parts. If you have all correct answers, score yourself one hundred (100). Deduct eight points from one hundred for each wrong answer. Thus if you have three wrong, you have a grade of seventy-six for this quiz. Enter your score on the line indicated on page 234.

ANSWERS:

1.–B; 2.–B; 3.–C; 4.–A; 5.–B; 6.–B; 7.–B; 8.–B; 9.–B; 10.–B; 11.–A; 12.–B.

Scoring directions and answers to quizzes for Chapters VIII and IX.

To be scored as two (2) quizzes of eight (8) parts each. If you have any wrong answers, deduct twelve points for each. Enter your scores on the line indicated on page 234.

ANSWERS:

1.–B; 2.–B; 3.–B; 4.–A; 5.–B; 6.–B; 7.–A; 8.–B;
9.–B; 10.–B; 11.–C; 12.–B; 13.–A; 14.–B; 15.–B; 16.–C.

Scoring directions and answers to quiz for **Chapter X.**

To be scored as one (1) quiz of fifteen (15) parts. If you have any wrong answers, deduct six points for each. Enter your score on the line indicated on page 234.

ANSWERS:

1.–B; 2.–B; 3.–B; 4.–A; 5.–B; 6.–C; 7.–B; 8.–A; 9.–B; 10.–A; 11.–B; 12.–A; 13.–B; 14.–B; 15.–B.

Scoring directions and answers to quiz for **Chapter XI.**

To be scored as one (1) quiz of six (6) parts. Deduct sixteen points each for wrong answers. Enter your score as indicated on page 234.

ANSWERS:

1.–B; 2.–A; 3.–C; 4.–C; 5.–C; 6.–C.

Scoring directions and answers to quiz for **Chapter XII.**

To be scored as one (1) quiz of sixteen (16) parts. If you have any wrong answers, deduct five points from one hundred for each. Check your answers against the photos of equipment and their proper terms on pages 111, 112 and 113. Enter your score on the line indicated on page 234.

Scoring directions and answers to quizzes for **Chapter XIII.**

To be scored as three (3) separate quizzes. In the first section (listing and explaining leg and hand aids, of which there are three leg and five hand aids) you will deduct twelve points for a completely wrong answer. If some part of an answer is incorrect, you must use you own judgment as to how much to take off from your score. Turn back to page 117, Chapter XIII, to check your answers.

*   *   *

Sections two and three are scored as two (2) quizzes of sixteen (16) parts each. Deduct six points for each wrong answer. Enter your scores on the lines indicated on page 234.

ANSWERS:

1. False—see page 118—paragraph 5
2. True—see page 119—paragraph 1
3. False—see page 119—paragraph 4
4. True—see page 119—paragraph 4
5. True—see page 120—paragraph 1
6. False—see page 120—paragraph 2
7. True—see page 120—paragraph 3
8. True—see page 120—paragraph 3
9. False—see page 120—paragraph 3
10. True—see page 120—paragraph 4
11. True—see page 120—paragraph 4
12. True—see page 121—paragraph 1
13. False—see page 121—paragraph 1
14. False—see page 121—paragraph 3
15. True—see page 122—paragraph 2
16. True—see page 122—paragraph 2

                                  *   *   *

17. False—see page 122—paragraph 2
18. False—see page 122—paragraph 5
19. True—see page 124—paragraph 1
20. False—see page 124—paragraph 2
21. True—see page 124—paragraph 5
22. True—see page 125—paragraph 3
23. True—see page 125—paragraph 6
24. True—see page 126—paragraph 2
25. True—see page 126—paragraph 4
26. False—see page 128—paragraph 2
27. True—see page 128—paragraph 3
28. False—see page 129—paragraph 1
29. True—see page 128—paragraph 4
30. True—see page 128—paragraph 4; page 129—paragraph 1
31. Check your drawing of a circle, half circle and a half circle in reverse against diagrams on page 127.
32. Check your drawing of a zigzag, serpentine, and a figure eight against diagrams on page 127.

Scoring directions and answers to quiz for Chapter XIV.

To be scored as one (1) quiz of ten (10) parts. Deduct ten points from one hundred for each wrong answer. Enter your score on the line indicated on page 235.

ANSWERS:

1. B; 2. C; 3. A; 4. A; 5. B; 6. B; 7. A; 8. B; 9. B; 10. C.

Scoring directions and answers to quizzes for Chapters XV and XVI.

To be scored as three (3) full value quizzes. Statements 1 through 27 will be scored as two (2) quizzes of thirteen (13) and fourteen (14) parts respectively. If you have any wrong answers in these sections, deduct seven points from one hundred for each. Enter your scores on the lines indicated on page 235.

ANSWERS:

1. False—see page 142—paragraph 4
2. True—see page 142—paragraph 5
3. False—see page 142—paragraph 6
4. False—see page 143—paragraph 2
5. False—see page 143—paragraph 4 (You never wear white pique stock or black boots with brown tweed jacket)
6. False—see page 146—paragraph 2
7. False—see page 143—paragraph 4
8. True—see page 146—paragraph 2
9. False—see page 143—paragraph 4 (With the black coat, you *must* wear the white stock)
10. True—see page 143—paragraph 4
11. False—see page 143—paragraph 4
12. True—see page 143—paragraph 4
13. False—see page 147—paragraph 6

*　　*　　*

14. False—see page 147—paragraph 8
15. True—see page 147—paragraph 9
16. False—see page 147—paragraph 10
17. False—see page 148—paragraph 1
18. False—see page 148—paragraph 1
19. True—see page 148—paragraph 4

20. True—see page 148—paragraph 6
21. True—see page 148—paragraph 7
22. False—see page 148—paragraph 7
23. False—see page 148—paragraph 8
24. True—see page 149—paragraph 1
25. False—see page 149—paragraph 2
26. False—see page 149—paragraph 4
27. False—see page 150—paragraph 1

*   *   *

Scoring directions for last section of quizzes for Chapters XV and XVI. In this section you have 25 words or phrases which would be expressed differently by one familiar with foxhunting terms. If you have any wrong answers, deduct four points from one hundred for each. If you score over ninety on this quiz, you may add five points to your score on any previous quiz in which you have not done as well. This is your "bonus" for mastering a difficult subject!

The foxhunting account should read as follows:

(1)   (2)   (3)
The first covert was blank (or "drawn blank") so the huntsman lifted his
                                   (4)   (5)
hounds through a field to another covert where (the) hounds found. The
              (6)   (7)
fox, a large dog fox, was viewed away (or "viewed") by all the members. Jester
              (8)   (9)
was the first to speak on finding the line (or simply "Jester challenged"). (The)
                                                        (10)
hounds were off in hot pursuit with a glorious burst of hound music.
              (11)
They carried the line (or "worked the line") all the way over to the river,
              (12)   (13)
where they lost. After about a ten minute check the field thought that once
                        (14)   (15)
again the hounds must have found (or recovered) when Jill spoke first (or
                                        (16)
"challenged") and the other hounds owned to it. It just happened that Jill
              (17)
was inclined to babble (or "fling her tongue" or be "mouthy").
                        (18)
It turned out that the pack was rioting on rabbit, so the huntsman got them
              (19)
back and rated them.
                        (20)
When the hounds once again recovered (or "found" or "found the line")
                                                        (21)
they ran for nearly an hour until he (the fox) finally went to ground over by
Johnson's creek. As the hunt was hacking home, (the) hounds jumped another

fox and this time after a fast chase of about 40 minutes they killed. The hunts-
(22)

man was particularly glad to have a kill that day as some of the young entry
(23)

had never been blooded.

(24)   (25)
The brush was given to the first lady to ride in at the kill; the mask to the

first gentleman.

Scoring directions and answers to quizzes for **Chapters XVII, XVIII and XIX.**

To be scored as two (2) quizzes, one of twelve (12) and the other of thirteen (13) parts. If you have any wrong answers, deduct eight points from one hundred for each. Enter your score on lines indicated on page 235.

ANSWERS:

  1. False—see page 170—paragraph 3
  2. True—see page 172—paragraph 2
  3. True—see page 183—paragraph 3
  4. False—see page 183—paragraph 4
  5. True—see page 173—Classes 4, 5 or 6
  6. True—see page 184—paragraph 1
  7. True—see page 173—Class 7; see also pages 185 through 188
  8. True—see page 174—Class 14
  9. True—see page 195—paragraph 1
 10. False—see page 195—paragraph 1
 11. True—see page 163—paragraph 4
 12. True—see page 174—Class 10; see also page 191—paragraph 2
 13. False—see page 194—paragraph 2
 14. True—see page 176—paragraph 1
 15. True—see page 176—paragraph 3; see also page 178—paragraph 1
 16. True—see page 176—paragraph 3
 17. False—see page 178—paragraph 1
 18. False—see page 179—paragraphs 1 and 2
 19. False—see page 178—paragraph 2
 20. False—see page 179—paragraph 5
 21. True—see page 189—paragraph 1
 22. False—see page 169—paragraphs 3 and 4
 23. True—see page 188—paragraph 3
 24. True—see page 195—paragraph 2
 25. True—see page 178—paragraphs 1 and 2; page 179—paragraphs 1, 2 and 3

Scoring directions and answers to quiz for Chapter XX.

To be scored as one (1) quiz of thirteen (13) parts. Deduct seven points from one hundred for each wrong answer. Enter your score on the line indicated on page 235.

ANSWERS:

 1. False—see page 202—paragraph 6; page 203—paragraph 2
 2. True—see page 203—paragraph 3
 3. True—see page 203—paragraph 3
 4. False—see page 203—paragraph 3
 5. False—see page 204—paragraph 5
 6. True—see page 204—paragraph 5
 7. True—see page 204—paragraph 5
 8. True—see page 205—paragraph 4
 9. True—see page 205—paragraph 4
10. True—see page 206—paragraph 1
11. True—see page 206—paragraph 1
12. False—see page 207—paragraph 3
13. True—see page 207—paragraph 3

Answers to quiz for Chapter XXI. Section 2—Evaluation.

1st place winner (Sally Hilton on *April Dawn*): Photo 5—page 222.

Rider jumping on an advanced level. Note that rider has heels well depressed and steps down in her stirrups in such a way that she has an excellent base of support. And since the base of support is good, the excellent "following through the air" becomes possible. In this particular picture there is really nothing to fault.

2nd place winner (Christine Solski on *Just Willie*): Photo 9—page 223.

Rider jumping on an advanced level. This rider too, has an excellent base of support, a strong position and achieves an excellent line from bit to elbow, following the gestures of the horse's head and neck through the air. However, we can not claim perfection of form in her case, as she has dropped her shoulders too low for classic style.

3rd place winner (Sophie Connery on *War Echo*): Photo 1—page 221.

Here the rider achieves a very nice line from bit to elbow, but she is not actually following *through the air*. She takes a little support from the sides of the horse's neck in what we call a jump on "an intermediate level." The rider looks slightly "behind." The lower leg should be a little further back; its present position, plus the rounded back, gives one the feeling that the rider may sit down before the jump is completed. (Contrast this leg position with that of the number two winner; there you know that the rider can stay up off the horse's back throughout all phases of the jump.)

4th place winner (Kit Cavendish on *Witchcraft*): Photo 4—page 222.

Here you see the rider pivoting on her knees with lower leg swinging back. The rider is too far out of the saddle for the height of the jump. Also, she is resting on her hands, and has "broken wrists"—that is, hands bent a little back, and the smooth line from bit to elbow very definitely broken.

5th place winner (Mary Lou Walters on *Little Mingo*): Photo 2—page 221.

This is the photo over which our group of "judges" at home disagreed the most. Obviously, the mare took off early, from her position over the jump as she begins the descent. The rider, in order to avoid being left, sat down on the horse but managed to lean forward. Sitting over a jump instead of remaining up out of the saddle is, of course, a fault as it interferes with the free movement of horse's back and quarters. Also, she should have more weight down in the stirrups; the foot apparently has slipped through the stirrup and heel is no longer down. However, she does manage to follow the gesture of the mare's head and neck, although not quite "through the air"; her hands touch the neck, though very lightly. I personally feel that hands and arms are excellent and that she made a very clever recovery from a situation in which she could have been badly left. The other point of view is that if she had stayed up out of the saddle, let the reins loop and grabbed the mane to avoid being left, she would interfere less with the mare's jump than she does by sitting. But I counter by saying that you have only to look at the extended head and neck of the horse and to see how boldly and confidently she is jumping to realize that the sitting down didn't upset her much. (We finally compromised on this fifth place decision—I had it higher and some of our group lower, so if you have it up a notch or two, or down a notch or two, it won't be surprising!)

6th place winner (Christine Solski on *Nitch Notch*): Photo 3—page 221.

Here is a rider catching mane who obviously, from her excellent over-all design, should jump on an advanced level. Actually, I happen to know the reason that she catches the mane. In the show ring, this horse comes in and "props," making sticky fences. It is next to impossible to follow through the air when the free forward movement is interrupted. However, one must judge what one sees, so we must mark Christine down to 6th place here when compared with the others. If we judge *what we see,* we would have to say, "rider with excellent seat, legs and base of support, but jumping on an elementary level." Contrast this picture with the same rider as the number 2 winner. This is a much prettier picture, but a less skillful jump. It is easier to get a good design of body, if the body is steadied by support from the hands.

7th place winner (Peggy Mann on *Glennwood*): Photo 6—page 222.

Here rider attempts to follow and managed to drop her hands instead. We suspect that she is not permitting the horse to extend his head and neck as freely as he would like to. Contrast this photo with that of the same horse in Chapter VI, jumping over cavaletti on loose reins and note the position of head and neck in each. Rider's back also is badly "humped" but she does manage to keep her seat out of the saddle.

8th place winner (Kit on *Trigger*): Photo 7—page 223.

Obviously a beginner jump, with the rider catching mane, and hands almost on the pony's ears!

9th place winner (Sally on *Penny Ante*): Photo 8—page 223.

Rider jumping on a beginner level, in attempting to use a crop over the jump, straightens out legs, drops shoulders, and worst of all, catches horse in the mouth.

Enter your quiz scores on the lines indicated. Divide the total by twenty-four to determine your over-all score on Theory of Riding.

Your scores for quiz preceding Chapter I (Two quiz value)	Score 1 _____
	Score 2 _____
Your scores for quizzes on Chapters II and III (Score as two quizzes)	Score 3 _____
	Score 4 _____
Your scores for quizzes on Chapters IV and V (Score as two quizzes)	Score 5 _____
	Score 6 _____
Your score for quizzes on Chapters VI and VII (Score as one quiz)	Score 7 _____
Your score for quizzes on Chapters VIII and IX (Score as two quizzes)	Score 8 _____
	Score 9 _____
Your score for quiz on Chapter X (Score as one quiz)	Score 10 _____
Your score for quiz on Chapter XI (Score as one quiz)	Score 11 _____
Your score for quiz on Chapter XII (Score as one quiz)	Score 12 _____
Your score for quizzes on Chapter XIII (Score as three quizzes)	Score 13 _____
	Score 14 _____
	Score 15 _____

Your score for quiz on Chapter XIV (Score as one quiz)   Score 16 _____

Your score for quizzes on Chapters XV and XVI (Score as three quizzes)   Score 17 _____

Score 18 _____

Score 19 _____

Your scores for quizzes on Chapters XVII, XVIII and XIX (Score as two quizzes)   Score 20 _____

Score 21 _____

Your score for quiz on Chapter XX (Score as one quiz)   Score 22 _____

Your score for quizzes on Chapter XXI (Score as two quizzes)   Score 23 _____

Score 24 _____

TOTAL _____

Total divided by twenty-four for your over-all grade on Theory of Riding   _____

_____